German Essays on Science in the 20th Century

The German Library: Volume 82

Volkmar Sander, General Editor

GERMAN ESSAYS ON SCIENCE IN THE 20th CENTURY

Edited by
Wolfgang Schirmacher

CONTINUUM • NEW YORK

1996
The Continuum Publishing Company
370 Lexington Avenue, New York, NY 10017

The German Library
is published in cooperation with Deutsches Haus,
New York University.
This volume has been supported by Inter Nationes, and a grant
from the funds of Stifterverband für die Deutsche Wissenschaft.

Printed in the United States of America

Library of Congress Cataloging-in-Publication Data

German essays on science in the 20th century /
edited by Wolfgang Schirmacher.
p. cm. — (German library ; 82)
Includes bibliographical references.
ISBN 0-8264-0746-3 (hardcover : alk. paper). —ISBN
0-8264-0747-1 (pbk. : alk. paper)
1. Physics—Germany—History—20th century. 2. Life sciences—
—Germany—History—20th century. 3. Social sciences—Germany—
—History—20th century. I. Schirmacher, Wolfgang. II. Series.
QC9.G3G47 1996
500—dc20 95-47851
CIP

Acknowledgments will be found on page 312,
which constitutes an extension of the copyright page.

Contents

Social Sciences, Law, and Culture

Introduction

Science in the Age of Its Criticism

The twentieth century has brought us to the imposing high point of the scientific-technological age and marks the beginning of a critical loss of confidence in the powers of science. German scientists such as Albert Einstein, Max Planck, Werner Heisenberg, Otto Hahn, and Lise Meitner laid the foundations for a revolution in our conception of the world the consequences of which were felt far beyond the academic scientific community. The Theory of Relativity, the Quantum Theory, and the Theory of Natural Radioactivity broke through the bounds of our everyday world and announced a manipulatable reality that was to function like the fabled golden goose. With the advent of nuclear power, we seemed to have an inexhaustible source of energy at our disposal. And the medical sciences, buoyed in the nineteenth century by the prospect of conquering many of the most terrible diseases, acquired even more powerful resources through their link to physics. With physics becoming the paradigm of all knowledge, the mathematization of the world attained fulfillment. It had begun with Descartes, continued on through Newtonian mechanics, and culminated in Heisenberg's quest for the "world formula." Nothing exists that cannot be clearly expressed in mathematical terms and that means that anything can be constructed by engineers. The moon landing in 1969, one small step for Neil Armstrong and a giant leap for mankind, was the jubilantly acclaimed consummation of an American belief in progress that refused to recognize any limitations.

Yet only a year later, with the near disaster of the Apollo 13 Mission, the euphoria came to an end even in the United States, and the dark side of science and technology made itself known. Since the age of Francis Bacon, knowledge has been understood as the power to alter nature; but not until the twentieth century was this potential exercised industrially, on a large scale. The apparently inexorable drive toward the application of scientific knowledge at all costs led to a dilemma that was to prove devastating. The first application of atomic energy was the bombing of Hiroshima and Nagasaki, a horrible and politically controversial instrument of mass murder against a civil population, and physics has yet to recover from this terrible occurrence. In the following decades a "gentle" nuclear energy was promoted, in vain; allegedly safe power plants were applauded, as if designed by Corbusier, in green pastures, safe for children. Yet the mistrust remained and intensified, all-too-well-founded fears were confirmed with the near-meltdowns in Harrisburg and Chernobyl: as if the two World Wars had not already demonstrated how scientific inventions could be transformed into weapons, inevitably destroying whatever remnants of humanitarian impulses may survive in wartime. Technologically-applied science proved itself a Moloch that devoured the children of its inventors, with cool indifference, as matter-of-factly as a trash compactor: sixty-million human beings lost their lives because the Western societies eagerly delivered themselves into the hands of the self-generating dynamics of scientific-technological progress.

The suspicion of science and its promises are not, however, a primarily intellectual distrust, but spring from the cultural memory of the industrialized nations upon which the atrocities of progress have left indelible marks. We have had to suppress these painful memories in order to be able to maintain and improve the standard of living we do not wish to give up. But we have paid with a dangerous loss of memory in our identity. And for this reason, too, the ego is no longer master of its own destiny as it is dependent upon something it deeply fears. In the same way, the glaring contradiction can be understood that in daily living, criticism of science and hostility toward technology can very well be compatible with an unquestioned utilization of science and technology. It takes only a new provocation to kindle latent anxieties and scientists who consider themselves our deliverers see themselves pilloried as enemies of humankind. The second half of the twentieth century offers an excellent example of this with gene technology, a field to which German Nobel Prize recipients such as Manfred Eigen and Christine Nüsslein-Volhard have made significant contributions. Instead of being proud that the biological sciences can now work with the fundamental "building block" of life and that medical science is in a position to treat the causes of hereditary diseases instead of having only recourse to offering a remedy of their symptoms, the critical public reacts with a fear that can often take irrational forms. Every genetically-altered plant is almost thought of as a harbinger of doom. But can we, *should we,* entrust this fundamental biological alteration of the human world to Frankenstein's zealous heirs among today's scientists?

Alienation of Science from the World

Philosophical minds among scientists, such as Werner Heisenberg, to name only one, recognized early on the danger of the mathematization of science, its consequent degree of abstraction that necessarily excludes the nonscientific community from discussion. The alienation of science from the "lifeworld" threatens its legitimacy. The trend toward ever-increasing specialization destroys the "unity of knowledge" (Hermann Weyl) and the search for scientific truth changes. In Max Weber's analysis, what had once been a "vocation" had become in the United States a "capitalistic and at the same time bureaucratic enterprise." Weber compared the German academic system of apprenticeship with the American way of carrying on scientific research and came to the somehow overoptimistic conclusion that the quest for knowledge as a vocation and the inner calling for science is possible in both systems, and depends entirely upon the inspiration and personality of the individual scientist. Strict specialization, therefore, would not necessarily exclude a "passionate devotion" of the individual who pursues "science for science's sake." But the reality is all too often a different matter completely. Professional success is then measured according to external criteria such as lab equipment and grants, with the real object seeming to lie in being quoted as often as possible by other scientists. Professionals secretly dream of being awarded a Nobel Prize, and original motivation of scientific research is forgotten, namely, the striving for the improvement of living conditions for all.

It is quite true, the ancient Greeks, indulged by their slave economy, considered a spiritual life to be the one good life, and toward the attainment of this goal saw little need of the application of their science in everyday living. *Techne* was a pure knowledge. Therefore, there existed no inner relation to the ecologically devastating deforestation of the Greek coastal-woodland regions, a shortsighted ravishing of nature that was dictated entirely by the needs of a rapidly developing shipping industry. Yet even in their day, the pragmatic Romans understood how senseless this division of theory and application was and in their empire demonstrated what Bacon formulated centuries later: *knowledge is power.* Since the founding fathers of modernity thus declared, it has been the avowed mission of science to wrest from nature its secrets in order to create human worlds, satisfying the needs of our bodies as well as our souls. Descartes thought man capable of becoming the master and rightful owner of an artificial nature. Spinoza described this fulfillment of humanity as *ethics,* whereas Leibniz laid the foundation for an absolute self-responsibility of the human individual with his monad.

As recently as the nineteenth century, science was an activity of gentlemen who read in the book of nature and aspired to great discoveries for the good of all humankind. With often absurdly limited technological means, basic laws of nature were discovered and an increasing number of new sciences were founded. Not until the advance of the industrial revolution, and especially during the era of large-scale scientific research, did the conception of science change completely and reveal a dependence upon technology, which had long remained hidden behind the striving for knowledge. But it then became apparent that the only questions science can ask are those allowed by its instruments, and the lofty art of speculative thought, which had stimulated knowledge since the time of Aristotle, was banished to the realm of philosophy. "Science does not think" (Heidegger), but rather explores according to stringent rules and acts in accord with the phenomenon under inquiry. The world view of physics became the culturally authoritative model—until far into the second half of the twentieth century—and even the fiercest critics still make reference to it. "To the facts!" was the battle cry, not only of Ernst Mach, a physicist and philosopher of science who inspired logical positivism as well as phenomenology. Ernst Mach favored a natural world view, "free of speculation and metaphysical ingredients" and stressed that phenomena can be understood only in terms of experience. Knowledge is derived from sensations, and, according to Mach, mechanics is the prototype of science. Renowned German physicists such as

Erwin Schrödinger, Albert Einstein, Max Planck, Otto Hahn, Werner Heisenberg, and Carl-Friedrich von Weizsäcker have, in addition, all been influential philosophers who established the "unity of nature" (von Weizsäcker) and the "principles of research" (Einstein), but nonetheless affirmed the "criticism of science" (Schrödinger). Planck praised the power of imagination, which cannot be reduced to causality, and offered veracity and reverence as methodological values. The "new science," which ended the period of classical physics, demanded a radical alteration in consciousness and the ability—as the mathematician Hermann Weyl phrased it—to combine a state of wonder with clarity. Einstein, who had become a household name, complained about people who unthinkingly use the wonders of science and technology without knowing more about their principles than a cow contentedly chewing its cud knows of botany. But the great physicists are usually also gifted writers, communicating their ideas clearly and with elegance. The responsibility of a scientist to educate the public on matters of science, especially as advocated by von Weizsäcker, was taken seriously by the German mandarins, as the essays in this volume demonstrate.

Following the philosopher Arthur Schopenhauer, Einstein believed we turn to science in order to rid ourselves of a cruel and boring everyday existence. As a scientist, Einstein's sole aim was to acquire an insight into the great riddle of the universe and to find an equation line, a discovery he could consider "something for eternity." The mathematician Kurt Gödel made certain his scientific search left the ivory tower. "Gödel's proof" stated that within any logical mathematical system there are propositions or questions that cannot be proved or disproved on the basis of the axioms within that system. The interdependence of language and reality fascinated Heisenberg who asked the Kantian questions with renewed vigor: *What is real? How can I know? What is matter?* Heisenberg's "uncertainty principle," which was not meant to be applied to everyday life, resonated with existential angst. It was Martin Heidegger, Heisenberg's philosophical partner in many dialogues, who formulated the problem: modern science has, as a theory, changed how we deal with reality in a sinister way. The building of the atomic bomb, a project in which most of the German physicists were unsuccessfully involved, proved the case. The discoverer of nuclear fission, Otto Hahn, at least managed during World War II to direct his work toward his utilization for peaceful purposes only. His closest associate, Lise Meitner, a rare female physicist in a male-dominated peer group, fled to neutral Sweden and refused to enter into the pact with the devil. Her crucial contribution to physics for which she felt "a kind of personal love" was purposely long overlooked.

Since the 1970s however, and in the shadow of the ecological crisis, the life sciences have replaced physics as a model, a development that has only just begun and that will undoubtedly continue on far into the next century. Robert Koch was the father figure within bacteriology. Educated in the nineteenth century, he was a fierce competitor of Louis Pasteur, using Ernst Abbe's new microscopes to detect even smaller organisms. The biochemical battle against cholera, always among the most devastating diseases, was one of the great success stories of science, and Koch was one of its heroes. Adolf Butenandt's discovery of sexual hormones opened a new avenue to research in biochemistry. Jakob von Uexküll, a zoologist, became influential in initiating environmental research as well as opening new paths in ethology. Konrad Lorenz, educated by the "gestalt of nature," found his research with geese useful in developing into a resolute critic of modern civilization. Manfred Eigen, together with his associate Ruthild Winkler-Oswatisch, succeeded in producing scientific best-sellers, informing the public on their new findings in evolution, transforming an extremely abstract subject matter into a readable and enjoyable form. Necessity and change are basic elements of the biochemical "game of life" as directed by the laws of nature. God may be shrewd, but is not, as Einstein mused, malicious.

In contrast, the social sciences, which experienced their heyday in midcentury, have now lost their cultural influence to a great extent. Influenced by Hegel, Comte, Marx, Dilthey, and Simmel, Max Weber, called the "Machiavelli of Heidelberg" (Raymond Aron), revolutionized sociology in terms of a systematic approach. Transdisciplinarity is the magic formula for the social sciences, law, and the humanities. Pointing to interdependencies in daily life proved to be Georg Simmel's strength, and Karl Vossler emphasized that languages must be studied in relation to their cultural history. Gustav Radbruch observed that every search for justice depended on moral values that are relative to time and place. Law and order are as necessary as the common good—this had been Radbruch's findings, helping him design a democratic and lawful government. Robert Bosch, an industrialist who was an advocate of European unity, managed to achieve good relations with his workers by treating them as equals. Culture is a product of public consciousness, von Weizsäcker concluded, and science contributes to this process in a significant way.

But the cultural climate has changed dramatically in the last decades. For all three sciences today, it is true that with the end of the modern age they have lost the formative power of the "great narratives" and have now found recognition in the postmodern world only as regional-language games.

The "end of metaphysics" (Heidegger) reveals itself worldwide as a crisis of confidence and is manifest in cultural postmodernity as a total breakdown of authority in society and private life. The authority of science as paradigm of truth is affected as well as technology, which served as the main vehicle for progress. Modern science, structured as applied technology, has lost its universal appeal. Even if we enjoy the sleek products of information technology, we don't "buy" the principle any longer. The contributions of technology are widely challenged and evaluated in terms of death or life. There seems to be an unbridgeable gap between science/technology on the one hand and postmodernity on the other. Technological science, particularly in the new form of gene technology, is to be strongly opposed by a culture following the diversity of life games and enjoying the complexity of unsolved riddles. Postmodernism allows us to see that problems do not have to be solved, but rather be celebrated as starting points for "otherness." The idea of authority through knowledge and technological skills is alien to a culture in which personal intensity and aesthetic experience emerge as new criteria of truth. How can there be a connection between logical argument, experimental proof and solved problems (characterizing science and technology), and "anything goes," which is the watchword of postmodernity? Waiting without expectations, acting without belief, an ironic world view—how could this be compatible with the seriousness and the goal-oriented commitment that science and technology demand?

The widespread perception is that scientists and engineers, once high priests of reason and stewards of progress, have now become lab operators and, in the view of radical critics, the "worst enemies of mankind." "Why do they hate us so much? Scientists never claimed to know anything for certain!" commented Mitchell Feigenbaum, one of the founders of Chaos Theory. This eminent scientist from Rockefeller University wanted no part of the misuse of scientific discoveries as tools to gain power in society. Feigenbaum has a point. A closer look reveals that research scientists and technological inventors are often eccentrics, hopeless misfits who never grew up, compulsive gamblers who risk the family fortune in the next bet with nature. It is a well-concealed fact that our creative scientists live in self-designed playhouses (with very expensive toys) guarded by burned-out older colleagues (serving as grant-proposal writers) who invent all the high goals and reasonable purposes in order to get funding. A step-by-step rational approach within accepted parameters, a systematic falsification of premises—these are merely daydreams of philosophers such as Karl Popper (who never worked in a lab, as his former student Paul K. Feyerabend pointed out). Surprisingly, genuine science is not the science we should have, according to theories of rationality, but the mess kids have made by enjoying themselves. Here are two recent examples. The crucial inventions in information technology were made by hackers, i.e., illegal users of information networks who served no accepted purpose. A number of them who became millionaires and responsible businessmen recently established a grant foundation for future hackers (whose games are now crimes and subject to FBI investigation) in order to protect the only source of creativity in this field. Second, regarding gene technology, today a major enterprise with billions of dollars at stake, the techno scientists have not yet achieved what they promised, but they do not really mind: by accident and as byproducts they have discovered information that will lead to cures for several still-incurable diseases such as Alzheimer's. They work randomly and contrary to planning, intuitively and in the course of a game, regardless of the given goals, and this professional freedom is typical of authentic science as well as of postmodernity as a transition period leading to artificial life.

Postmodern science reveals authentic science as the life-style of the scientists involved. Science in this understanding still remains a game of life and death, but played by innocent children and not under the authority of a "means-to-an-end rationality" (Weber). This basic innocence of science is mirrored in the postmodern culture, where it appears as a kind of Socratic ignorance—I know that I don't know and, therefore, I know more than anyone who claims knowledge. Postmodernity knows what failed in the attempt to keep the promise of a humane life, but is reluctant to identify a new order in chaos. Yet a philosophy of difference—preparing us for artificial life—does not suggest there is no order. Rather, it is highly possible that we shall never understand it, or, at least, that we need first to effect a fundamental change in our way of understanding, from discursive knowledge to intuitive wisdom, as Spinoza teaches us.

Even if we consider that science playing the knowledge game with very expensive toys is a sound description and suits the postmodern condition, how can this be true of a technology that determines the way science is implemented? Who needs an airplane pilot with a postmodern mind, or a surgeon who would suddenly enjoy removing your liver instead of carrying out the planned operation on your stomach? "Anything goes" seems to be bad advice for technology, as it very easily leads to: *Nothing works!* Or is this bleak view caused by an understanding that judges technology by anthropocentric standards of fulfilling given goals, acting as our servants and slaves, being ontologically second-rate to man? Consider another understanding of technology. We live through our technologies the artificial life assigned by nature. The techniques of walking and breathing are not fundamentally different from information technology or gene technology. We are responsible for all of our technologies and—after a lifelong aesthetic education are able to differentiate between those that failed and those fulfilled.

Postmodernity is a cultural condition that does not mean that "anything" can happen all the time, randomly and without meaningful connections. On the contrary, "anything goes" addresses the creative potential of a human being and celebrates the diversity of our life technologies. There is no ideological fixation of goals and expectations compelling one to do the wrong thing or act as one would rather not as a self-responsible person. Anything is within reach if one can live it to its fullest and if one's whole person is involved, not merely the self-deceiving mind. For Weizsäcker, this prudent action should lead to a "culture" as "public consciousness." In this sense, why would an airplane captain wish to destroy the plane, or the surgeon harm the patient instead of optimally fulfilling the technology at hand? (Of course, it would be better not to allow a psychopath to fly a jumbo jet!) From a postmodern viewpoint, we acknowledge that technology fulfills itself. This is seldom compatible with anthropocentric goals that we traditionally impose on technology. The optimum of technology, as well as the depth of scientific knowledge, reveals itself in its own time, and we need to learn to appreciate rather than to press forward. The artificial-life question is not whether artificial-life systems exhibit life-like behavior. Instead, scientists must be keenly aware that the touchstone of a truly artificial life—as with any life form imaginable—is its potential for allowing a good life.

For his invaluable help in the selection of the essays in this volume and for its preparation for print, I wish to thank my research associate Sven Nebelung.

W. S.
Translated by Virginia Cutrufelli

PHYSICS AS SCIENTIFIC WORLD VIEW

Ernst Mach

Philosophical and Scientific Thought

1. Lower animals living under simple, constant and favorable conditions adapt themselves to immediate circumstances through their innate reflexes. This usually suffices to maintain individual and species for a suitable period. An animal can withstand more intricate and less stable conditions only if it can adapt to a wider range of spatial and temporal surroundings. This requires a farsightedness in space and time which is met first by more perfect sense organs, and with mounting demands by a development in the life of the imagination. Indeed an organism that possesses memory has wider spatial and temporal surroundings in its mental field of vision than it could reach through its senses. It perceives, as it were, even those regions that adjoin the directly visible, seeing the approach of prey or foe before any sense organ announces them. What guarantees to primitive man a measure of advantage over his animal fellows is doubtless only the strength of his individual memory, which is gradually reinforced by the communicated memory of forebears and tribe. Likewise, what essentially marks progress in civilization is that noticeably wider regions of space and time are drawn within the scope of human attention. With the partial relief that a rising civilization affords, to begin with through division of labor, development of trades

and so on, the individual's imaginative life is focused on a smaller range of facts and gains in strength, while that of society as a whole does not lose in scope. Gradually the activity of thinking thus invigorated may itself become a calling. Scientific thought arises out of popular thought, and so completes the continuous series of biological development that begins with the first simple manifestations of life.

2. The goal of the ordinary imagination is the conceptual completion and perfection of a partially observed fact. The hunter imagines the way of life of the prey he has just sighted, in order to choose his own behavior accordingly. The farmer considers the proper soil, sowing and maturing of the fruit of plants that he intends to cultivate. This trait of mental completion of a fact from partial data is common to ordinary and scientific thought. Galileo, too, merely wants to represent to himself the trajectory as a whole, given the initial speed and direction of a projected stone. However, there is another feature that often very significantly distinguishes scientific from ordinary thought: the latter, at least in its beginnings, serves practical ends, and first of all the satisfaction of bodily needs. The more vigorous mental exercise of scientific thought fashions its own ends and seeks to satisfy itself by removing all intellectual uneasiness: having grown in the service of practical ends, it becomes its own master. Ordinary thought does not serve pure knowledge, and therefore suffers from various defects that at first survive in scientific thought, which is derived from it. Science only very gradually shakes itself free from these flaws. Any glance at the past will show that progress in scientific thought consists in constant correction of ordinary thought. As civilization grows, however, so scientific thought reacts on those modes of thought that serve only practical ends: ordinary thought becomes increasingly restricted and replaced by technical thought which is pervaded by science.

3. The representation in thought of facts or the adaption of thought to fact, enables the thinker mentally to complete partially observed facts, insofar as completion is determined by the observed part. Their determination consists in the mutual dependence of factual features, so that thought has to aim at these. Since ordinary thinking and even incipient scientific

thought must make do with a rather crude adaption of thoughts to facts, the former do not quite agree amongst each other. Mutual adaption of thoughts is therefore the further task to be solved in order to attain full intellectual satisfaction. This last endeavor, which involves logical clarification of thinking though reaching far beyond this goal, is the outstanding mark that distinguishes scientific from ordinary thought. The latter is enough so long as it roughly serves the realization of practical ends.

4. Scientific thought presents itself in two seemingly different forms: as philosophy and as specialist research. The philosopher seeks to orient himself as completely and comprehensively as possible in relation to the totality of facts, which necessarily involves him in building on material borrowed from the special sciences. The special scientist is at first concerned only with finding his way about a smaller area of facts. Since, however, facts are always somewhat arbitrarily and forcibly defined with a view to the momentary intellectual aim, these boundary lines are constantly shifting as scientific thought advances: in the end the scientist too comes to see that the results of all other special enquiries must be taken into account, for the sake of orientation in his own field. Clearly in this way special enquirers also collectively aim at a total picture through amalgamation of all special fields. Since this is at best imperfectly attainable, this effort leads to more or less covert borrowings from philosophical thought. The ultimate end of all research is thus the same. This shows itself also in the fact that the greatest philosophers, such as Plato, Aristotle, Descartes, Leibniz and others have opened up new ways of specialist enquiry, while scientists like Galileo, Newton, Darwin and others have greatly furthered philosophic thought without being called philosophers.

Yet it is true that what the philosopher regards as a possible starting point appears to the scientist as a distant goal of his work; but this difference of view need not and indeed does not prevent enquirers from learning from each other. Through its many attempts to summarize the most general features of large areas, philosophy has gained ample experience in this line, even learning gradually to recognize and avoid some of its own mistakes that the philosophically untrained scientist is almost bound to commit even today. However, philosophy has furnished science with some positive notions of value too, for example ideas of conservation. Philosophers in their turn take from special sciences foundations that are sounder than anything from ordinary thought. Science, to him, is an example of a careful, solid and successful structure, whose excessive onesidedness at the same time affords him useful lessons. Indeed, every philosopher has his own private view of science, and every scientist his private philosophy. However, these private scientific views are usually somewhat outdated and it is extremely rare that a scientist can respect the occasional scientific pronouncement of philosophers; whereas most scientists today adhere to a materialist philosophy of 150 years' standing, whose inadequacy has long since been recognized not only by professional philosophers but by any layman not too cut off from philosophic thought. Few philosophers today take part in the work of science, and only exceptionally do scientists address their own intellectual attention to philosophical questions: yet such efforts are essential for mutual understanding, since mere reading is here useless to either side.

Surveying the age-old paths that philosophers and scientists have trodden, we find that they are often well cleared. At some points however, they seem to be blocked by quite natural and instinctive philosophical and scientific prejudices that have remained as waste from old experiments and unsuccessful work. It would be advisable at times to clear these heaps of waste, or to sidestep them.

5. Not only humanity but each individual on reaching full consciousness finds within himself a view of the world to which he has not contributed deliberately. He accepts this as a gift of nature and civilization: everyone must begin here. No thinker can do more than start from this view, extend and correct it, use his forebears' experience and avoid their mistakes as best he may, in short: carefully to tread the same path again on his own. What, then, is this world view? I find myself surrounded by moveable bodies in space, some inanimate, others plants, animals and men. My body, likewise moveable in space, is for me a visible and touchable object of sense perception occupying a part of sensible space alongside and outside other bodies, just as they do. My body differs from

those of other people in certain individual features but above all in that when objects touch my body peculiar feelings supervene that I do not observe when other bodies are touched. My body is not quite as accessible to my eyes as the bodies of others. I can see only a small part of my head, at least directly. In general my body appears to me under a perspective quite different from that of all others: towards them I cannot take up that optical point of view. Similarly for touch and the other senses. For example, I hear my voice quite differently from that of others. Besides, I find memories, hopes, fears, drives, desires, a will and so on, of whose development I am as innocent as of the existence of the bodies in my surroundings. The foregoing considerations and the movement of the one definite body issuing from that will mark that body as mine. When I observe the behavior of other human bodies, not only practical needs but also a close analogy force me, even against my will, to hold that memories, hopes, fears, motives, wishes, and will similar to those associated with my body are bound up with other human and animal bodies. The behavior of other people further compels me to assume that my body and other objects exist as immediately for them as their bodies and other objects do for me; whereas my memories, desires and the like are for them the result of the same sort of irresistible analogical inference as theirs for me. The totality of what is immediately given in space for all may be called the physical, whereas what is immediately given only to one while others must infer it by analogy may provisionally be called the mental. The totality that is given immediately only to one we shall call also his ego, in the restricted sense. We note Descartes's opposition of matter to mind, extension to thought. This is the natural basis of dualism, which may stand for a whole range of transitions from mere materialism to pure spiritualism, depending on how we value the physical and the mental, taking one as basic and the other derived. The dualist contrast may however become so acute as to exclude, contrary to any natural view, all contact between physical and mental; this gives rise to such monstrosities as "occasionalism" or "pre-established harmony."

6. The findings in my spatial surroundings depend on one another. A magnetic needle is set in motion as soon as another magnet comes close enough. A body becomes warm near fire

and cold when in contact with ice. A sheet of paper in a dark room becomes visible by the flame of a lamp. The behavior of other people forces me to assume that in all this their findings resemble mine. A grasp of these mutual dependences within our findings and our experiences is of the greatest interest to us, both practically for the satisfaction of needs and theoretically for the mental completion of incomplete findings. In observing these dependences amongst bodies I can treat men and animals as though inanimate by abstracting from everything obtained by analogy. But I observe again that my body essentially influences this finding. A body can throw a shadow on a sheet of white paper; but if I have just been looking at a rather bright object, I shall see on the paper a spot similar to the shadow. By suitable position of the eyes I may see a body double, or two very similar bodies as three. If I have just turned round suddenly, I may see mechanically moving bodies as at rest and vice versa. If I close my eyes optical findings cease altogether. Analogous tactual or thermal findings and so on may be induced by corresponding bodily influences. If my neighbor conducts the same experiments on his body this does not alter my findings, although I learn from reports and have to assume by analogy that his findings are similarly modified.

The constituents of my spatial findings thus generally depend not only on one another but also on findings as to my body, and likewise for everybody. If one places excessive emphasis on the latter dependence while underrating the former, one may easily come to regard all findings as mere products of one's own body, that is as "subjective." However, the spatial boundaries of our own body are always present and we see that findings outside them depend on one another as well as on findings inside them. The investigation of external dependences is indeed much simpler and further advanced than that of cross-boundary ones. Still, we may expect these last to be of the same kind as the first, as we infer with noticeably growing certainty from research on the bodies of men and animals external to us. A developed physiology, increasingly based on physics, can unravel the subjective conditions of a finding. Naïve subjectivism, which construed variant findings of one person under variable conditions and of different persons as so many cases of appearance in contrast with a hypothetical constant reality, is no longer admissible. For what matters is only a full grasp of all conditions of a finding: that alone is of practical or theoretical interest.

7. As to the sum of my physical findings, these I can analyse into what are at present unanalysable elements: colors, sounds, pressures, temperatures, smells, spaces, times and so on. These elements depend both on external and internal circumstances; when the latter are involved, and only then, we may call these elements sensations. Since another's sensations are no more directly given to me than mine to him, I am entitled to regard the elements of the mental as the same as those into which I have analysed the physical. Thus the mental and physical have common elements and are not in stark opposition as commonly supposed. This becomes even clearer if we can show that memories, ideas, feelings, will and concepts can be built up from traces left behind by sensations and are therefore comparable with them. If now I call the sum of my mental aspect, sensations included, my ego in the widest sense (in contrast with the restricted ego), then in this sense I could say that my ego contains the world (as sensation and idea). Still, we must not overlook that this conception does not exclude others equally legitimate. This solipsist position seems to abolish the world as independent, blurring the contrast between it and ego. The boundary nevertheless remains, only it no longer runs round the restricted ego but through the extended one, that is through "consciousness." Indeed we could not have derived the solipsist position without observing the boundary and the analogy between my own and others' ego. Those who say that we cannot go beyond the ego therefore mean the extended ego, which already contains a recognition of the world and other minds. Nor is confining oneself to the "theoretical" solipsism of the enquirer any more acceptable: there are no isolated enquirers, each has practical ends of his own, can learn from others and works for their guidance too.

8. In making our physical findings we are subject to many errors and delusions. A straight rod dipped into water at an angle is seen bent, and the inexperienced might think that it will turn out to feel bent too. The virtual image in a concave mirror looks tangible. An object in glaring light is regarded as white and we are amazed to find that under moderate illumination

we find it is black. The shape of a tree trunk in the dark reminds us of the figure of a man and we imagine him to be in front of us. All such "delusions" rest on the fact that we do not know or fail to observe the conditions under which the finding is made, or that we suppose them to be other than they are. Besides, the imagination rounds off incomplete findings in the way that is most familiar to it, thus occasionally falsifying them. What in ordinary thought leads to the opposition between illusion and reality, between appearance and object, is the confusion between findings under the most various conditions with findings under very definite and specific conditions. Once this opposition has emerged, it tends to invade philosophy as well, and is not easily dislodged. The weird and unknowable "thing-in-itself" behind appearances is the ordinary object's unmistakeable twin, having lost all other significance. After misconstruing the boundary between the internal and external and thereby imposing the stamp of illusion on the ego's entire context, have we any further need for an unknowable something outside the confines that the ego can never transcend? Is it any more than a relapse into ordinary thought to see some solid core behind "delusive" appearances?

When we consider elements like red, green, hot, cold, and the rest, which are physical and mental in virtue of their dependence on both external and internal circumstances, and are in both respects immediately given and identical, the question as to illusion and reality loses its sense. Here we are simultaneously confronted by the elements of the real world and of the ego. The only possible further question of interest concerns their functional interdependence, in the mathematical sense. Such a connection might be called an object, though not an unknowable one: with every new observation or scientific theorem it becomes better known. If we look at the restricted ego without prejudice, it too turns out to be a functional connection between these elements, except that its form is here a little different from what we are used to in the physical field: consider the way ideas and their connections differ from physical elements. We need no unknown and unknowable something behind these processes, nor would it help in the least toward better understanding. Yet there is something all but unexplored standing behind the ego, namely our body; but every new observation in physiology and psychology makes the ego better known to us: introspection and experiment in psychology, brain anatomy and psychopathology, already the source of many valuable explanations, here work strongly in the direction of physics in the widest sense, combining with it into a more penetrating grasp of the world. We may expect all sensible questions gradually to approach being answerable.

9. In examining the mutual dependence of varying ideas one hopes to grasp mental processes and in particular one's own experiences and actions. One who still needs an observing and acting subject, has failed to see that he could have saved himself the whole trouble of the enquiry, for he has now gone full circle. It reminds us of the farmer who went to a factory to have the working of steam engines explained to him and then asked "Where are the horses that drive the machines?" It was Herbart's main merit to have examined the processes of ideas as such, yet even he spoiled his whole psychology by starting from the assumption that the soul is simple. Only lately have we begun to accept a psychology without soul.

10. In pushing the analysis of experience as far as currently untranscendable elements our main advantage is that the two problems of the "unfathomable" thing and the equally "unexplorable" ego are presented in their simplest and clearest form, which is precisely what makes it easy to see them as sham problems. By elimination of what it is senseless to explore, what the special sciences can really explore emerges all the more clearly: the complex interdependence of the elements. While groups of such elements may be called things or bodies, it turns out that there are strictly speaking no isolated objects: they are only fictions for a preliminary enquiry, in which we consider strong and obvious links but neglect weaker and less noticeable ones. The same distinction of degree gives rise also to the opposition of world to ego: an isolated ego exists no more than an isolated object: both are provisional fictions of the same kind.

11. Our considerations offer little or nothing to the philosopher: they are not designed to solve one, or seven, or nine cosmic riddles; they merely lead to removing false problems that hinder scientific enquiry, while leaving the rest to positive re-

search. We offer only a negative rule for scientific research which need not concern the philosopher, especially if he already possesses (or thinks he does) secure foundations for a world view. If then our account is to be judged primarily from a scientific standpoint, this cannot mean that philosophers are not to criticize it, modify it to suit their needs or even reject it altogether. However, for the scientist it is quite a secondary matter whether his ideas fit into some given philosophic system or not, so long as he can use them with profit as a starting point for research. For the scientist is not so fortunate as to possess unshakeable principles, he has become accustomed to regarding even his safest and best-founded views and principles as provisional and liable to modification through experience. Indeed, the greatest advances and discoveries have been possible only through this attitude.

12. To the scientist likewise, our account can show at best an ideal, whose gradual and approximate realization remains the task of future research. The finding out of the direct connections between the elements is so complex a task that it cannot be solved all at once but only step by step. It was much easier to ascertain a rough and ready outline of the way in which whole collections of elements or bodies depend on one another, and it was rather a matter of chance and practical need which elements seemed the more important, which were focused on and which remained unnoticed. The individual enquirer is in the midst of developing science and must start with his predecessors' incomplete findings which at best he can correct and perfect according to his ideal. In gratefully adopting for his own work the help and hints contained in these preliminaries, he often adds the errors of predecessors and contemporaries to his own. A return to a quite naïve point of view, even if it were possible, would afford to one who had shed all the views of his contemporaries not only the advantage of freedom from prejudice, but also the drawback of confusion arising from the complexity of the task and the impossibility of even starting any enquiry. If therefore we seem here to be returning to a primitive standpoint, in order to conduct the enquiry along new and better paths, this is an artificial simplemindedness that does not give up the advantages gained through long periods of growing civilization, but on the contrary uses insights

presupposing a fairly high level of thought as to physics, physiology and psychology. Only at such a level is a resolution into "elements" conceivable. We are thus returning to the starting points of inquiry with the deeper and richer insight produced by previous inquiry. A certain stage of mental development must be reached before scientific considerations can start at all, but no science can use ordinary concepts in their vagueness: it must return to their beginning and origin in order to make the concepts more precise and pure. Should this be forbidden only to psychology and epistemology?

13. If we have to investigate a set of multiply interdependent elements there is only one method at our disposal: the method of variation. We simply have to observe the change of every element for changes in any other: it makes little difference whether these latter changes occur "spontaneously" or are brought about through our "will." The dependences are ascertained by "observation" and "experiment." Even if elements were linked only in pairs, being otherwise independent, the systematic study of these links would be troublesome enough: a simple mathematical argument shows that for elements interdependent in groups of three, four and so on, the task soon becomes practically inexhaustible. Any provisional neglect of less noticeable dependences, any anticipation of obvious connections, must therefore be felt as making the task significantly easier: both these simplifications were first discovered instinctively, under the influence of practical requirements, needs, and mental constitution, and afterwards used with conscious skill and method by scientists. Without such moves, which might well count as blemishes, science could neither have arisen nor grown. Scientific research is somewhat like unravelling complicated tangles of strings, in which luck is almost as vital as skill and accurate observation. Research to the inquirer is just as exciting as the pursuit of a rare beast over difficult terrain is to the hunter.

If one wants to investigate the interdependence of any elements, those whose influence is plain but felt as disturbing the enquiry had best be kept as constant as possible. That is the first and foremost way of making research easier. Since we know that every element depends both on external and internal elements we are led to begin by studying the concomitances of external elements while leaving internal ones (those of the observer himself) under conditions that remain constant as far as possible. By examining the interdependence of the luminosity of bodies, or their temperatures, or motion, under conditions that remain as far as possible the same for one or even different observers taking part, we make physical knowledge as free as possible from the influence of our own individual bodies. To complete this we have to study internal and cross-boundary physiological and psychological connections, a task significantly facilitated by the prior physical investigations. This division of labor too has arisen instinctively, and we need merely become conscious of its advantages to go on using it methodically. Scientific research is full of examples of analogous divisions in smaller fields of investigation.

14. Following these introductory remarks let us now look more closely at the leading themes of scientific inquiry. In this we lay no claims to completeness, and indeed would rather guard against premature philosophizing and systematizing. Let us take an attentive walk through the field of scientific inquiry and observe the detailed behavior of the inquirer. By what means has our knowledge of nature actually grown in the past, and what are the prospects for further growth in the future? The inquirer's behavior has developed instinctively in practical activity and popular thought, and has merely been transferred to the field of science where in the end it has been developed into a conscious method. To meet our requirements we shall not need to go beyond the empirically given. We shall be satisfied if we can reduce the features of the inquirer's behavior to actually observable ones in our own physical and mental life (features that recur in practical life and in the action and thought of peoples); and if we can show that this behavior really leads to practical and intellectual advantages. A natural basis for this purpose is a general consideration of our physical and mental life.

Translated by Paul Foulkes

Hermann Weyl

Knowledge as Unity

Fourteen years ago when our neighboring university in the city of brotherly love celebrated its bicentennial, I delivered a talk on "The Mathematical Way of Thinking," the opening sentences of which sound like an anticipation of our present theme. "By the mental process of thinking," I said then, "we try to ascertain truth; it is our mind's effort to bring about its own enlightenment by evidence. Hence, just as truth itself and the experience of evidence, it is something fairly uniform and universal in character. Appealing to the light of our innermost self, it is neither reducible to a set of mechanically applicable rules, nor is it divided into water-tight compartments like historical, philosophical, or mathematical thinking. True, nearer the surface there are certain techniques and differences; for instance, the procedures of fact-finding in the courtroom and in a physical laboratory are conspicuously different." The same conviction was more forcefully expressed by the father of Western philosophy, Descartes, who said: "The sciences taken all together are identical with human wisdom, which always remains one and the same, however applied to different subjects, and suffers no more differentiation proceeding from them than the light of the Sun experiences from the variety of the things it illumines."

But it is easier to state this thesis in general terms than to defend it in detail when one begins to survey the various branches of human knowledge. Ernst Cassirer, whose last years were so intimately connected with Columbia University, set out to dig for the root of unity in man by a method of his own, first developed in his great work, *Philosophie der symbolischen Formen,* of which the lucid *Essay on Man,* written much later in this country, is a revised and condensed version. In it he tries to answer the question "What is man?" by a penetrating analysis of man's cultural activities and creations: language, myth, religion, art, history, science. As a common feature of all of them he finds the symbol, symbolic representation. He sees in them "the threads which weave the symbolic net, the tangled net of human experience." "Man," he says, "no longer lives in a merely physical universe, he lives in a symbolic universe."

Since "reason is a very inadequate term with which to comprehend the forms of man's cultural life in all their richness and variety," the definition of man as the *animal rationale* had better be replaced by defining him as an *animal symbolicum.* Investigation of these symbolic forms on the basis of appropriate structural categories should ultimately tend towards displaying them as "an organic whole tied together not by a *vinculum substantiale* but a *vinculum functionale.*" Cassirer invites us to look upon them "as so many variations on a common theme," and sets as the philosopher's task "to make this theme audible and understandable." Yet, much as I admire Cassirer's analyses, which betray a mind of rare universality, culture, and intellectual experience, their sequence, as one follows them in his book, resembles more a suite of *bourrées,* sarabands, minuets and *gigues* than variations on a single theme. In the concluding paragraph he himself emphasizes "the tensions and frictions, the strong contrasts and deep conflicts between the various powers of man, that cannot be reduced to a common denominator." He then finds consolation in the thought that "this multiplicity and disparateness does not denote discord or disharmony," and his last word is that of Heraclitus, accepting "harmony in contrariety, as in the case of the bow and the lyre." Perhaps man cannot hope to be more than that; but am I wrong when I feel that Cassirer quits with a promise unfulfilled?

1

In this dilemma let me now first take cover behind the shield of that special knowledge in which I have experience through my own research: the natural sciences, including mathematics. Even here doubts about their methodical unity have been raised. This however seems unjustified to me. Following Galileo, one may describe the method of science in general terms as a combination of passive observation refined by active experiment with that symbolic construction to which theories ultimately reduce. Physics is the paragon. Hans Driesch and the holistic school have claimed for biology a methodical approach different from and transcending that of physics. However nobody doubts that the laws of physics hold for the body of an animal or for myself as well as for a stone. Driesch's attempts to prove that the organic processes are incapable of mechanical explanation rest on much too narrow a notion of mechanical or physical explanations of nature. Here quantum physics has opened new possibilities.

On the other side, wholeness is not a feature limited to the organic world. Every atom is already a whole of quite definite structure; its organization is the foundation of possible organizations and structures of the utmost complexity. I do not suggest that we are safe against surprises in the future development of science. Not so long ago we had a pretty startling one in the transition from classical to quantum physics. Similar future breaks may greatly affect epistemological interpretation, as this one did the notion of causality; but there are no signs that the basic method itself, symbolic construction combined with experience, will change.

It is to be admitted that on the way to their goal of symbolic construction scientific theories pass through preliminary stages, in particular the classifying or morphological stage. Linnaeus's classification of plants and Cuvier's comparative anatomy are early examples; comparative linguistics or jurisprudence are analogues in the historical sciences. The features which natural science determines by experiments repeatable at any place and any time are universal; they have that empirical necessity which is possessed by the laws of nature. But beside this domain of the necessary there remains a domain of the contingent. The one cosmos of stars and diffuse matter, sun and earth, and the plants and animals living on earth are accidental or singular phenomena. We are interested in their evolution. Primitive thinking even puts the question "How did it come about?" before the question "How is it?"

All history in the proper sense is concerned with the development of one singular phenomenon, human civilization on earth. Yet if the experience of natural science accumulated in her own history has taught one thing, it is that knowledge of the laws and of the inner constitution of things must be far advanced before one may hope to understand or hypothetically reconstruct their genesis. For want of such knowledge as is now slowly being gathered by genetics, the speculations on pedigrees and phylogeny let loose by

Darwinism in the last decades of the nineteenth century were mostly premature. Kant and Laplace had the firm basis of Newton's gravitational law on which to advance their hypotheses about the origin of the planetary systems.

2

After this brief glance at the methods of natural science, which are the same in all its branches, it is time now to point out the limits of science. The riddle posed by the double nature of the ego certainly lies beyond those limits. On the one hand, I am a real individual man, born of a mother and destined to die, carrying out real physical and psychical acts, one among many—far too many, I may think when boarding a subway during rush hours. On the other hand, I am vision open to reason, a self-penetrating light, immanent sense-giving consciousness, or whatever you choose to call it, and as such am unique. Therefore I can say to myself both "I think; I am real and conditioned" and "I think, and in my thinking I am free." More clearly than in acts of volition, the decisive point in the problem of freedom comes out, as Descartes remarked, in theoretical acts. Take for instance the statement $2 + 2 = 4$; not by blind natural causality, but because I see that $2 + 2 = 4$, does this judgment form itself in me as a real psychic act and my lips form the words "two and two make four." Reality or the realm of being is not closed, but open toward meaning in the ego, where meaning and being are merged in indissoluble union—though science will never tell us how. We do not see through the real origin of freedom.

And yet nothing is more familiar and disclosed more often than this mysterious "marriage of light and darkness," of self-transparent consciousness and real being. The access is my knowledge of myself from within, by which I am aware of my acts of perception, thought, volition, feeling, and doing, in a manner entirely different from the theoretical knowledge that represents the parallel cerebral processes in symbols. This inner awareness of myself is the basis for the more or less intimate understanding of my fellow men, whom I acknowledge as beings of my own kind. Granted that I do not know of their consciousness in the same manner that I know of my own; nevertheless my interpretative understanding of it is an apprehension of indisputable adequacy. As hermeneutic interpretation it is as characteristic for the historical, as symbolic construction is for the natural sciences. Its illumining light not only falls on my fellow men; it also reaches, though with ever-increasing dimness and incertitude, deep into the animal kingdom. Kant's narrow opinion that we can feel compassion but cannot share joy with other living creatures is justly ridiculed by Albert Schweitzer who asks, "Did he never see a thirsty ox coming home from the fields drink?"

It is idle to disparage this hold on nature "from within" as anthropomorphic and to elevate the objectivity of theoretical construction, though one must admit that understanding for the very reason that it is concrete and full lacks the freedom of the "hollow symbol." Both roads run, as it were, in opposite directions: what is darkest for theory, man, is most luminous for understanding from within; and to the elementary inorganic processes that are most easily approachable by theory, interpretation finds no access whatever. In biology the latter may serve as a guide to important problems, although it will not provide an objective theory as their solution. Such teleological statements as "the hand is there to grasp, the eye to see" compel us to discover what internal material organization enables hand and eye to perform these functions according to physical laws which hold for them as for any inanimate object.

3

Realizing that sensuous qualities are but effects of external agents on our sense organs and hence mere apparitions, Democritus said: "Sweet and bitter, cold and warm, as well as the colors, all these exist but in opinion and not in reality; what really exists are unchangeable particles, atoms, which move in empty space." Following his lead, the founders of modern science, Kepler, Galileo, Newton, Huygens, with the approval of the philosophers, Descartes, Hobbes, Locke, discarded the sense qualities, on account of their subjectivity, as building material of the objective world which our perceptions reflect. But they clung to the objectivity of space, time, matter, and hence of motion and the corresponding geometric and kinematic concepts. Thus Huygens, who developed the undulatory theory of light, could say with the best of conscience that colored light beams are in reality oscillations of an ether consisting of tiny particles. But soon the objectivity of space and time also became suspect.

Today we find it hard to realize why their intuition was thought particularly trustworthy. Fortunately, Descartes's analytic geometry had provided the tool which enabled us to get rid of them and to replace them by numbers, that is, mere symbols. At the same time one learned how to introduce such concealed characters, as the inertial mass of a body, not by defining them explicitly but by postulating certain simple laws to which one subjects the observation of reacting bodies. The upshot of it all is a purely symbolic construction that uses as its material nothing but mind's free creations: symbols.

The monochromatic beam of light which for Huygens was in reality an ether wave has now become a formula expressing a certain undefined symbol F, called electromagnetic field, as a mathematically defined function of four other symbols, x, y, z, and t, called space-time coordinates. It is evident that now the words "in reality" must be put between quotation marks. Who could seriously pretend that the symbolic construct *is* the true real world? Objective being, reality, becomes elusive, and science no longer claims to erect a sublime, truly objective world above the Slough of Despond in which our daily life moves. Of course, in some way one must establish the connection between the symbols and our perceptions. Here the symbolically expressed laws of nature rather than any explicit intuitive definitions of the significance of the symbols play a fundamental role, as also do the concretely described procedures of observation and measurement.

In this manner a theory of nature emerges which only as a whole can be confronted with experience, while the individual laws of which it consists, when taken in isolation have no verifiable content. This is not in accord with the traditional idea of truth which looks at the relation between being and knowing from the side of being, and which may perhaps be formulated as follows: "A statement points to a fact, and it is true if the fact to which it points is just what it states." The truth of physical theory is of a different brand.

Quantum theory has gone even a step farther. It has shown that observation always amounts to an uncontrollable intervention, since measurement of one quantity irretrievably destroys the possibility of measuring certain other quantities. Thereby the objective being which we hope to construct as one big piece of cloth, each time tears off; what is left in our hands are rags.

The notorious man-in-the-street with his common sense will undoubtedly feel a little dizzy when he sees what thus becomes of that reality which seems to surround him in such firm, reliable, and unquestionable shape in his daily life. But we must point out to him that the constructions of physics are only a natural prolongation of operations which his own mind performs, though mainly unconsciously, in perception when, for example, the solid shape of a body constitutes itself as the common source of its various perspective views. For a person who can assume any one of a continuum of possible positions, these views are conceived as appearances of an entity on the next higher level of objectivity, that of the three-dimensional body. Carry on this constitutive process in which one rises from level to level and one will come to the symbolic constructs of physics. The whole edifice rests on a foundation essential to all reasonable thinking: of our complete experience it uses only that which is unmistakably *aufweisbar.*

I hope I will be pardoned by using the German word. I will explain it by reference to the foundations of mathematics. We have come to realize that isolated statements of classical mathematics in most cases make as little sense as do the statements of physics. Thus it has become necessary to change mathematics from a system of meaningful propositions into a game of formulas which is played according to certain rules. The formulas are composed of certain clearly distinguishable symbols, as concrete as the men on a chess board. Intuitive reasoning is required and used merely for establishing the consistency of the game—a task which so far has only partially been accomplished and which we may never succeed in finishing. The visible tokens employed as symbols must be, to borrow David Hilbert's words, "recognizable with certainty, independently of time and place, and independently of minor differences and the material conditions of their execution (e.g., whether written by pencil on paper or by chalk on blackboard)." It is also essential that they should be reproducible wherever and whenever needed.

Here is the prototype of what we consider as *aufweisbar*, something to which we can point *in concreto*. The inexactitude which is inseparable from continuity and thus clings inevitably to any spatial configuration is overcome here in principle, since only clearly distinguishable marks are used and slight modifications are ignored "as not affecting their identity." Of course, even so, errors are not excluded. When putting such symbols one behind the other in a formula, like letters in a printed word, one obviously employs space and spatial intuition in a way quite different from a procedure that makes space in the sense of Euclidean geometry with its exact straight lines one of the bases on which knowledge rests, as Kant does. The *Aufweisbare* we start with is not such a pure distillate, it is much more concrete.

Also the physicist's measurements, for example, the reading of a pointer, are operations performed in the *Aufweisbaren*—although here one has to take the approximate character of all measurements into account. Physical theory sets the mathematical formulas consisting of symbols into relation with the results of concrete measurements.

4

At this juncture I wish to mention two collections of essays by the mathematician and philosopher, Kurt Reidemeister, published in 1953 and 1954 under the titles *Geist und Wirklichkeit* and *Die Unsachlichkeit der Existenzphilosophie*. The most important of the essays is the "Prolegomena zu einer kritischen Philosophie," in the first volume. Reidemeister is a positivist inasmuch as he maintains the irremissible nature of the factual which science determines; he ridicules (rightly, I think) such profound-sounding but hollow evocations as Martin Heidegger indulges in, especially in his last publications. On the other hand, by his insistence that science does not make use of our full experience but selects from it that which is *aufweisbar,* Reidemeister makes room for such other types of experience as are claimed by the windbags of profundity as their proper territory: the experience of the indisposable significant in contrast to the disposable factual.

Here belongs the intuition through and in which the beautiful, whether incorporated in a vase, a piece of music, or a poem, appears and becomes transparent, and the reasonable experience governing our dealings and communications with other people, for instance, the ease with which we recognize and answer a smile. Of course, the physical and the esthetic properties of a sculpture are related to each other; the sculptor is exacting with respect to the geometric properties of his work because the desired esthetic effect depends on them. The same connection is perhaps even more obvious in the field of acoustics. Reidemeister, however, urges us to admit our *Nicht-Wissen,* our not knowing how to combine these two sides of theory into one unified realm of being—just as we cannot see through the union of I, the conditioned individual, and I who through thinking am free.

This *Nicht-Wissen* is the protecting wall behind which Reidemeister wants to save the indisposable significant from the grasp of hollow profundity and restore our inner freedom for a genuine apprehension of ideas. Perhaps I overrate Reidemeister's attempt, which no doubt is still in a pretty sketchy state, when I say that, just as Kant's philosophy was based on and made to fit Newton's physics, so his attempt takes the present status of the foundations of mathematics as its lead. And as Kant supplements his *Critique of Pure Reason* by one of practical reason and of esthetic judgment, so Reidemeister's analysis leaves room for other experiences than those science makes use of, in particular for the hermeneutic understanding and interpretation on which history is based.

The first philosopher who fully realized the significance of hermeneutics as the basic method of history was Wilhelm Dilthey. He traced it back to the exegesis of the Holy Scriptures. The chapter on history in Cassirer's *Essay on Man* is one of the most successful recent treatments. He rejects the assumption of a special historical logic or reason as advanced by Wilhelm Windelband or more recently and much more impetuously by Ortega y Gasset. According to him, the essential difference between history and such branches of science as paleontology which deal with singular phenomena lies in the necessity for the historian to interpret his "petrefacts," his monuments and documents, as having symbolic content.

5

Finally, I come to this conclusion: at the basis of all knowledge there lies, first, intuition, mind's ordinary act of seeing what is given, limited in the sciences to the *Aufweisbare,* but in fact extending far beyond. How far one should go in including the *Wesensschau* of Edmund Husserl's phenomenology, I prefer to leave in the dark. Beside intuition there lie, second, understanding and expression. Even in Hilbert's formalized mathematics one must understand directions given in words on how to handle the symbols and formulae. Expression is the active counterpart of passive understanding. Beside these there lies, third, the thinking of the possible. In science a very stringent form of it is exercised when by thinking out the possibilities of the mathematical game, we try to make sure that the game will never lead to a contradiction; a much freer form is the imagination by which theories are conceived. Here, of course, lies a source of subjectivity for the direction in which science develops. As Albert Einstein once admitted, there is no logical path leading from experience to theory, and yet the decision as to which theories are adopted turns out ultimately to be unambiguous. Imagination of the possible is of equal importance for the historian who tries to reenliven the past.

On the basis of intuition, understanding, and thinking of the possible, we have in science certain practical actions, namely the construction of symbols and formulae on the mathematical side, the construction of the measuring devices on the empirical side. There is no analogue for this in history. Here its place is taken by hermeneutic interpretation which ultimately springs from the inner awareness and knowledge of myself. Therefore the work of a great historian depends on the richness and depth of his own inner experience. Cassirer finds wonderful words of praise for Leopold von Ranke's intellectual and imaginative nonemotional sympathy, the universality of which enabled him to write the history of the Popes and of the Reformation, of the Ottomans and the Spanish Monarchy.

Being and knowing, where should we look for unity? I have tried to make clear that the shield of being is broken beyond repair. We need not shed too many tears about it. Even the world of our daily life is not *one,* to the extent people are inclined to assume; it would not be difficult to show up some of its cracks. Only in knowing may there be unity. Indeed, mind in the fullness of its experience has unity. Whoever says "I" points to it. But just because it is unity, I am unable to describe it otherwise than by such characteristic actions of the mind mutually supporting each other as I have enumerated. Here I feel that I am closer to the unity of the luminous center than where Cassirer hoped to catch it in the complex symbolic creations which his lumen built up on the history of mankind. For these—and in particular myth, religion, and, alas, philosophy—are rather turbid filters for the light of truth, by virtue or perhaps I should say by vice of man's infinite capacity for self-deception.

What then besides turbidity can be expected from such a brief philosophical essay as this? If it is aimless, let me make a confession before I ask your pardon. The reading of Reidemeister's essay has caused me to think over the old epistemological problems with which my own writings have dealt in the past, and I have not yet won through to a new clarity. Indecision of mind does not make for coherence, but would one not cease to be a philosopher if he ceased to live in a state of wonder and mental suspense?

Translator unknown

Erwin Schrödinger

Science, Art, and Play

With man, as with every other species, the primary aim of thought and action is to satisfy his needs and to preserve his life. Unless the conditions of life are excessively unfavorable, there remains a surplus force; and this is true even of animals. Even with animals, this surplus manifests itself in play; an animal when playing is conscious of the fact that its activity is not directed towards any aim or towards the satisfaction of the needs of life. A ball of wool interests and amuses the kitten, but it does not hope to find any hidden dainty within. The dog continues to roll the beslavered stone and his eyes implore us to throw it again: "Put an aim before me; I have none and would like to have one." With man the same surplus of force produces an intellectual play by the side of the physical play or sport. Instances of such intellectual play are games in the ordinary sense, like card games, board games, dominoes, or riddles, and I should also count among them every kind of intellectual activity as well as Science; and if not the whole of Science at any rate the advance guard of Science, by which I mean research work proper.

Play, art and science are the spheres of human activity where action and aim are not as a rule determined by the aims imposed by the necessities of life; and even in the exceptional instances where this is the case, the creative artist or the investigating scientist soon forget this fact—as indeed they must forget it if their work is to prosper. Generally, however, the aims are chosen freely by the artist or student himself, and are superfluous; it would cause no immediate harm if these aims were not pursued. What is operating here is a surplus force remaining at our disposal beyond the bare struggle for existence: art and science are thus luxuries like sport and play, a view more acceptable to the beliefs of former centuries than to the present age. It was a privilege of princes and flourishing republics to draw artists and scientists within their sphere, and to give them a living in exchange for an activity which yielded nothing save entertainment, interest and repute for the prince or the city. In every age such procedure has been regarded as a manifestation of internal strength and health, and the rulers and peoples have been envied who could afford to indulge in this noble luxury, this source of pure and lofty pleasure.

If this view is accepted we are compelled to see the chief and lofty aim of science to-day, as in every other age, in the fact that it enhances the general joy of living. It is the duty of a teacher of science to impart to his listeners knowledge which will prove useful in their professions; but it should also be his intense desire to do it in such a way as to cause them pleasure. It should cause him at least as much satisfaction to speak before an audience of working men who have taken an hour off their leisure time in the hope of obtaining an intellectual joy as to speak before the engineers of an industrial undertaking who may be supposed to be chiefly concerned with the practical exploitation of the most recent results of scientific investigation. I need not here speak of the quality of the pleasures derived from pure knowledge; those who have experienced it will know that it contains a strong esthetic element and is closely related to that derived from the contemplation of a work of art. Those who have never experienced it cannot understand it; but that is no reason why they should "withdraw weeping from our community," since it may be supposed that they find compensation elsewhere within the sphere of art—as, for example, in the free and vigorous exercise of a well-trained body in sport, play or dance. Speaking generally, we may say that all this belongs to the same category—to the free unfolding of noble powers which remain available, beyond purely utilitarian activities, to cause pleasure to the individual and to others.

It might be objected that after all there is a considerable difference between scientific and artistic and even more between scientific and playful activity, the difference residing in the fact that scientific activity has a powerful influence on the practical shaping of life and the satisfaction of its needs. It might be said that it had eminently contributed to material well-being and that the doctor's and the engineer's skill and the judge's and statesman's wisdom are the fruit it bears; and it may be urged that, on a serious view, these fruits in which the whole of mankind can share are of a higher value than the pleasures of study and discovery, which are open to a few privileged men and their listeners and readers. It might, on the other hand, be felt that the equation of these pleasures with art is slightly arrogant. Moreover, are we seriously to regard the practical results of science as the acceptable by-products of learned leisure? Should not rather the joys of research be regarded as the pleasant accompaniment of a work which in itself, so far from being playful, is entirely grave and devoted to practical aims?

Judgments of value are problematical. There can be no discussion as to the thanks due by mankind to modern surgery, and to the men who have combated epidemic diseases. Yet it should not be forgotten that the advances of surgery were an antidote desperately needed against the advances of applied science, which would be almost unbearable without the relief provided by the surgeon's ready hand. I do not wish to speak ill of the advances of applied science; indeed it seems to me that one of the chief claims to fame of modern applied science is that it disregards material welfare and personal security and promotes and even creates purely intellectual values which exist for their own sake and not for any given material purpose. I have here in mind chiefly, because this seems to me to be the most important point, the overcoming of distances in order to promote communication and understanding. I admit that this overcoming of distances has its material aspects. A merchant in Hamburg can reach New York in four days; he learns the exchange quotations daily on board by wireless, can give instructions to his office, and so on. But are we, mankind in general, really interested so very much in the rapidity of business transactions? I venture to deny it. What we really have at heart is something very different. What really gives us pleasure is something very different: far more people than formerly can visit different countries; the nations are brought nearer to each other, can appreciate each other's civilizations, and learn to understand each other. Daring men can penetrate into the polar ice without our being compelled to feel anxiety during months and years; for we receive signals from them, we know where they are, and we can render them assistance. Last, not least, the pure technical pleasure of overcoming difficulties, the pleasure of succeeding, apart from practical advantages, is continually winning a greater place, not only in the minds of those immediately concerned, for these probably experienced it at all times, but also in the minds of entire peoples. The Zeppelin and the Blue Ribbon of the Atlantic obtained for Germany a reputation kindred to that obtained by Walther, Tasso, and Ariosto for the courts where they wrote their poetry.

These and similar considerations lead to the conviction that science with all its consequences is not such a desperately serious affair and that, all things considered, it contributes less to material well-being than is generally assumed, while it contributes more than is generally assumed to purely ideal pleasures. True, its effect on the multitude is generally indirect and the occasions are rare when science can give joy to the many by laying before it its immediate results: indeed, this happens only in those cases where it lays before the community a work of art. At any rate those who have stood with bated breath and trembling knees before the two thousand years' old dream of beauty created of white marble which the industry of archeologists has erected in the Berlin Museum will consider that at least as far as the science of archeology is concerned the question as to why it is being pursued has been answered. As a rule the way to the masses is long and less direct and in certain rare cases it may appear as though a complete barrier existed. However, we would ask that the right to exist should be acknowledged even for these distant blossoms on the Tree of Knowledge; our reason being that they must first fertilize each other in order that other branches shall be able to bear such obvious fruits, palpable to the entire community, as the Graf Zeppelin or the Pergamon Altar.

From a certain standpoint, indeed, the number of individuals sharing in a given cultural achievement is really irrelevant. The truth is that arithmetic cannot be applied to matters of the mind any more than to any other manifestation of life: multiplication here becomes impossible. Once a thought has flashed in the thinker's brain it is in existence and is not increased in value by the fact that a hundred other brains follow it. This argument is correct; yet the fact must be remembered that we are not dealing with a single achievement of civilization or a single sphere of ideas, but with a multiplicity; and for this reason it is desirable even from the purely esoteric and scientific point of view that the approaches to these intellectual treasures should be facilitated and thrown open to the greatest possible number of persons, even if they partake of them less completely than the "initiated." In this manner there is an increasing chance that a number of cultural values may become the property, in favorable circumstances, of one individual; and this amounts to a real "multiplication" of cultural values, and indeed to more than that. When thoughts fructify they lead to new and undreamed of developments.

It is sometimes said that physics is today in a stage of transformation and revolution; a stage described by some as a crisis. Such a stage is one of abnormal activity and of enhanced vital power. Linguistically the expression "crisis" (the Greek χρίσις equals "decision") is appropriate; yet it is misleading if it suggests anything resembling a crisis in a business undertaking, a cabinet, or in the course of a disease. In these cases we are thinking of a dangerous stage of decision followed by complete collapse; whereas in science we mean that new facts or ideas have occurred which compel us to take up a definite position in questions which had hitherto been open or, more frequently, had never passed beyond a kind of vague awareness. It is precisely our desire to be compelled to take up a definitive position; and in the exact sciences such a compulsion is frequently enough brought about deliberately by so-called crucial experiments. The more important the issue happens to be, the "worse" the "crisis" will be; and the more certainly will it lead to an extension and illumination of our scientific knowledge. I admit that the critical stage itself bears a certain similarity to the feverish stages of an illness, which is due to the sudden upsetting of opinions which had hitherto been regarded as secure; a learned delirium is no rarity. But the comparison is invalid unless we add that in the case of science the disease guarantees the patient a freer, happier, and more intensive life on his recovery. To infer from the crisis in individual sciences that there is such a thing as a general twilight of science is a mistake resting upon a confusion of words.

But though we have grasped that this critical stage is not abnormal, and still less is any harbinger of disaster, we are still faced by the question why it is that the transvaluation of all values, which is really a permanent phenomenon, has taken such an acute form not in one science, but in many, and perhaps in most. Such is the case in mathematics, chemistry, astronomy and psychology. Can this be an accident?

In experimental science facts of the greatest importance are rarely discovered accidentally: more frequently new ideas point the way toward them. The ideas which form the background of the individual sciences have an internal inter-connection, but they are also firmly connected with each other and with the ideas of the age in a far more primitive manner. This inter-connection consists in the simple fact that a far from negligible and steadily growing percentage of the men who devote themselves to scientific studies are also human beings who share in the general world of ideas of the age. The influence of these ideas can often be traced into unexpected ramifications. Thus some years ago astronomy was threatened with a kind of arterio-sclerosis due to the fact that no crisis was on the horizon; and it was saved from this phenomenon of old age, not so much by the perfection of its instruments and by the progress made by physics in the interpretation of astral spectra, as by a new and a wholly independent idea. It was suggested that really new discoveries could be reached not by careful study of individual stars, but by comparative statistics applied to vast groups of stars. This idea, which is so clearly connected with other tendencies of the times, has opened up vast new tracts and has extended our apprehension of space almost to infinity.

Our age is possessed by a strong urge toward the criticism of traditional customs and opinions. A new spirit is arising which is unwilling to accept anything on authority, which does not so much permit as demand independent, rational thought on every subject, and which refrains from hampering any attack based upon such thought, even though it be directed against things which formerly were considered to be sacrosanct as you please. In my opinion this spirit is the common cause underlying the crisis of every science today. Its results can only be advantageous: no scientific structure falls entirely into ruin: what is worth preserving preserves itself and requires no protection.

In my opinion this is true not only of science: it is of a far more universal application. There is never any need to oppose the assaults of the spirit of the age: that which is fit to live will successfully resist.

Translator unknown

Albert Einstein

Principles of Research

In the temple of Science are many mansions, and various indeed are they that dwell therein and the motives that have led them thither. Many take to science out of a joyful sense of superior intellectual power; science is their own special sport to which they look for vivid experience and the satisfaction of ambition; many others are to be found in the temple who have offered the products of their brains on this altar for purely utilitarian purposes. Were an angel of the Lord to come and drive all the people belonging to those two categories out of the temple, it would be noticeably emptier, but there would still be some men, of both present and past times, left inside. Our Planck is one of them, and that is why we love him.

I am quite aware that we have just now lightheartedly expelled in imagination many excellent men who are largely, perhaps chiefly, responsible for the building of the temple of Science; and in many cases our angel would find it a pretty ticklish job to decide. But of one thing I feel sure: if the types we have just expelled were the only types there were, the temple would never have existed, any more than one can have a wood consisting of nothing but creepers. For these people any sphere of human activity will do, if it comes to a point; whether they become officers, tradesmen or scientists depends on circumstances. Now let us have another look at those who have found favor with the angel. Most of them are somewhat odd, uncommunicative, solitary fellows, really less like each other, in spite of these common characteristics, than the hosts of the rejected. What has brought them to the temple? That is a difficult question and no single answer will cover it. To begin with I believe with Schopenhauer that one of the strongest motives that lead men to art and science is escape from everyday life with its painful crudity and hopeless dreariness, from the fetters of one's own ever shifting desires. A finely tempered nature longs to escape from personal life into the world of objective perception and thought; this desire may be compared with the townsman's irresistible longing to escape from his noisy, cramped surroundings into the silence of high mountains, where the eye ranges freely through the still, pure air and fondly traces out the restful contours apparently built for eternity. With this negative motive there goes a personal one. Man tries to make for himself in the fashion that suits him best a simplified and intelligible picture of the world; he then tries to some extent to substitute this cosmos of his for the world of experience, and thus to overcome it. This is what the painter, the poet, the speculative philosopher and the natural scientist do, each in his own fashion. He makes this cosmos and its construction the pivot of his emotional life, in order to find in this way the peace and security which he cannot find in the narrow whirlpool of personal experience.

What place does the theoretical physicist's picture of the world occupy among all these possible pictures? It demands the highest possible standard of rigorous precision in the description of relations, such as only the use of mathematical language can give. In regard to his subject matter, on the other hand, the physicist has to limit himself very severely: he must content himself with describing the most simple events which can be brought within the domain of our experience; all events of a more complex order are beyond the power of the human intellect to reconstruct with the subtle accuracy and logical perfection which the theoretical physicist demands. Supreme purity, clarity and certainty at the cost of completeness. But what can be the attraction of getting to know such a tiny section of nature thoroughly, while one leaves everything subtler and more complex shyly and timidly alone? Does the product of such a modest effort deserve to be called by the proud name of a theory of the Universe?

In my belief the name is justified; for the general laws on which the structure of theoretical physics is based claim to be valid for any natural phenomenon whatsoever. With them, it ought to be possible to arrive at the description, that is to say, the theory, of every natural process, including life, by means of pure deduction, if that process of deduction were not far beyond the capacity of the human intellect. The physicist's renunciation of completeness for his cosmos is therefore not a matter of fundamental principle.

The supreme task of the physicist is to arrive at those universal elementary laws from which the cosmos can be built up by pure deduction. There is no logical path to these laws; only intuition, resting on sympathetic understanding of experience, can reach them. In this methodological uncertainty, one might suppose that there were any number of possible systems of theoretical physics all with an equal amount to be said for them; and this opinion is no doubt correct, theoretically. But evolution has shown that at any given moment, out of all conceivable constructions, a single one has always proved itself absolutely superior to all the rest. Nobody who has really gone deeply into the matter will deny that in practice the world of phenomena uniquely determines the theoretical system, in spite of the fact that there is no logical bridge between phenomena and their theoretical principles; this is what Leibniz described so happily as a "pre-established harmony." Physicists often accuse epistemologists of not paying sufficient attention to this fact. Here, it seems to me, lie the roots of the controversy carried on some years ago between Mach and Planck.

The longing to behold this pre-established harmony is the source of the inexhaustible patience and endurance with which Planck has devoted himself, as we see, to the most general problems of our science, refusing to let himself be diverted to more grateful and more easily attained ends. I have often heard colleagues try to attribute this attitude of his to extraordinary will-power and discipline—wrongly, in my opinion. The state of mind which enables a man to do work of this kind is akin to that of the religious worshiper or the lover; the daily effort comes from no deliberate intention or program, but straight from the heart. There he sits, our beloved Planck, and smiles inside himself at my childish playing-about with the lantern of Diogenes. Our affection for him needs no threadbare explanation. May the love of science continue to illumine his path in the future and lead him to the solution of the most important problem in present-day physics, which he has himself posed and done so much to solve. May he succeed in uniting the quantum theory and electrodynamics in a single logical system.

Translated by Alan Harris

What Is the Theory of Relativity?

I gladly accede to the request of your colleague to write something for the *Times* on relativity. After the lamentable breakdown of the old active intercourse between men of learning, I welcome this opportunity of expressing my feelings of joy and gratitude towards the astronomers and physicists of England. It is thoroughly in keeping with the great and proud traditions of scientific work in your country that eminent scientists should have spent much time and trouble, and your scientific institutions have spared no expense, to test the implications of a theory which was perfected and published during the War in the land of your enemies. Even though the investigation of the influence of the gravitational field of the sun on light rays is a purely objective matter, I cannot forbear to express my personal thanks to my English colleagues for their work; for without it I could hardly have lived to see the most important implication of my theory tested.

We can distinguish various kinds of theories in physics. Most of them are constructive. They attempt to build up a picture of the more complex phenomena out of the materials of a relatively simple formal scheme from which they start out. Thus the kinetic theory of gases seeks to reduce mechanical, thermal and diffusional processes to movements of molecules—i.e., to build them up out of the hypothesis of molecular motion. When we say that we have succeeded in understanding a group of natural processes, we invariably mean that a constructive theory has been found which covers the processes in question.

Along with this most important class of theories there exists a second, which I will call "principle-theories." These employ the analytic, not the synthetic, method. The elements which form their basis and starting-point are not hypothetically constructed but empirically discovered ones, general characteristics of natural processes, principles that give rise to mathematically formulated criteria which the separate processes or the theoretical representations of them have to satisfy. Thus the science of thermodynamics seeks by analytical means to deduce necessary connections, which separate events have to satisfy, from the universally experienced fact that perpetual motion is impossible.

The advantages of the constructive theory are completeness, adaptability and clearness, those of the principle theory are logical perfection and security of the foundations.

The theory of relativity belongs to the latter class. In order to grasp its nature, one needs first of all to become acquainted with the principles on which it is based. Before I go into these, however, I must observe that the theory of relativity resembles a building consisting of two separate stories, the special theory and the general theory. The special theory, on which the general theory rests, applies to all physical phenomena with the exception of gravitation; the general theory provides the law of gravitation and its relations to the other forces of nature.

It has, of course, been known since the days of the ancient Greeks that in order to describe the movement of a body, a second body is needed to which the movement of the first is referred. The movement of a vehicle is considered in reference to the earth's surface, that of a planet to the totality of the visible fixed stars. In physics the body to which events are spatially referred is called the coordinate system. The laws of the mechanics of Galileo and Newton, for instance, can only be formulated with the aid of a coordinate system.

The state of motion of the coordinate system may not, however, be arbitrarily chosen, if the laws of mechanics are to be valid (it must be free from rotation and acceleration). A coordinate system which is admitted in mechanics is called an "inertial system." The state of motion of an inertial system is according to mechanics not one that is determined uniquely by nature. On the contrary, the following definition holds good: a coordinate system that is moved uniformly and in a straight line relatively to an inertial system is likewise an inertial system. By the "special principle of relativity" is meant the generalization of this definition to include any natural event whatever: thus, every universal law of nature which is valid in relation to a coordinate system C, must also be valid, as it stands, in relation to a coordinate system C′, which is in uniform translatory motion relatively to C.

The second principle, on which the special theory of relativity rests, is the "principle of the constant velocity of light in vacuo." This principle asserts that light in vacuo always has a definite velocity of propagation (independent of the state of motion of the observer or of the source of the light). The confidence which physicists place in this principle springs from the successes achieved by the electrodynamics of Clerk Maxwell and Lorentz.

Both the above-mentioned principles are powerfully supported by experience, but appear not to be logically reconcilable. The special theory of relativity finally succeeded in reconciling them logically by a modification of kinematics—i.e., of the doctrine of the laws relating to space and time (from the point of view of physics). It became clear that to speak of the simultaneity of two events had no meaning except in relation to a given coordinate system, and that the shape of measuring devices and the speed at which clocks move depend on their state of motion with respect to the coordinate system.

But the old physics, including the laws of motion of Galileo and Newton, did not fit in with the suggested relativist kinematics. From the latter, general mathematical conditions issued, to which natural laws had to conform, if the above-mentioned two principles were really to apply. To these, physics had to be adapted. In particular, scientists arrived at a new law of motion for (rapidly moving) mass points, which was admirably confirmed in the case of electrically charged particles. The most important upshot of the special theory of relativity concerned the inert mass of corporeal systems. It turned out that the inertia of a system necessarily depends on its energy-content, and this led straight to the notion that inert mass is simply latent energy. The principle of the conservation of mass lost its independence and became fused with that of the conservation of energy.

The special theory of relativity, which was simply a systematic development of the electrodynamics of Clerk Maxwell and Lorentz, pointed beyond itself, however. Should the independence of physical laws of the state of motion of the coordinate system be restricted to the uniform translatory motion of coordinate systems in respect to each other? What has nature to do with our coordinate systems and their state of motion? If it is necessary for the purpose of describing nature, to make use of a coordinate system arbitrarily introduced by us, then the choice of its state of motion ought to be subject to no restriction; the laws ought to be entirely independent of this choice (general principle of relativity).

The establishment of this general principle of relativity is made easier by a fact of experience that has long been known, namely that the weight and the inertia of a body are controlled by the same constant. (Equality of inertial and gravitational mass.) Imagine a coordinate system which is rotating uniformly with respect to an inertial system in the Newtonian manner. The centrifugal forces which manifest themselves in relation to this system must, according to Newton's teaching, be regarded as effects of inertia. But these centrifugal forces are, exactly like the forces of gravity, proportional to the masses of the bodies. Ought it not to be possible in this case to regard the coordinate system as stationary and the centrifugal forces as gravitational forces? This seems the obvious view, but classical mechanics forbid it.

This hasty consideration suggests that a general theory of relativity must supply the laws of gravitation, and the consistent following up of the idea has justified our hopes.

But the path was thornier than one might suppose, because it demanded the abandonment of Euclidean geometry. This is to say, the laws according to which fixed bodies may be arranged in space, do not completely accord with the spatial laws attributed to bodies by Euclidean geometry. This is what we mean when we talk of the "curvature of space." The fundamental concepts of the "straight line," the "plane," etc., thereby lose their precise significance in physics.

In the general theory of relativity the doctrine of space and time, or kinematics, no longer figures as a fundamental independent of the rest of physics. The geometrical behavior of bodies and the motion of clocks rather depend on gravitational fields, which in their turn are produced by matter.

The new theory of gravitation diverges considerably, as regards principles, from Newton's theory. But its practical results agree so nearly with those of Newton's theory that it is difficult to find criteria for distinguishing them which are accessible to experience. Such have been discovered so far:

(1) In the revolution of the ellipses of the planetary orbits round the sun (confirmed in the case of Mercury).
(2) In the curving of light rays by the action of gravitational fields (confirmed by the English photographs of eclipses).
(3) In a displacement of the spectral lines towards the red end of the spectrum in the case of light transmitted to us from stars of considerable magnitude.

The chief attraction of the theory lies in its logical completeness. If a single one of the conclusions drawn from it proves wrong, it must be given up; to modify it without destroying the whole structure seems to be impossible.

Let no one suppose, however, that the mighty work of Newton can really be superseded by this or any other theory. His great and lucid ideas will retain their unique significance for all time as the foundation of our whole modern conceptual structure in the sphere of natural philosophy.

Note: Some of the statements in your paper concerning my life and person owe their origin to the lively imagination of the writer. Here is yet another application of the principle of relativity for the delectation of the reader:—Today I am described in Germany as a "German savant," and in England as a "Swiss Jew." Should it ever be my fate to be represented as a *bête noire,* I should, on the contrary, become a "Swiss Jew" for the Germans and a "German savant" for the English.

Translated by Alan Harris

Max Planck

The Universe in the Light of Modern Physics

1

Physics is an exact science and hence depends upon measurement, while all measurement itself requires sense perception. Consequently all the ideas employed in physics are derived from the world of sense perception. It follows from this that the laws of physics ultimately refer to events in the world of the senses; and in view of this fact many scientists and philosophers tend to the belief that at bottom physics is concerned exclusively with this particular world. What they have in mind, of course, is the world of man's senses. On this view, for example, what is called an "object" in ordinary parlance is, when regarded from the standpoint of physics, simply a combination of different sense data localized in one place. It is worth pointing out that this view cannot be refuted by logic, since logic itself is unable to lead us beyond the confines of our own senses; it cannot even compel one to admit the independent existence of others outside oneself.

In physics, however, as in every other science, common sense alone is not supreme; there must also be a place for reason. Further, the mere absence of logical contradiction does not necessarily imply that everything is reasonable. Now reason tells us that if we turn our back upon a so-called object and cease to attend to it, the object still continues to exist. Reason tells us further that both the individual man and mankind as a whole, together with the entire world which we apprehend through our senses, is no more than a tiny fragment in the vastness of nature, whose laws are in no way affected by any human brain. On the contrary, they existed long before there was any life on earth, and will continue to exist long after the last physicist has perished.

It is considerations of this kind, and not any logical argument, that compel us to assume the existence of another world of reality behind the world of the senses; a world which has existence independent of man, and which can only be perceived indirectly through the medium of the world of the senses, and by means of certain symbols which our senses allow us to apprehend. It is as though we were compelled to contemplate a certain object in which we are interested through spectacles of whose optical properties we were entirely ignorant.

If the reader experiences difficulty in following this argument, and finds himself unable to accept the idea of a real world which at the same time is expressly asserted to lie beyond our senses, we might point out that there is a vast difference between a physical theory complete in every detail, and the construction of such a theory. In the former case the content of the theory can be analyzed exactly, so that it is possible to prove at every point that the notions which we apply to the world of sense are adequate to the formulation of this theory; in the latter case we must develop a theory from a number of individual measurements. The second problem is very much more difficult, while the history of physics shows that whenever it has been solved, this has been done on the assumption of a real world independent of our senses; and it seems reasonably certain that this will continue to be the case in the future.

But besides the world of sense and the real world, there is also a third world which must be carefully distinguished from these: the world of physics. It differs from the two others because it is a deliberate hypothesis put forward by a finite human mind; and as such, it is subject to change and to a kind of evolution. Thus the function of this world of physics may be described in two ways, according as it is related to the real world, or to the world of the senses. In the first case the problem is to apprehend the real world as completely as possible; in the second, to describe the world of the senses in the simplest possible terms. There is no need, however, to assign superior merit to either of these formulations, since each of them, taken by itself alone, is incomplete and unsatisfactory. On the one hand, the real world cannot be apprehended directly at all; while on the other no definite answer is possible to the question: Which is the simplest description of a given number of interdependent sense perceptions? In the history of physics it has happened more than once that, of two descriptions, one was for a time considered the more complicated but was later discovered to be the simpler of the two.

The essential point therefore is that these two formulations of the problem, when practically applied, shall be complementary to each other and not contradictory. The first is an indispensable aid to the groping imagination of the investigator, supplying him with ideas without which his work remains unfruitful; the second provides him with a firm foundation of facts. In actual practice individual physicists are influenced in their investigations by their personal preference for metaphysical, or for positivist, ideas. But besides the metaphysicians and the positivists there is a third group of students who investigate the world from the physical point of view. They differ from the first two groups in being interested not so much in the relation between the world of physics, on the one hand, and the real world and the world of sense data, on the other, as in the internal consistency and logical structure of the world of physics. These men form the axiomatic school, whose activity is as necessary and useful as is that of the others. At the same time, they are equally exposed to the danger of specialization which, in their case, would lead to a barren formalism taking the place of a fuller understanding of the world of physics. For as soon as contact with reality has been lost, physical law ceases to be felt as the relation between a number of magnitudes which have been ascertained independently of one another, and becomes a mere definition by which one of these magnitudes is derived from the others. In this method there is a particular attraction, due to the fact that a physical magnitude can be defined far more exactly by means of an equation than by means of measurement. But at the same time, this method amounts to a renunciation of the true meaning of magnitude; while it must also be remembered that confusion and misunderstanding result when the same name is retained in order to denote a changed meaning.

We see, then, how physicists are at work in different directions and from different standpoints in elaborating a systematic view of the world of physics. Nevertheless the aim of all these endeavors is the same, and consists in establishing a law which connects the events of the world of sense with one another and with those of the real world. Naturally, these different tendencies predominated in turn at different stages of history. Whenever the physical world presented a stable appearance, as in the second half of the last century, the metaphysical view tended to predominate, and it was believed that a complete grasp of the real world was relatively near. Conversely, in times of change and insecurity like the present, positivism tends to occupy the foreground; for in such times a careful student will tend to seek support where he can find real security; and this is to be found precisely in the events of the world of the senses.

Now if we consider the different forms which the view of the physical world has taken in the course of history, and if we look for the peculiarities which characterized these changes, two facts will strike us with special force. First, it is plain that when regarded as a whole, all the changes in the different views of the world of physics do not constitute a rhythmical swing of the pendulum. On the contrary, we find a clear course of evolution making more or less steady progress in a definite direction; progress which is best described by saying that it adds to the content of the world of sense, rendering our knowledge more profound and giving us a firmer grasp of it. The most striking instance of this is found in the practical application of physics. Not even the most confirmed skeptic can deny that we see and hear at a greater distance and command greater forces and speeds than an earlier generation; while it is equally certain that this progress is an enduring increase of knowledge, which is in no danger of being described as an error and rejected at any future date.

Secondly, it is a very striking fact that the impulse toward simplification and improvement of the world picture of physics was due in each instance to some kind of novel observation—that is, to some event in the world of sense. But at the same moment the structure of this physical world consistently moved farther and farther away from the world of sense and lost its former anthropomorphic character. Still further, physical sensations have been progressively eliminated, as for example in physical optics, in which the human eye no longer plays any part at all. Thus the physical world has become progressively more and more abstract; purely formal mathematical operations play a growing part, while qualitative differences tend to be explained more and more by means of quantitative differences.

Now we have already pointed out that the physical view of the world has been continually perfected and also related to the world of sense. If this fact is added to those mentioned in the last paragraph, the result is extraordinarily striking; at first, indeed, it appears completely paradoxical. Of this apparent paradox there is, in my opinion, only one rational explanation. This consists in saying that as the view of the physical world is perfected, it simultaneously recedes from the world of sense; and this process is tantamount to an approach to the world of reality. I have no logical proof on which to base this opinion; it is impossible to demonstrate the existence of the real world by purely rational methods: but at the same time it is equally impossible ever to refute it by logical methods. The final decision must rest upon a common-sense view of the world, and the old maxim still remains true that that world view is the best which is the most fruitful. Physics would occupy an exceptional position among all the other sciences if it did not recognize the rule that the most far-reaching and valuable results of investigation can only be obtained by following a road leading to a goal which is theoretically unobtainable. This goal is the apprehension of true reality.

2

What changes have taken place in the physical view of the world during the last twenty years? We all know that the changes which have occurred during this period are among the most profound that have ever risen in the evolution of any science; we also know that the process of change has not yet come to an end. Nevertheless, it would appear that in this flux of change certain characteristic forms of the structure of this new world are beginning to crystallize; and it is certainly worth while to attempt a description of these forms, if only in order to suggest certain improvements.

If we compare the old theory with the new, we find that the process of tracing back all qualitative distinctions to quantitative distinctions has been advanced very considerably. All the various chemical phenomena, for example, have now been explained by numerical and spatial relations. According to the modern view there are no more than two ultimate substances, namely, positive and negative electricity. Each of these consists of a number of minute particles, similar in nature and with similar charges of an opposite character; the positive particle is called the proton, the negative the electron. Every chemical atom that is electrically neutral consists of a number of protons cohering with one another, and of a similar number of electrons, some of which are firmly fixed to the protons, together with which they form the nucleus of the atom, while the rest revolve around the nucleus.

Thus the hydrogen atom, the smallest of all, has one proton for nucleus and one electron revolving round the nucleus; while the largest atom, uranium, contains 238 protons and 238 electrons; but only 92 electrons revolve round the nucleus while the others are fixed in it. Between these two atoms lie all the other elements, with many kinds of different combinations. The chemical properties of an element depend, not on the total number of its protons or electrons, but on the number of revolving electrons, which yield the atomic number of the element.

Apart from this important advance, which is however merely the successful application of an idea first evolved many centuries ago, there are two completely new ideas which distinguish the modern conception of the world from its predecessor; these are the theory of relativity, and the quantum theory. It is these two ideas which are peculiarly characteristic of the new world of physics. The fact that they appeared in science almost simultaneously is something of a coincidence; for their content, as well as their practical effect upon the structure of the physical view of the world, are entirely different.

The theory of relativity seemed at first to introduce a certain amount of confusion into the traditional ideas of time and space; in the long run, however, it has proved to be the completion and culmination of the structure of classical physics. To express the positive results of the special theory of relativity in a single word, it might be described as the fusion of time and space in one unitary concept. It is not, of course, asserted that time and space are absolutely similar in nature; their relation resembles that between a real number and an imaginary number, when these are combined together to form the unified concept of a complex number. Looked at in this way, Einstein's work for physics closely resembles that of Gauss for mathematics. We might further continue the comparison by saying that the transition from the special to the general theory of relativity is the counterpart in physics to the transition from linear functions to the general theory of functions in mathematics.

Few comparisons are entirely exact, and the present is no exception to the rule. At the same time it gives a good idea of the fact that the introduction of the theory of relativity into the physical view of the world is one of the most important steps toward conferring unity and completeness. This appears clearly in the results of the theory of relativity, especially in the fusing of momentum and energy, in the identification of the concept of mass with the concept of energy, of inertial with ponderable mass, and in the reduction of the laws of gravitation to Riemann's geometry.

Brief though these main outlines are, they contain a vast mass of new knowledge. The new ideas mentioned apply to all natural events great and small, beginning with radioactive atoms emanating waves and corpuscles, and ending with the movements of celestial bodies millions of light-years away.

The last word on the theory of relativity probably still remains to be said. Surprises may yet await us, especially when we consider that the problem of amalgamating electrodynamics with mechanics has not yet been definitely solved. Again, the cosmological implications of the theory of relativity have not yet been fully cleared up, the chief reason being that everything depends upon the question whether or not the matter of outer space possesses a finite density; this question has not yet been answered. But whatever reply is eventually given to these questions, nothing will alter the fact that the principle of relativity has advanced the classical physical theory to its highest stage of completion, and that its world view is rounded off in a very satisfactory manner.

This fact will perhaps be a sufficient reason for devoting no more time to the theory of relativity; I might also point out that there are many treatises on the theory adapted to the requirements of readers of every kind.

3

The idea of the universe as thus far described appeared almost perfectly adapted to its purpose; but this state of affairs has suddenly been upset by the quantum theory. Here again I shall attempt to describe the characteristic idea of this hypothesis in one word. We may say, then, that its essence consists in the fact that it introduces a new and universal constant, namely the elementary quantum of action. It was this constant which, like a new and mysterious messenger from the real world, insisted on turning up in every kind of measurement, and continued to claim a place for itself. On the other hand, it seemed so incompatible with the traditional view of the universe provided by physics that it eventually destroyed the framework of this older view.

For a time it seemed that a complete collapse of classical physics was not beyond the bounds of possibility; gradually, however, it appeared, as had been confidently expected by all who believed in the steady advance of science, that the introduction of the quantum theory led not to the destruction of physics, but to a somewhat profound reconstruction, in the course of which the whole science was rendered more universal. For if the quantum of action is assumed to be infinitely small, quantum physics becomes merged in classical physics. In fact the foundations of the structure of classical physics not only proved unshakeable, but actually were rendered firmer through the incorporation of the new ideas. The best course, therefore, will be first to examine the latter.

It will be best to begin by enumerating the essential component features. These are the universal constants, e.g., the gravitational constant, the velocity of light, the mass and charge of electrons and protons. These are perhaps the most tangible symbols of a real world, and they retain their meaning unchanged in the new view of the universe. Further, we may mention the great principles of the conservation of energy and of momentum, which, although they were under suspicion for a time, have eventually emerged unimpaired. It should be emphasized that in this process of transition these principles were proved to be something more than mere definitions, as some members of the axiomatic school would like to believe. Further, we may mention the main laws of thermodynamics, and especially the second law, which through the introduction of an absolute value for entropy obtained a more exact formulation than it possessed in classical physics. Lastly we may point to the principle of relativity, which has proved itself a reliable and eloquent guide in the new regions of quantum physics.

The question may now be asked whether modern physics differs at all from the older physics, if all these foundations of classical physics have remained untouched. It is easy to find an answer to this question by examining the elementary quantum of action somewhat more closely. It implies that in principle an equation can be established between energy and frequency; $E = hv$.* It is this equation which classical physics utterly fails to explain. The fact itself is so baffling because energy and frequency possess different

---

*In this equation E stands for energy, and v for frequency, that is, the number of vibrations per second. For example, light vibrations range from about 400 million million per second to about 800 million million. h represents Planck's constant, discovered by the author of this work. It is an unchanging or invariable quantity, and extremely minute, its value being 655 preceded by 26 decimal places. [*Trans.*]

dimensions; energy is a dynamic magnitude, whereas frequency is a kinematic magnitude. This fact in itself, however, does not contain a contradiction. The quantum theory postulates a direct connection between dynamics and kinematics; this connection is due to the fact that the unit of energy, and consequently the unit of mass, are based upon the units of length and of time; thus the connection, so far from being a contradiction, enriches and rounds off the classical theory. There is, nevertheless, a direct contradiction, which renders the new theory incompatible with the classical theory. The following considerations make clear this contradiction. Frequency is a local magnitude, and has a definite meaning only for a certain point in space; this is true alike of mechanical, electric, and magnetic vibrations, so that all that is requisite is to observe the point in question for a sufficient time. Energy, on the other hand, is an additive quantity; so that according to the classical theory it is meaningless to speak of energy at a certain point, since it is essential to state the physical system the energy of which is under discussion; just as it is similarly impossible to speak of a definite velocity unless the system be indicated to which velocity is referred. Now we are at liberty to choose whatever physical system we please, either little or great; and consequently the value of the energy is always to a certain extent arbitrary. The difficulty, then, consists in the fact that this arbitrary energy is supposed to be equated with a localized frequency. The gulf between these two concepts should now be clearly apparent: and in order to bridge this gulf a step of fundamental importance must be taken. This step does imply a break with those assumptions which classical physics has always regarded and employed as axiomatic.

Hitherto it had been believed that the only kind of causality with which any system of physics could operate was one in which all the events of the physical world—by which, as usual, I mean not the real world but the world view of physics—might be explained as being composed of local events taking place in a number of individual and infinitely small parts of space. It was further believed that each of these elementary events was completely determined by a set of laws without respect to the other events; and was determined exclusively by the local events in its immediate temporal and spatial vicinity. Let us take a concrete instance of sufficiently general application. We will assume that the physical system under consideration consists of a system of particles, moving in a conservative field of force of constant total energy. Then according to classical physics each individual particle at any time is in a definite state; that is, it has a definite position and a definite velocity, and its movement can be calculated with perfect exactness from its initial state and from the local properties of the field of force in those parts of space through which the particle passes in the course of its movement. If these data are known, we need know nothing else about the remaining properties of the system of particles under consideration.

In modern mechanics matters are wholly different. According to modern mechanics, merely local relations are no more sufficient for the formulation of the law of motion than would be the microscopic investigation of the different parts of a picture in order to make clear its meaning. On the contrary, it is impossible to obtain an adequate version of the laws for which we are looking, unless the physical system is regarded *as a whole*. According to modern mechanics, each individual particle of the system, in a certain sense, at any one time, exists simultaneously in every part of the space occupied by the system. This simultaneous existence applies not merely to the field of force with which it is surrounded but also to its mass and its charge.

Thus we see that nothing less is at stake here than the concept of the particle—the most elementary concept of classical mechanics. We are compelled to give up the earlier essential meaning of this idea; only in a number of special borderline cases can we retain it. But if we pursue the line of thought indicated above, we shall find what is that we can substitute for the concept of the particle in more general cases.

The more accurately the position of the configuration point is ascertained, the less accurate is the amount of momentum; and conversely. These two kinds of uncertainty are thus in a certain sense complementary; this complementariness is limited by the fact that momentum can under certain conditions be defined with absolute accuracy in wave mechanics, whereas the position of a configuration point always remains uncertain within a finite region.

Now this relation of uncertainty, established by Heisenberg, is something quite unheard of in classical mechanics. It had always been known, of course, that every measurement is subject to a certain amount of inaccuracy; but it had always been assumed that an improvement in method would lead to an improvement in accuracy, and that this process could be carried on indefinitely. According to Heisenberg, however, there is a definite limit to the accuracy obtainable. What is most curious is that this limit does not affect position and velocity separately, but only the two when combined together. In principle, either taken by itself can be measured with absolute accuracy, but only at the cost of the accuracy of the other.

Strange as this assertion may seem, it is definitely established by a variety of facts. I will give one example to illustrate this. The most direct and accurate means of ascertaining the position of a particle consists in the optical method, when the particle is looked at with the naked eye or through a microscope, or else is photographed. Now for this purpose the particle in question must be illuminated. If this is done the definition becomes more accurate; consequently the measurement becomes more exact in proportion as the light waves employed become shorter and shorter. In this sense, then, any desired degree of accuracy can be attained. On the other hand there is also a disadvantage, which affects the measurement of velocity. Where the masses in question have a certain magnitude, the effect of light upon the illuminated object may be disregarded. But the case is altered if a very small mass, e.g., a single electron, is selected; because each ray of light, which strikes the electron and is reflected by it, gives it a distinct impulse; and the shorter the light wave the more powerful is this impulse. Consequently, the shorter the light wave the more accurately is it possible to determine position; but at the same moment measurement of velocity becomes proportionately inaccurate; and similarly in analogous instances.

On the view which has just been set out, classical mechanics, which is based on the assumption of unchanging and accurately measurable corpuscles moving with a definite velocity, forms one ideal limiting case. This ideal case is actually realized when the observed system possesses a relatively considerable energy. When this happens, the distinct characteristic energy values will lie close to each other, and a relatively small region of energy will contain a considerable number of high wave frequencies (i.e., of short wave lengths); through the superposition of these a small wave group with definite momentum can be delimited comparatively accurately within the configuration space. In this case, wave mechanics merges with the mechanics of particles; Schrödinger's differential equation becomes the classical differential equation of Hamilton and Jacobi, and the wave group travels in configuration space in accordance with the same laws which govern the motion of a system of particles according to classical mechanics. But this state of affairs is of a limited duration; for the individual material waves are not interfering continually in the same manner, and consequently the wave group will disintegrate more or less quickly; the position of the relative configuration point will become more and more uncertain, and finally the only quantity remaining that is accurately defined is the wave function ψ.

The question now arises whether these conclusions correspond with experience. Since the quantum of action is so small, this question can be answered only within the framework of atomic physics; consequently the methods employed will always be extremely delicate. At present we can only say that hitherto no fact has been discovered which throws doubt on the applicability in physics of all these conclusions.

The fact is that since the wave equation was first formulated, the theory has been developing at a most remarkable rate. It is impossible within the framework of a small volume to mention all the extensions and applications of the theory which have been evolved within recent years. I shall confine myself to the so-called stress of protons and electrons; the formulation of quantum mechanics in terms of relativity; the application of the theory to molecular problems, and the treatment of the so-called many-body problem, i.e., its application to a system containing a number of exactly similar particles. Here statistical questions, relating to the number of possible states within a system, having a given energy, are particularly important; they also have a bearing on the calculation of the entropy of the system.

Finally, I cannot here enter in detail upon the physics of light quanta. In a certain sense this study has developed in the opposite direction from the physics of particles. Originally Maxwell's theory of electromagnetic waves dominated this region, and it was not seen until later that we must assume the existence of discrete light particles; in other words that the electromagnetic waves, like the material waves, must be interpreted as waves of probability.

Perhaps there is no more impressive proof of the fact that a pure wave theory cannot satisfy the demands of modern physics any more than a pure corpuscular theory. Both theories, in fact, represent extreme limiting cases. The corpuscular theory, which is the basis of classical mechanics, does justice to the configuration of a system, but fails to determine the values of its energy and of momentum; conversely the wave theory, which is characteristic of classical electrodynamics, can give an account of energy and momentum, but excludes the idea of the localization of light particles. The standard case is represented by the intermediate region, where both theories play equally important parts; this region can be approached from either side, although at present a close approach is impossible. Here many obscure points await solution, and it remains to be seen which of the various methods employed for their solution best leads to the goal. Among them we may mention the matrix calculus invented by Heisenberg, Born, and Jordan, the wave theory due to De Broglie and Schrödinger, and the mathematics of the *q* numbers introduced by Dirac.

4

If we attempt to draw a comprehensive conclusion from the above description and to obtain an insight into the distinguishing characteristics of our new picture of the world, the first impression will no doubt be somewhat unsatisfactory. First of all it will appear surprising that wave mechanics, which itself is in complete contradiction to classical mechanics, nevertheless makes use of concepts drawn from the classical corpuscular theory; e.g., the concept of the coordinates and momentum of a particle, and of the kinetic and potential energy of a system of particles. The contradiction is the more surprising since it afterward proved impossible simultaneously to determine exactly the position and momentum of a particle. At the same time these concepts are absolutely essential to wave mechanics; for without them it would be impossible to define configuration space and ascertain its measurements.

There is another difficulty attached to the wave theory, consisting in the fact that material waves are not as easy to bring before the imagination as are acoustic or electromagnetic waves; for they exist in configuration space instead of ordinary space, and their period of vibration depends on the choice of the physical system to which they belong. The more extensive this system is assumed to be, the greater will be its energy, and with this the frequency.

It must be admitted that these are serious difficulties. It will be possible, however, to overcome them if two conditions are fulfilled: the new theory must be free from internal contradictions; and its applied results must be definite and of some significance for measurement. At the present time opinions are somewhat divided whether these requirements are fulfilled by quantum mechanics, and if so, to what extent. For this reason I propose to discuss this fundamental point further.

It has frequently been pointed out that quantum mechanics confines itself on principle to magnitudes and quantities which can be observed, and to questions which have a meaning within the sphere of physics. This observation is correct; but in itself it must not be considered a special advantage of the quantum theory as opposed to other theories. For the question whether a physical magnitude can in principle be observed, or whether a certain question has a meaning as applied to physics, can never be answered a priori, but only from the standpoint of a given theory. The distinction between the different theories consists precisely in the fact that according to one theory a certain magnitude can in principle be observed, and a certain question have a meaning as applied to physics; while according to the other theory this is not the case. For example, according to the theories of Fresnel and Lorentz, with their assumption of a stationary ether, the absolute velocity of the earth can in principle be observed; but according to the theory of relativity it cannot; again, the absolute acceleration of a body can be in principle observed according to Newtonian mechanics, but according to relativity mechanics it cannot. (Similarly the problem of the construction of a *perpetuum mobile* had a meaning before the principle of the conservation of energy was introduced, but ceased to have a meaning after its introduction.) The choice between these two opposed theories depends not upon the nature of the theories in themselves, but upon experience. Hence it is not sufficient to describe the superiority of quantum mechanics, as opposed to classical mechanics, by saying that it confines itself to quantities and magnitudes which can in principle be observed, for in its own way this is true also of classical mechanics. We must indicate the particular magnitudes or quantities which, according to quantum mechanics, are or are not in principle observed; after this has been done it remains to demonstrate that experience agrees with the assertion.

Now this demonstration has in fact been completed, e.g., with respect to Heisenberg's principle of uncertainty, so far as seems possible at the present moment, and to this extent it can be looked upon as proving the superiority of wave mechanics.

In spite of these considerable successes, the principle of uncertainty which is characteristic of quantum physics has caused considerable hesitation, because the definition of magnitudes and quantities which are continually in use is in principle treated as being inexact by this theory. This dissatisfaction is increased by the fact that the concept of probability has been introduced in the interpretation of the equations used in quantum mechanics; for this seems to imply a surrender of the demands of strict causality in favor of a form of indeterminism. Today, indeed, there are eminent physicists who under the compulsion of facts are inclined to sacrifice the principle of strict causality in the physical view of the world.

If such a step should actually prove necessary the goal of physicists would become more remote; and this would be a disadvantage whose importance it is impossible to overestimate. For in my opinion, so long as any choice remains, determinism is in all circumstances preferable to indeterminism, simply because a definite answer to a question is always preferable to an indefinite one.

So far as I can see, however, there is no ground for such a renunciation. For there always remains the possibility that the reason why it is impossible to give a definite answer resides, not in the nature of the theory, but in the manner in which the question is asked. If a question is inadequately formulated physically, the most perfect physical theory can give no definite answer; a fact widely known in classical statistics and frequently discussed. For example, if two elastic spheres strike one another in a plane, while their velocities before impact and the laws of impact are known in all their details, it still remains impossible to state their velocities after impact. The fact is that, in order to calculate the four unknown components of the velocities of the two spheres after impact, we have only three equations derived from the conservation of energy and the two components of momentum. From this, however, we do not infer that there is no causality governing impact phenomena; what we do say is that certain essential data are missing which are requisite for their complete determination.

In order to apply these considerations to the problems of quantum physics, we must now return to the arguments dealt with in the Introduction.

If it is really true that, in its perpetual changes, the structure of the physical world view moves further and further away from the world of the senses, and correspondingly approaches the real world (which, as we saw, cannot in principle be apprehended at all), then it plainly follows that our view of the world must be purged progressively of all anthropomorphic elements. Consequently we have no right to admit into the physical world view any concepts based in any way upon human mensuration. In fact this is not the case with Heisenberg's principle of uncertainty: this was reached from the consideration that the elements of the new view of the world are not material corpuscles, but simple periodic material waves which correspond to the physical system under consideration—a conclusion obtained in accordance with the mathematical principle that it is impossible to determine a definite particle with definite momentum by means of superposition of simple periodic waves having a finite length. The principle has nothing whatever to do with any measurement, while the material waves are definitely determined by means of the mathematical problem of boundary values relating to the case in question. Here there is no question of indeterminism.

The question of the relation between the material waves and the world of sense is a different one. For this relation renders it possible for us to become acquainted with physical events; if a system were completely cut off from its surroundings we could never know of its existence.

At first glance it appears that this question has nothing to do with physics, since it belongs partly to physiology and partly to psychology. These objections, however, lead to no real difficulty. It is always possible to imagine suitably constructed instruments being substituted for human senses, e.g., self-registering apparatus like a sensitive film, which registers the impressions derived from the environment, and is thus capable of furnishing evidence about the events taking place in these surroundings. If such instruments are included within the physical system which we propose to consider, and if all other influences are eliminated, then we have a physical system cut off from the rest of the world of which we can discover something by means of measurement; although it is true that we must take into account the structure of the measuring instruments, and the reaction which they might conceivably have upon the events which we desire to measure.

If we possessed an instrument reacting to a simple periodic material wave in the same way as a resonator reacts to a sound wave, then we would be in a position to measure individual material waves and thus to analyze their behavior. This is not the case; the fact is that the indications given by such instruments as we possess, e.g., the darkening of a photographic film, do not allow us to make a safe inference about all the details of the process under examination. We have no right, however, to infer from this that the laws of material waves are indeterminate.

Another and more direct attempt might be made to substantiate the assumption of indeterminism from the fact that, according to wave mechanics, the events within a system of particles cut off from the outside world are not determined in any way by the initial state of the system, i.e., by the initial configuration and initial momentum. There is not even an approximate determination; for the wave group corresponding to the initial state will in time disintegrate generally and fall apart into individual waves of probability.

On closer consideration, however, we see that in this instance the element of indeterminism is due to the manner in which the question is asked. The question is based upon corpuscular mechanics; and in corpuscular mechanics the initial state governs the course of the event for all time. But in wave mechanics such a question has no place, if only because the final result is on principle affected with a finite inaccuracy due to the principle of uncertainty.

Since the times of Leibniz, on the other hand, another form of question in classical mechanics has been known which in this sphere leads to a definite answer. An event is completely determined for all time if, apart from the configuration at a certain time, we know, not the momentum, but the configuration of the same system at a different instant. In this case the principle of variation, or principle of least action, is used in order to calculate the event. To take the previous example, where two elastic spheres meet in a plane, if we know the initial and final position of the spheres and the interval between those two positions, then the three unknown qualities, namely the two local coordinates and the time coordinate of impact, are completely determined by the three equations of conservation.

This changed formulation of the problem differs from the previous formulation because it is immediately applicable to wave mechanics. It is true, as we saw, that a given configuration can never be defined with complete accuracy by the wave theory; but on the other hand it is theoretically possible to reduce the uncertainty below any desired limit, and thus to determine the event in question with any desired degree of accuracy. Further, the disintegration of wave groups is no evidence in favor of indeterminism, since it is equally possible for a wave group to conglomerate: in both the wave theory and the corpuscular theory the *direction* of the process is immaterial. Any movement might equally well take place in the opposite direction.

When the above formulation of the problem is adopted a given wave group generally, of course, exists only at the two selected instants: in the intervening period, as well as before and after the process, the different elementary waves will exist separately. But whether they are described as material waves or as waves of probability, in either case they will be completely determined. This is the explanation of the apparent paradox, that when a physical system passes by a definite process from one definite configuration during a definite time into some other definite configuration, the question what its configurations are during the intervening period has no physical significance; similarly on this view there is no meaning in the question of what is the track of light quantum emitted from a point source and absorbed at a given point on an observation screen.

It should at the same time be emphasized that on this view the meaning of determinism is not exactly what it is in classical physics. In the latter the configuration is determined; in quantum physics, the material waves. The distinction is important, because the connection between the configuration and the world of sense is far more direct than that between the material waves and the sense-world. To this extent the relation between the physical world view and the world of sense appears to be considerably looser in modern physics.

This is undoubtedly a disadvantage; but it is the price that must be paid in order to preserve the determinism of our world view. And further, this step appears to lie in the general direction in which physics is actually developing; this has been pointed out on more than one occasion, since in the course of its progressive evolution, the structure of the physical view of the world is moving farther and farther away from the world of sense, and assuming more and more abstract forms. Indeed, the principle of relativity seems actually to demand such a view; for on this principle time stands on the same level with space, whence it follows that, if a finite space is required for the causal description of a physical process, a finite temporal interval must also be used in order to complete the description.

On the other hand, it may well be that the suggested formulation of the question is too one-sided, and too anthropomorphic to furnish satisfactory material for a new theory of the structure of the physical world; it may be that we shall have to look for some other formulation. In any case many complex problems remain to be solved, and many obscure points to be cleared up.

In view of the peculiar difficulties of the position which has been reached by theoretical physics, a feeling of doubt persists whether the theory, with all its radical innovations, is really on the right path. The answer to this decisive question depends wholly upon the degree of necessary contact with the sense-world which the physical world view maintains in the course of its incessant advance. If this contact is lost even the most perfect world view would be no better than a bubble ready to burst at the first puff of wind. There is, fortunately, no cause for apprehension, at least in this respect: indeed we may assert without exaggeration that there was no period in the history of physics when theory and experience were linked so closely together as they are now. Conversely, it was the facts learned from experiments that shook and finally overthrew the classical theory. Each new idea and each new step were suggested to investigators, where it was not actually thrust upon them, as the result of measurements. The theory of relativity was led up to by Michelson's experiments on optical interference, and the quantum theory by Lummer's, Pringsheim's, Rubens's, and Kurlbaum's measurements of the spectral distribution of energy; by Lenard's experiments on the photoelectric effect; and by Franck and Hertz's experiments on the impact of electrons. It would lead me too far if I were to enter on the numerous and surprising results which have compelled physical theory to abandon the classical standpoint and to enter on a definite new course.

We can only hope that no change will take place in this peaceful international collaboration. It is in this reciprocal action of experiment and theory—which is at once a stimulus to and a check upon progress—that we see the surest and indeed the only guarantee of the future advance of physics.

What will be the ultimate goal? I had occasion at the beginning to point out that research in general has a twofold aim—the effective domination of the world of sense, and the complete understanding of the real world; and that both these aims are in principle unattainable. But it would be a mistake to be discouraged on this account. Both our theoretical and practical tangible results are too great to warrant discouragement; and every day adds to them. Indeed, there is perhaps some justification for seeing in the very fact that this goal is unattainable, and the struggle unending, a blessing for the human mind in its search after knowledge. For it is in this way that its two noblest impulses—enthusiasm and reverence—are preserved and inspired anew.

Translated by W. H. Johnston

Werner Heisenberg

Quantum Theory and the Structure of Matter

The concept of matter has undergone a great number of changes in the history of human thinking. Different interpretations have been given in different philosophical systems. All these different meanings of the word are still present in a greater or lesser degree in what we conceive in our time as the word "matter."

The early Greek philosophy from Thales to the Atomists, in seeking the unifying principle in the universal mutability of all things, had formed the concept of cosmic matter, a world substance which experiences all these transformations, from which all individual things arise and into which they become again transformed. This matter was partly identified with some specific matter like water or air or fire; only partly, because it had no other attribute but to be the material from which all things are made.

Later, in the philosophy of Aristotle, matter was thought of in the relation between form and matter. All that we perceive in the world of phenomena around us is formed matter. Matter is in itself not a reality but only a possibility, a "potentia"; it exists only by means of form. In the natural process the "essence," as Aristotle calls it, passes over from mere possibility through form into actuality. The matter of Aristotle is certainly not a specific matter like water or air, nor is it simply empty space; it is a kind of indefinite corporeal substratum, embodying the possibility of passing over into actuality by means of the form. The typical examples of this relation between matter and form in the philosophy of Aristotle are the biological processes in which matter is formed to become the living organism, and the building and forming activity of man.

The statue is potentially in the marble before it is cut out by the sculptor.

Then, much later, starting from the philosophy of Descartes, matter was primarily thought of as opposed to mind. There were the two complementary aspects of the world, "matter" and "mind," or, as Descartes put it, the "res extensa" and the "res cogitans." Since the new methodical principle of natural science, especially of mechanics, excluded all tracing of corporeal phenomena back to spiritual forces, matter could be considered as a reality of its own independent of the mind and of any supernatural powers. The "matter" of this period is "formed matter," the process of formation being interpreted as a causal chain of mechanical interactions; it has lost its connection with vegetative soul of Aristotelian philosophy, and therefore the dualism between matter and form is no longer relevant. It is this concept of matter which constitutes by far the strongest component in our present use of the word "matter."

Finally, in the natural science of the nineteenth century another dualism has played some role, the dualism between matter and force. Matter is that on which forces can act; or matter can produce forces. Matter, for instance, produces the force of gravity, and this force acts on matter. Matter and force are two distinctly different aspects of the corporeal world. In so far as the forces may be formative forces this distinction comes closer to the Aristotelian distinction of matter and form. On the other hand, in the most recent development of modern physics this distinction between matter and force is completely lost, since every field of force contains energy and in so far constitutes matter. To every field of force there belongs a specific kind of elementary particles with essentially the same properties as all other atomic units of matter.

When natural science investigates the problem of matter it can do so only through a study of the forms of matter. The infinite variety and mutability of the forms of matter must be the immediate object of the investigation and the efforts must be directed toward finding some natural laws, some unifying principles that can serve as a guide through this immense field. Therefore, natural science—and especially physics—has concentrated its interest for a long period on an analysis of the structure of matter and of the forces responsible for this structure.

Since the time of Galileo the fundamental method of natural science had been the experiment. This method made it possible to pass from general experience to specific experience, to single out characteristic events in nature from which its "laws" could be studied more directly than from general experience. If one wanted to study the structure of matter one had to do experiments with matter. One had to expose matter to extreme conditions in order to study its transmutations there, in the hope of finding the fundamental features of matter which persist under all apparent changes.

In the early days of modern natural science this was the object of chemistry, and this endeavor led rather early to the concept of the chemical element. A substance that could not be further dissolved or disintegrated by any of the means at the disposal of the chemist—boiling, burning, dissolving, mixing with other substances, etc.—was called an element. The introduction of this concept was a first and most important step toward an understanding of the structure of matter. The enormous variety of substances was at least reduced to a comparatively small number of more fundamental substances, the "elements," and thereby some order could be established among the various phenomena of chemistry. The word "atom" was consequently used to designate the smallest unit of matter belonging to a chemical element, and the smallest particle of a chemical compound could be pictured as a small group of different atoms. The smallest particle of the element iron, e.g., was an iron atom, and the smallest particle of water, the water molecule, consisted of one oxygen atom and two hydrogen atoms.

The next and almost equally important step was the discovery of the conservation of mass in the chemical process. For instance, when the element carbon is burned into carbon dioxide the mass of the carbon dioxide is equal to the sum of the masses of the carbon and the oxygen before the process. It was this discovery that gave a quantitative meaning to the concept of matter: independent of its chemical properties matter could be measured by its mass.

During the following period, mainly the nineteenth century, a number of new chemical elements were discovered; in our time this number has reached one hundred. This development showed quite clearly that the concept of the chemical element had not yet reached the point where one could understand the unity of matter. It was not satisfactory to believe that there are very many kinds of matter, qualitatively different and without any connection between one another.

In the beginning of the nineteenth century some evidence for a connection between the different elements was found in the fact that the atomic weights of different elements frequently seemed to be integer multiples of a smallest unit near to the atomic weight of hydrogen. The similarity in the chemical behavior of some elements was another hint leading in the same direction. But only the discovery of forces much stronger than those applied in chemical processes could really establish the connection between the different elements and thereby lead to a closer unification of matter.

These forces were actually found in the radioactive process discovered in 1896 by Becquerel. Successive investigations by Curie, Rutherford and others revealed the transmutation of elements in the radioactive process. The *a*-particles are emitted in these processes as fragments of the atoms with an energy about a million times greater than the energy of a single atomic particle in a chemical process. Therefore, these particles could be used as new tools for investigating the inner structure of the atom. The result of Rutherford's experiments on the scattering of *a*-rays was the nuclear model of the atom in 1911. The most important feature of this well-known model was the separation of the atom into two distinctly different parts, the atomic nucleus and the surrounding electronic shells. The nucleus in the middle of the atom occupies only an extremely small fraction of the space filled by the atom (its radius is about a hundred thousand times smaller than that of the atom), but contains almost its entire mass. Its positive electric charge, which is an integer multiple of the so-called elementary charge, determines the number of the surrounding electrons—the atom as a whole must be electrically neutral—and the shapes of their orbits.

This distinction between the atomic nucleus and the electronic shells at once gave a proper explanation of the fact that for chemistry the chemical elements are the last units of matter and that very much stronger forces are required to change the elements into each other. The chemical bond between neighboring atoms is due to an interaction of the electronic shells, and the energies of this interaction are comparatively small. An electron that is accelerated in a discharge tube by a potential of only several volts has sufficient energy to excite the electronic shells to the emission of radiation, or to destroy the chemical bond in a molecule. But the chemical behavior of the atom, though it consists of the behavior of its electronic shells, is determined by the charge of the nucleus. One has to change the nucleus if one wants to change the chemical properties, and this requires energies about a million times greater.

The nuclear model of the atom, however, if it is thought of as a system obeying Newton's mechanics, could not explain the stability of the atom. As has been pointed out in an earlier chapter, only the application of quantum theory to this model through the work of Bohr could account for the fact that, for example, a carbon atom after having been in interaction with other atoms or after having emitted radiation always finally remains a carbon atom with the same electronic shells as before. This stability could be explained simply by those features of quantum theory that prevent a simple objective description in space and time of the structure of the atom.

In this way one finally had a first basis for the understanding of matter. The chemical and other properties of the atoms could be accounted for by applying the mathematical scheme of quantum theory of the electronic shells. From this basis one could try to extend the analysis of the structure of matter in two opposite directions. One could either study the interaction of atoms, their relation to larger units like molecules or crystals or biological objects; or one could try through the investigation of the atomic nucleus and its components to penetrate to the final unity of matter. Research has proceeded on both lines during the past decades and we shall in the following pages be concerned with the role of quantum theory in these two fields.

The forces between neighboring atoms are primarily electric forces, the attraction of opposite and the repulsion of equal charges; the electrons are attracted by the nuclei and repelled from each other. But these forces act not according to the laws of Newtonian mechanics but those of quantum mechanics.

This leads to two different types of binding between atoms. In the one type the electron of one atom passes over to the other one, for example, to fill up a nearly closed electronic shell. In this case both atoms are finally charged and form what the physicist calls ions, and since their charges are opposite they attract each other.

In the second type one electron belongs in a way characteristic of quantum theory to both atoms. Using the picture of the electronic orbit, one might say that the electron goes around both nuclei spending a comparable amount of time in the one and in the other atom. This second type of binding corresponds to what the chemists call a valency bond.

These two types of forces, which may occur in any mixture, cause the formation of various groupings of atoms and seem to be ultimately responsible for all the complicated structures of matter in bulk that are studied in physics and chemistry. The formation of chemical compounds takes place through the formation of small closed groups of different atoms, each group being one molecule of the compound. The formation of crystals is due to the arrangement of the atoms in regular lattices. Metals are formed when the atoms are so tightly packed that their outer electrons can leave their shells and wander through the whole crystal. Magnetism is due to the spinning motion of the electron, and so on.

In all these cases the dualism between matter and force can still be retained, since one may consider nuclei and electrons as the fragments of matter that are kept together by means of the electromagnetic forces.

While in this way physics and chemistry have come to an almost complete union in their relations to the structure of matter, biology deals with structures of a more complicated and somewhat different type. It is true that in spite of the wholeness of the living organism a sharp distinction between animate and inanimate matter can certainly not be made. The development of biology has supplied us with a great number of examples where one can see that specific biological functions are carried by special large molecules or group or chains of such molecules, and there has been an increasing tendency in modern biology to explain biological processes as consequences of the laws of physics and chemistry. But the kind of stability that is displayed by the living organism is of a nature somewhat different from the stability of atoms or crystals. It is a stability of process or function rather than a stability of form. There can be no doubt that the laws of quantum theory play a very important role in the biological phenomena. For instance, those specific quantum-theoretical forces that can be described only inaccurately by the concept of chemical valency are essential for the understanding of the big organic molecules and their various geometrical patterns; the experiments on biological mutations produced by radiation show both the relevance of the statistical quantum-theoretical laws and the existence of amplifying mechanisms. The close analogy between the working of our nervous system and the functioning of modern electronic computers stresses again the importance of single elementary processes in the living organism. Still all this does not prove that physics and chemistry will, together with the concept of evolution, someday offer a complete description of the living organism. The biological processes must be handled by the experimenting scientist with greater caution than processes of physics and chemistry. As Bohr has pointed out, it may well be that a description of the living organism that could be called complete from the standpoint of the physicist cannot be given, since it would require experiments that interfere too strongly with the biological functions. Bohr has described this situation by saying that in biology we are concerned with manifestations of possibilities in that nature to which we belong rather than with outcomes of experiments which we can ourselves perform. The situation of complementarity to which this formulation alludes is represented as a tendency in the methods of modern biological research which, on the one hand, makes full use of all the methods and results of physics and chemistry and, on the other hand, is based on concepts referring to those features of organic nature that are not contained in physics or chemistry, like the concept of life itself.

So far we have followed the analysis of the structure of matter in one direction: from the atom to the more complicated structures consisting of many atoms; from atomic physics to the physics of solid bodies, to chemistry and to biology. Now we have to turn to the opposite direction and follow the line of research from the outer parts of the atom to the inner parts and from the nucleus to the elementary particles. It is this line which will possibly lead to an understanding of the unity of matter. Here we need not be afraid of destroying characteristic structures by our experiments. When the task is set to test the final unity of matter we may expose matter to the strongest possible forces, to the most extreme conditions, in order to see whether any matter can ultimately be transmuted into any other matter.

The first step in this direction was the experimental analysis of the atomic nucleus. In the initial period of these studies, which filled approximately the first three decades of our century, the only tools available for experiments on the nucleus were the *a*-particles emitted from radioactive bodies. With the help of these particles Rutherford succeeded in 1919 in transmuting nuclei of light elements; he could, for instance, transmute a nitrogen nucleus into an oxygen nucleus by adding the *a*-particle to the nitrogen nucleus and at the same time knocking out one proton. This was the first example of processes on a nuclear scale that reminded one of chemical processes, but led to the artificial transmutation of elements. The next substantial progress was, as is well known, the artificial acceleration of protons by means of high-tension equipment to energies sufficient to cause nuclear transmutation. Voltages of roughly one million volts are required for this purpose and Cockcroft and Walton in their first decisive experiment succeeded in transmuting nuclei of the element lithium into those of helium. This discovery opened up an entirely new line of research, which may be called nuclear physics in the proper sense and which very soon led to a qualitative understanding of the structure of the atomic nucleus.

The structure of the nucleus was indeed very simple. The atomic nucleus consists of only two kinds of elementary particles. The one is the proton which is at the same time simply the hydrogen nucleus; the other is called neutron, a particle which has roughly the mass of the proton but is electrically neutral. Every nucleus can be characterized by the number of protons and neutrons of which it consists. The normal carbon nucleus, for instance, consists of six protons and six neutrons. There are other carbon nuclei, less frequent in number (called isotopic to the first ones), that consist of six protons and seven neutrons, etc. So one had finally reached a description of matter in which, instead of the many different chemical elements, only three fundamental units occurred: the proton, the neutron, and the electron. All matter consists of atoms and therefore is constructed from these three fundamental building stones. This was not yet the unity of matter, but certainly a great step toward unification and—perhaps still more important—simplification. There was of course still a long way to go from the knowledge of the two building stones of the nucleus to a complete understanding of its structure. The problem here was somewhat different from the corresponding problem in the outer atomic shells that had been solved in the middle of the twenties. In the electronic shells the forces between the particles were known with great accuracy, but the dynamic laws had to be found, and were found in quantum mechanics. In the nucleus the dynamic laws could well be supposed to be just those of quantum mechanics, but the forces between the particles were not known beforehand; they had to be derived from the experimental properties of the nuclei. This problem has not yet been completely solved. The forces have probably not such a simple form as the electrostatic forces in the electronic shells and therefore the mathematical difficulty of computing the properties from complicated forces and the inaccuracy of the experiments make progress difficult. But a qualitative understanding of the structure of the nucleus has definitely been reached.

Then there remained the final problem, the unity of matter. Are these fundamental building stones—proton, neutron and electron—final indestructible units of matter, atoms in the sense of Democritus, without any relation except for the forces that act between them or are they just different forms of the same kind of matter? Can they again be transmuted into each other and possibly into other forms of matter as well? An experimental attack on this problem requires forces and energies concentrated on atomic particles much larger than those that have been necessary to investigate the atomic nucleus. Since the energies stored up in atomic nuclei are not big enough to provide us with a tool for such experiments, the physicists have to rely either on the forces in cosmic dimensions or on the ingenuity and skill of the engineers.

Actually, progress has been made on both lines. In the first case the physicists make use of the so-called cosmic radiation. The electromagnetic fields on the surface of stars extending over huge spaces are under certain circumstances able to accelerate charged atomic particles, electrons and nuclei. The nuclei, owing to their greater inertia, seem to have a better chance of remaining in the accelerating field for a long distance, and finally when they leave the surface of the star into empty space they have already traveled through potentials of several thousand million volts. There may be a further acceleration in the magnetic fields between the stars; in any case the nuclei seem to be kept within the space of the galaxy for a long time by varying magnetic fields, and finally they fill this space with what one calls cosmic radiation. This radiation reaches the earth from the outside and consists of nuclei of practically all kinds, hydrogen and helium and many heavier elements, having energies from roughly a hundred or a thousand million electron volts to, again in rare cases, a million times this amount. When the particles of this cosmic radiation penetrate into the atmosphere of the earth they hit the nitrogen atoms or oxygen atoms of the atmosphere or may hit the atoms in any experimental equipment exposed to the radiation.

The other line of research was the construction of big accelerating machines, the prototype of which was the so-called cyclotron constructed by Lawrence in California in the early thirties. The underlying idea of these machines is to keep by means of a big magnetic field the charged particles going round in circles a great number of times so that they can be pushed again and again by electric fields on their way around. Machines reaching up to energies of several hundred million electron volts are in use in Great Britain, and through the cooperation of twelve European countries a very big machine of this type is now being constructed in Geneva which we hope will reach up to energies of twenty-five-billion electron volts. The experiments carried out by means of cosmic radiation or of the big accelerators have revealed new interesting features of matter. Besides the three fundamental building stones of matter—electron, proton, and neutron—new elementary particles have been found which can be created in these processes of highest energies and disappear again after a short time. The new particles have similar properties as the old ones except for their instability. Even the most stable ones have lifetimes of roughly only a millionth part of a second, and the lifetimes of others are even a thousand times smaller. At the present time about twenty-five different new elementary particles are known; the most recent one is the negative proton.

These results seem at first sight to lead away from the idea of the unity of matter, since the number of fundamental units of matter seems to have again increased to values comparable to the number of different chemical elements. But this would not be a proper interpretation. The experiments have at the same time shown that the particles can be created from other particles or simply from the kinetic energy of such particles, and they can again disintegrate into other particles. Actually the experiments have shown the complete mutability of matter. All the elementary particles can, at sufficiently high energies, be transmuted into other particles, or they can simply be created from kinetic energy and can be annihilated into energy, for instance, into radiation. Therefore, we have here actually the final proof for the unity of matter. All the elementary particles are made of the same substance, which we may call energy or universal matter; they are just different forms in which matter can appear.

If we compare this situation with the Aristotelian concepts of matter and form, we can say that the matter of Aristotle, which is mere "potentia," should be compared to our concept of energy, which gets into "actuality" by means of the form, when the elementary particle is created.

Modern physics is of course not satisfied with only qualitative description of the fundamental structure of matter; it must try on the basis of careful experimental investigations to get a mathematical formulation of those natural laws that determine the "forms" of matter, the elementary particles and their forces. A clear distinction between matter and force can no longer be made in this part of physics, since each elementary particle not only is producing some forces and is acted upon by forces, but it is at the same time representing a certain field of force. The quantum-theoretical dualism of waves and particles makes the same entity appear both as matter and as force.

All the attempts to find a mathematical description for the laws concerning the elementary particles have so far started from the quantum theory of wave fields. Theoretical work on theories of this type started early in the thirties. But the very first investigations on this line revealed serious difficulties the roots of which lay in the combination of quantum theory and the theory of special relativity. At first sight it would seem that the two theories, quantum theory and the theory of relativity, refer to such different aspects of nature that they should have practically nothing to do with each other, that it should be easy to fulfill the requirements of both theories in the same formalism. A closer inspection, however, shows that the two theories do interfere at one point, and that it is from this point that all the difficulties arise.

The theory of special relativity had revealed a structure of space and time somewhat different from the structure that was generally assumed since Newtonian mechanics. The most characteristic feature of this newly discovered structure is the existence of a maximum velocity that cannot be surpassed by any moving body or any travelling signal, the velocity of light. As a consequence of this, two events at distant points cannot have any immediate causal connection if they take place at such times that a light signal starting at the instant of the event on *one* point reaches the other point only after the time the other event has happened there; and vice versa. In this case the two events may be called simultaneous. Since no action of any kind can reach from the one event at the one point in time to the other event at the other point, the two events are not connected by any causal action.

For this reason any action at a distance of the type, say, of the gravitational forces in Newtonian mechanics was not compatible with the theory of special relativity. The theory had to replace such action by actions from point to point, from one point only to the points in an infinitesimal neighborhood. The most natural mathematical expressions for actions of this type were the differential equations for waves or fields that were invariant for the Lorentz transformation. Such differential equations exclude any direct action between "simultaneous" events.

Therefore, the structure of space and time expressed in the theory of special relativity implied an infinitely sharp boundary between the region of simultaneousness, in which no action could be transmitted, and the other regions, in which a direct action from event to event could take place.

On the other hand, in quantum theory the uncertainty relations put a definite limit on the accuracy with which positions and momenta, or time and energy, can be measured simultaneously. Since an infinitely sharp boundary means an infinite accuracy with respect to position in space and time, the momenta or energies must be completely undetermined, or in fact arbitrarily high momenta and energies must occur with overwhelming probability. Therefore, any theory which tries to fulfill the requirements of both special relativity and quantum theory will lead to mathematical inconsistencies, to divergences in the region of very high energies and momenta. This sequence of conclusions may perhaps not seem strictly binding, since any formalism of the type under consideration is very complicated and could perhaps offer some mathematical possibilities for avoiding the clash between quantum theory and relativity. But so far all the mathematical schemes that have been tried did in fact lead either to divergences, i.e., to mathematical contradictions, or did not fulfill all the requirements of the two theories. And it was easy to see that the difficulties actually came from the point that has been discussed.

The way in which the convergent mathematical schemes did not fulfill the requirements of relativity or quantum theory was in itself quite interesting. For instance, one scheme, when interpreted in terms of actual events in space and time, led to a kind of time reversal; it would predict processes in which suddenly at some point in space particles are created, the energy of which is later provided for by some other collision process between elementary particles at some other point. The physicists are convinced from their experiments that processes of this type do not occur in nature, at least not if the two processes are separated by measurable distances in space and time. Another mathematical scheme tried to avoid the divergences through a mathematical process which is called renormalization; it seemed possible to push the infinities to a place in the formalism where they could not interfere with the establishment of the well-defined relations between those quantities that can be directly observed. Actually this scheme has led to very substantial progress in quantum electrodynamics, since it accounts for some interesting details in the hydrogen spectrum that had not been understood before. A close analysis of this mathematical scheme, however, has made it probable that those quantities which in normal quantum theory must be interpreted as probabilities can under certain circumstances become negative in the formalism of renormalization. This would prevent the consistent use of the formalism for the description of matter.

The final solution of these difficulties has not yet been found. It will emerge someday from the collection of more and more accurate experimental material about the different elementary particles, their creation and annihilation, the forces between them. In looking for possible solutions of the difficulties one should perhaps remember that such processes with time reversal as have been discussed before could not be excluded experimentally, if they took place only within extremely small regions of space and time outside the range of our present experimental equipment. Of course one would be reluctant to accept such processes with time reversal if there could be at any later stage of physics the possibility of following experimentally such events in the same sense as one follows ordinary atomic events. But here the analysis of quantum theory and of relativity may again help us to see the problem in a new light.

The theory of relativity is connected with a universal constant in nature, the velocity of light. This constant determines the relation between space and time and is therefore implicitly contained in any natural law which must fulfill the requirements of Lorentz invariance. Our natural language and the concepts of classical physics can apply only to phenomena for which the velocity of light can be considered as practically infinite.

When we in our experiments approach the velocity of light we must be prepared for results which cannot be interpreted in these concepts.

Quantum theory is connected with another universal constant of nature, Planck's quantum of action. An objective description for events in space and time is possible only when we have to deal with objects or processes on a comparatively large scale, where

Planck's constant can be regarded as infinitely small. When our experiments approach the region where the quantum of action becomes essential we get into all those difficulties with the usual concepts that have been discussed in earlier chapters of this volume.

There must exist a third universal constant in nature. This is obvious for purely dimensional reasons. The universal constants determine the scale of nature, the characteristic quantities that cannot be reduced to other quantities. One needs at least three fundamental units for a complete set of units. This is most easily seen from such conventions as the use of the c-g-s system (centimetre, gram, second system) by the physicist. A unit of length, one of time and one of mass, is sufficient to form a complete set; but one must have at least three units. One could also replace them by units of length, velocity and mass; or by units of length, velocity and energy, etc. But at least three fundamental units are necessary. Now, the velocity of light and Planck's constant of action provide only two of these units. There must be a third one, and only a theory which contains this third unit can possibly determine the masses and other properties of the elementary particles. Judging from our present knowledge of these particles the most appropriate way of introducing the third universal constant would be by the assumption of a universal length the value of which should be roughly IO^{-13} cm, that is, somewhat smaller than the radii of the light atomic nuclei. When from such three units one forms an expression which in its dimension corresponds to a mass, its value has the order of magnitude of the masses of the elementary particles.

If we assume that the laws of nature *do* contain a third universal constant of the dimension of a length and of the order of IO^{-13} cm, then we would again expect our usual concepts to apply only to regions in space and time that are large as compared to the universal constant. We should again be prepared for phenomena of a qualitatively new character when we in our experiments approach regions in space and time smaller than the nuclear radii. The phenomenon of time reversal, which has been discussed and which so far has only resulted from theoretical considerations as a mathematical possibility, might therefore belong to these smallest regions. If so, it could probably not be observed in a way that would permit a description in terms of the classical concepts. Such processes would probably, so far as they can be observed and described in classical terms, obey the usual time order.

But all these problems will be a matter of future research in atomic physics. One may hope that the combined effort of experiments in the high energy region and of mathematical analysis will someday lead to a complete understanding of the unity of matter. The term "complete understanding" would mean that the forms of matter in the sense of Aristotelian philosophy would appear as results, as solutions of a closed mathematical scheme representing the natural laws for matter.

Translator unknown

Language and Reality in Modern Physics

Throughout the history of science, new discoveries and new ideas have always caused scientific disputes, have led to polemical publications criticizing the new ideas, and such criticism has often been helpful in their development; but these controversies have never before reached that degree of violence which they attained after the discovery of the theory of relativity and in a lesser degree after quantum theory. In both cases the scientific problems have finally become connected with political issues, and some scientists have taken recourse to political methods to carry their views through. This violent reaction on the recent development of modern physics can only be understood when one realizes that here the foundations of physics have started moving; and that this motion has caused the feeling that the ground would be cut from science. At the same time it probably means that one has not yet found the correct language with which to speak about the new situation and that the incorrect statements published here and there in the enthusiasm about the new discoveries have caused all kinds of misunderstanding. This is indeed a fundamental problem. The improved experimental technique of our time brings into the scope of science new aspects of nature which cannot be described in terms of the common concepts. But in what language, then, should they be described? The first language that emerges from the process of scientific clarification is in theoretical physics usually a mathematical language, the mathematical scheme, which allows one to predict the results of experiments. The physicist may be satisfied when he has the mathematical scheme and knows how to use it for the interpretation of the experiments. But he has to speak about his results also to nonphysicists who will not be satisfied unless some explanation is given in plain language, understandable to anybody. Even for the physicist the description in plain language will be a criterion of the degree of understanding that has been reached. To what extent is such a description at all possible? Can one speak about the atom itself? This is a problem of language as much as of physics, and therefore some remarks are necessary concerning language in general and scientific language specifically.

Language was formed during the prehistoric age among the human race as a means for communication and as a basis for thinking. We know little about the various steps in its formation; but language now contains a great number of concepts which are a suitable tool for more or less unambiguous communication about events in daily life. These concepts are acquired gradually without critical analysis by using the language, and after having used a word sufficiently often we think that we more or less know what it means. It is of course a well-known fact that the words are not so clearly defined as they seem to be at first sight and that they have only a limited range of applicability. For instance, we can speak about a piece of iron or a piece of wood, but we cannot speak about a piece of water. The world *piece* does not apply to liquid substances. Or, to mention another example: In discussions about the limitations of concepts, Bohr likes to tell the following story: "A little boy goes into a grocer's shop with a penny in his hand and asks: 'Could I have a penny's worth of mixed sweets?' The grocer takes two sweets and hands them to the boy saying: 'Here you have two sweets. You can do the mixing yourself.'" A more serious example of the problematic relation between words and concepts is the fact that the words "red" and "green" are used even by people who are colorblind, though the ranges of applicability of these terms must be quite different for them from what they are for other people.

This intrinsic uncertainty of the meaning of words was of course recognized very early and has brought about the need for definitions, or—as the word *definition* says—for the setting of boundaries that determine where the word is to be used and where not. But definitions can be given only with the help of other concepts, and so one will finally have to rely on some concepts that are taken as they are, unanalyzed and undefined.

In Greek philosophy the problem of the concepts in language has been a major theme since Socrates, whose life was—if we can follow Plato's artistic representation in his dialogues—a continuous discussion about the content of the concepts in language and about the limitations in modes of expression. In order to obtain a solid basis for scientific thinking, Aristotle in his logic started to analyze the forms of language, the formal structure of conclusions and deductions independent of their content. In this way, he reached a degree of abstraction and precision that had been unknown up to that time in Greek philosophy, and he thereby contributed immensely to the clarification, to the establishment of order in our methods of thought. He actually created the basis for the scientific language.

On the other hand, this logical analysis of language again involves the danger of an oversimplification. In logic the attention is drawn to very special structures, unambiguous connections between premises and deductions, simple patterns of reasoning, and all the other structures of language are neglected. These other structures may arise from associations between certain meanings of words; for instance, a secondary meaning of a word which passes only vaguely through the mind when the word is heard may contribute essentially to the content of a sentence. The fact that every word may cause many only half-conscious movements in our mind can be used to represent some part of reality in the language much more clearly than by the use of the logical patterns. Therefore, the poets have often objected to this emphasis in language and in thinking on the logical pattern, which—if I interpret their opinions correctly—can make language less suitable for its purpose. We may recall for instance the words in Goethe's *Faust* which Mephistopheles speaks to the young student (quoted from the translation by Anna Swanwick):

> Waste not your time, so fast it flies;
> Method will teach you time to win;
> Hence, my young friend, I would advise,
> With college logic to begin.
> Then will your mind be so well brac'd,
> In Spanish boots so tightly lac'd,
> That on 'twill circumspectly creep,
> Thought's beaten track securely keep,
> Nor will it, ignis-fatuus like,

Into the path of error strike.
Then many a day they'll teach you how
The mind's spontaneous acts, till now
As eating and as drinking free,
Require a process;—one, two, three!
In truth the subtle web of thought
Is like the weaver's fabric wrought,
One treadle moves a thousand lines,
Swift dart the shuttles to and fro,
Unseen the threads unnumber'd flow,
A thousand knots one stroke combines.
Then forward steps your sage to show,
And prove to you it must be so;
The first being so, and so the second,
The third and fourth deduc'd we see;
And if there were no first and second,
Nor third nor fourth would ever be.
This, scholars of all countries prize,
Yet 'mong themselves no weavers rise.
Who would describe and study aught alive,
Seeks first the living spirit thence to drive:
Then are the lifeless fragments in his hand,
There only fails, alas!—the spirit-band.

This passage contains an admirable description of the structure of language and of the narrowness of the simple logical patterns.

On the other hand, science must be based upon language as the only means of communication and there, where the problem of unambiguity is of greatest importance, the logical patterns must play their role. The characteristic difficulty at this point may be described in the following way. In natural science we try to derive the particular from the general, to understand the particular phenomenon as caused by simple general laws. The general laws when formulated in the language can contain only a few simple concepts—else the law would not be simple and general. From these concepts are derived an infinite variety of possible phenomena, not only qualitatively but with complete precision with respect to every detail. It is obvious that the concepts of ordinary language, inaccurate and only vaguely defined as they are, could never allow such derivations. When a chain of conclusions follows from given premises, the number of possible links in the chain depends on the precision of the premises. Therefore, the concepts of the general laws must in natural science be defined with complete precision, and this can be achieved only by means of mathematical abstraction.

In other sciences the situation may be somewhat similar in so far as rather precise definitions are also required; for instance, in law. But here the number of links in the chain of conclusions need not be very great, complete precision is not needed, and rather precise definitions in terms of ordinary language are sufficient.

In theoretical physics we try to understand groups of phenomena by introducing mathematical symbols that can be correlated with facts, namely, with the results of measurements. For the symbols we use names that visualize their correlation with the measurement. Thus the symbols are attached to the language. Then the symbols are interconnected by a rigorous system of definitions and axioms, and finally the natural laws are expressed as equations between the symbols. The infinite variety of solutions of these equations then corresponds to the infinite variety of particular phenomena that are possible in this part of nature. In this way the mathematical scheme represents the group of phenomena so far as the correlation between the symbols and the measurements goes. It is this correlation which permits the expression of natural laws in the terms of common language, since our experiments consisting of actions and observations can always be described in ordinary language.

Still, in the process of expansion of scientific knowledge the language also expands; new terms are introduced and the old ones are applied in a wider field or differently from ordinary language. Terms such as "energy," "electricity," "entropy" are obvious examples. In this way we develop a scientific language which may be called a natural extension of ordinary language adapted to the added fields of scientific knowledge.

During the past century a number of new concepts have been introduced in physics, and in some cases it has taken considerable time before the scientists have really grown accustomed to their use. The term *electromagnetic field*, for instance, which was to some extent already present in Faraday's work and which later formed the basis of Maxwell's theory, was not easily accepted by the physicists, who directed their attention primarily to the mechanical motion of matter. The introduction of the concept really involved a change in scientific ideas as well, and such changes are not easily accomplished.

Still, all the concepts introduced up to the end of the last century formed a perfectly consistent set applicable to a wide field of experience, and, together with the former concepts, formed a language which not only the scientists but also the technicians and engineers could successfully apply in their work. To the underlying fundamental ideas of this language belonged the assumptions that the order of events in time is entirely independent of their order in space, that Euclidean geometry is valid in real space, and that the events "happen" in space and time independently of whether they are observed or not. It was not denied that every observation had some influence on the phenomenon to be observed but it was generally assumed that by doing the experiments cautiously this influence could be made arbitrarily small. This seemed in fact a necessary condition for the ideal of objectivity which was considered as the basis of all natural science.

Into this rather peaceful state of physics broke quantum theory and the theory of special relativity as a sudden, at first slow and then gradually increasing, movement in the foundations of natural science. The first violent discussions developed around the problems of space and time raised by the theory of relativity. How should one speak about the new situation? Should one consider the Lorentz contradiction of moving bodies as a real contradiction or only as an apparent contradiction? Should one say that the structure of space and time was really different from what it had been assumed to be or should one only say that the experimental results could be connected mathematically in a way corresponding to this new structure, while space and time, being the universal and necessary mode in which things appear to us, remain what they had always been? The real problem behind these many controversies was the fact that no language existed in which one could speak consistently about the new situation. The ordinary language was based upon the old concepts of space and time and this language offered the only unambiguous means of communication about the setting up and the results of the measurements. Yet the experiments showed that the old concepts could not be applied everywhere.

The obvious starting point for the interpretation of the theory of relativity was therefore the fact that in the limiting case of small velocities (small compared with the velocity of light) the new theory was practically identical with the old one. Therefore, in this part of the theory it was obvious in which way the mathematical symbols had to be correlated with the measurements and with the terms of ordinary language; actually it was only through this correlation that the Lorentz transformation had been found. There was no ambiguity about the meaning of the words and the symbols in this region. In fact this correlation was already sufficient for the application of the theory to the whole field of experimental research connected with the problem of relativity. Therefore, the controversial questions about the "real" or the "apparent" Lorentz contradiction, or about the definition of the word "simultaneous" etc., did not concern the facts but rather the language.

With regard to the language, on the other hand, one has gradually recognized that one should perhaps not insist too much on certain principles. It is always difficult to find general convincing criteria for which terms should be used in the language and how they should be used. One should simply wait for the development of the language, which adjusts itself after some time to the new situation. Actually in the theory of special relativity this adjustment has already taken place to a large extent during the past fifty years. The distinction between "real" and "apparent" contradiction, for instance, has simply disappeared. The word *simultaneous* is used in line with the definition given by Einstein, while for the wider definition discussed in an earlier chapter the term "at a space-like distance" is commonly used, etc.

In the theory of general relativity the idea of a non-Euclidean geometry in real space was strongly contradicted by some philosophers who pointed out that our whole method of setting up the experiments already presupposed Euclidean geometry.

In fact if a mechanic tries to prepare a perfectly plane surface, he can do it in the following way. He first prepares three surfaces of, roughly, the same size which are, roughly, plane. Then he tries to bring any two of the three surfaces into contact by putting them against each other in different relative positions. The degree to which this contact is possible on the whole surface is a measure of the degree of accuracy with which the surfaces can be called "plane." He will be satisfied with his three surfaces only if the contact between any two of them is complete everywhere. If this happens one can prove mathematically that Euclidean geometry holds on the three surfaces. In this way, it was argued, Euclidean geometry is just *made* correct by our own measures.

From the point of view of general relativity, of course, one can answer that this argument proves the validity of Euclidean geometry only in small dimensions, in the dimensions of our experimental equipment. The accuracy with which it holds in this region is so high that the above process for getting plane surfaces can always be carried out. The extremely slight deviations from Euclidean geometry which still exist in this region will not be realized since the surfaces are made of material which is not strictly rigid but allows for very small deformations and since the concept of "contact" cannot be defined with complete precision. For surfaces on a cosmic scale the process that has been described would just not work; but this is not a problem of experimental physics.

Again, the obvious starting point for the physical interpretation of the mathematical scheme in general relativity is the fact that the geometry is very nearly Euclidean in small dimensions; the theory approaches the classical theory in this region. Therefore, here the correlation between the mathematical symbols and the measurements and the concepts in ordinary language is unambiguous. Still, one can speak about a non-Euclidean geometry in large dimensions. In fact a long time before the theory of general relativity had even been developed the possibility of a non-Euclidean geometry in real space seems to have been considered by the mathematicians, especially by Gauss in Göttingen. When he carried out very accurate geodetic measurements on a triangle formed by three mountains—the Brocken in the Harz Mountains, the Inselberg in Thuringia, and the Hohenhagen near Göttingen—he is said to have checked very carefully whether the sum of the three angles was actually equal to 180 degrees; and that he considered a difference which would prove deviations from Euclidean geometry as being possible. Actually he did not find any deviations within his accuracy of measurement.

In the theory of general relativity the language by which we describe the general laws actually now follows the scientific language of the mathematicians, and for the description of the experiments themselves we can use the ordinary concepts, since Euclidean geometry is valid with sufficient accuracy in small dimensions.

The most difficult problem, however, concerning the use of the language arises in quantum theory. Here we have at first no simple guide for correlating the mathematical symbols with concepts of ordinary language; and the only thing we know from the start is the fact that our common concepts cannot be applied to the structure of the atoms. Again the obvious starting point for the physical interpretation of the formalism seems to be the fact that the mathematical scheme of quantum mechanics approaches that of classical mechanics in dimensions which are large as compared to the size of the atoms. But even this statement must be made with some reservations. Even in large dimensions there are many solutions of the quantum-theoretical equations to which no analogous solutions can be found in classical physics. In these solutions the phenomenon of the "interference of probabilities" would show up, as was discussed in the earlier chapters; it does not exist in classical physics. Therefore, even in the limit of large dimensions the correlation between the mathematical symbols, the measurements, and the ordinary concepts is by no means trivial. In order to get to such an ambiguous correlation one must take another feature of the problem into account. It must be observed that the system which is treated by the methods of quantum mechanics is in fact a part of a much bigger system (eventually the whole world); it is interacting with this bigger system; and one must add that the microscopic properties of the bigger system are (at least to a large extent) unknown. This statement is undoubtedly a correct description of the actual situation. Since the system could not be the object of measurements and of theoretical investigations, it would in fact not belong to the world of phenomena if it had no interactions with such a bigger system of which the observer is a part. The interaction with the bigger system with its undefined microscopic properties then introduces a new statistical element into the description—both the quantum-theoretical and the classical one—of the system under consideration. In the limiting case of the large dimensions this statistical element destroys the effects of the "interference of probabilities" in such a manner that now the quantum-mechanical scheme really approaches the classical one in the limit. Therefore, at this point the correlation between the mathematical symbols of quantum theory and the concepts of ordinary language is unambiguous, and this correlation suffices for the interpretation of the experiments. The remaining problems again concern the language rather than the facts, since it belongs to the concept "fact" that it can be described in ordinary language.

But the problems of language here are really serious. We wish to speak in some way about the structure of the atoms and not only about the "facts"—the latter being, for instance, the black spots on a photographic plate or the water droplets in a cloud chamber. But we cannot speak about the atoms in ordinary language.

The analysis can now be carried further in two entirely different ways. We can either ask which language concerning the atoms has actually developed among the physicists in the thirty years that have elapsed since the formulation of quantum mechanics. Or we can describe the attempts for defining a precise scientific language that corresponds to the mathematical scheme.

In answer to the first question one may say that the concept of complementarity introduced by Bohr into the interpretation of quantum theory has encouraged the physicists to use an ambiguous rather than an unambiguous language, to use the classical concepts in a somewhat vague manner in conformity with the principle of uncertainty, to apply alternatively different classical concepts which would lead to contradictions if used simultaneously. In this way one speaks about electronic orbits, about matter waves and charge density, about energy and momentum, etc., always conscious of the fact that these concepts have only a very limited range of applicability. When this vague and unsystematic use of the language leads into difficulties, the physicist has to withdraw into the mathematical scheme and its unambiguous correlation with the experimental facts.

This use of the language is in many ways quite satisfactory, since it reminds us of a similar use of the language in daily life or in poetry. We realize that the situation of complementarity is not confined to the atomic world alone; we meet it when we reflect about a decision and the motives for our decision or when we have the choice between enjoying music and analyzing its structure. On the other hand, when the classical concepts are used in this manner, they always retain a certain vagueness, they acquire in their relation to "reality" only the same statistical significance as the concepts of classical thermodynamics in its statistical interpretation. Therefore, a short discussion of these statistical concepts of thermodynamics may be useful.

The concept "temperature" in classical thermodynamics seems to describe an objective feature of reality, an objective property of matter. In daily life it is quite easy to define with the help of a thermometer what we mean by stating that a piece of matter has a certain temperature. But when we try to define what the temperature of an atom could mean we are, even in classical physics, in a much more difficult position. Actually we cannot correlate this concept "temperature of the atom" with a well-defined property of the atom but have to connect it at least partly with our insufficient knowledge of it. We can correlate the value of the temperature with certain statistical expectations about the properties of the atom, but it seems rather doubtful whether an expectation should be called objective. The concept "temperature of the atom" is not much better defined than the concept "mixing" in the story about the boy who bought mixed sweets.

In a similar way in quantum theory all the classical concepts are, when applied to the atom, just as well and just as little defined as the "temperature of the atom"; they are correlated with statistical expectations; only in rare cases may the expectation become the equivalent of certainty. Again, as in classical thermodynamics, it is difficult to call the expectation objective. One might perhaps call it an objective tendency or possibility, a "potentia" in the sense of Aristotelian philosophy. In fact, I believe that the language actually used by physicists when they speak about atomic events produces in their minds similar notions as the concept "potentia." So the physicists have gradually become accustomed to considering the electronic orbits, etc., not as reality but rather as a kind of "potentia." The language has already adjusted itself, at least to some extent, to this true situation. But it is not a precise language in which one could use the normal logical patterns; it is a language that produces pictures in our mind, but together with them the notion that the pictures have only a vague connection with reality, that they represent only a tendency toward reality.

The vagueness of this language in use among the physicists has therefore led to attempts to define a different precise language which follows definite logical patterns in complete conformity with the mathematical scheme of quantum theory. The result of these attempts by Birkhoff and Neumann and more recently by Weizsäcker can be stated by saying that the mathematical scheme of quantum theory can be interpreted as an extension or modification of classical logic. It is especially one fundamental principle of classical logic which seems to require a modification. In classical logic it is assumed that, if a statement has any meaning at all, either the statement or the negation of the statement must be correct. Of "here is a table" or "here is not a table," either the first or the second statement must be correct. "Tertium non datur," a third possibility does not exist. It may be that we do not know whether the statement or its negation is correct; but in "reality" one of the two is correct.

In quantum theory this law "tertium non datur" is to be modified. Against any modification of this fundamental principle one can of course at once argue that the principle is assumed in common language and that we have to speak at least about our eventual modification of logic in the natural language. Therefore, it would be a self-contradiction to describe in natural language a logical scheme that does not apply to natural language. There, however, Weizsäcker points out that one may distinguish various levels of language.

One level refers to the objects—for instance, to the atoms or the electrons. A second level refers to statements about objects. A third level may refer to statements about statements about objects, etc. It would then be possible to have different logical patterns at the different levels. It is true that finally we have to go back to the natural language and thereby to the classical logical patterns. But Weizsäcker suggests that classical logic may be in a similar manner a priori to quantum logic, as classical physics is to quantum theory. Classical logic would then be contained as a kind of limiting case in quantum logic, but the latter would constitute the more general logical pattern.

The possible modification of the classical logical pattern shall, then, first refer to the level concerning the objects. Let us consider an atom moving in a closed box which is divided by a wall into two equal parts. The wall may have a very small hole so that the atom can go through. Then the atom can, according to classical logic, be either in the left half of the box or in the right half. There is no third possibility: "teritum non datur." In quantum theory, however, we have to admit—if we use the words "atom" and "box" at all—that there are other possibilities which are in a strange way mixtures of the two former possibilities. This is necessary for explaining the results of our experiments. We could, for instance, observe light that has been scattered by the atom. We could perform three experiments: first the atom is (for instance, by closing the hole in the wall) confined to the left half of the box, and the intensity distribution of the scattered light is measured; then it is confined to the right half and again the scattered light is measured; and finally the atom can move freely in the whole box and again the intensity distribution of the scattered light is measured. If the atom would always be in either the left half or the right half of the box, the final intensity distribution should be a mixture (according to the fraction of time spent by the atom in each of the two parts) of the two former intensity distributions. But this is in general not true experimentally. The real intensity distribution is modified by the "interference of probabilities"; this has been discussed before.

In order to cope with this situation, Weizsäcker has introduced the concept *degree of truth*. For any simple statement in an alternative like "The atom is in the left (or in the right) half of the box" a complex number is defined as a measure for its "degree of truth." If the number is 1, it means that the statement is true; if the number is 0, it means that it is false. But other values are possible. The absolute square of the complex number gives the probability for the statement's being true; the sum of the two probabilities referring to the two parts in the alternative (either "left" or "right" in our case) must be unity. But each pair of complex numbers referring to the two parts of the alternative represents, according to Weizsäcker's definitions, a "statement" which is certainly true if the numbers have just these values; the two numbers, for instance, are sufficient for determining the intensity distribution of scattered light in our experiment. If one allows the use of the term "statement" in this way one can introduce the term "complementarity" by the following definition: Each statement that is not identical with either of the two alternative statements—in our case with the statements: "the atom is in the left half" or "the atom is in the right half of the box"—is called complementary to these statements. For each complementary statement the question whether the atom is left or right is not decided. But the term "not decided" is by no means equivalent to the term "not known." "Not known" would mean that the atom is "really" left or right, only we do not know where it is. But "not decided" indicates a different situation, expressible only by a complementary statement.

This general logical pattern, the details of which cannot be described here, corresponds precisely to the mathematical formalism of quantum theory. It forms the basis of a precise language that can be used to describe the structure of the atom. But the application of such a language raises a number of difficult problems of which we shall discuss only two here: the relation between the different "levels" of language and the consequences for the underlying ontology.

In classical logic the relation between the different levels of language is a one-to-one correspondence. The two statements, "The atom is in the left half" and "It is true that the atom is in the left half," belong logically to different levels. In classical logic these statements are completely equivalent, i.e., they are either both true or both false. It is not possible that the one is true and the other false. But in the logical pattern of complementarity this relation is more complicated. The correctness or incorrectness of the first statement still implies the correctness or incorrectness of the second statement. But the incorrectness of the second statement does not imply the incorrectness of the first statement. If the second statement is incorrect, it may be undecided whether the atom is in the left half; the atom need not necessarily be in the right half. There is still complete equivalence between the two levels of language with respect to the correctness of a statement, but not with respect to the incorrectness. From this connection one can understand the persistence of the classical laws in quantum theory: wherever a definite result can be derived in a given experiment by the application of the classical laws the result will also follow from quantum theory, and it will hold experimentally.

The final aim of Weizsäcker's attempt is to apply the modified logical patterns also in the higher levels of language, but these questions cannot be discussed here.

The other problem concerns the ontology that underlies the modified logical patterns. If the pair of complex numbers represents a "statement" in the sense just described, there should exist a "state" or a "situation" in nature in which the statement is correct. We will use the word *state* in this connection. The "states" corresponding to complementary statements are then called "coexistent states" by Weizsäcker. This term "coexistent" describes the situation correctly; it would in fact be difficult to call them "different states," since every state contains to some extent also the other "coexistent states." This concept of "state" would then form a first definition concerning the ontology of quantum theory. One sees at once that this use of the word "state," especially the term "coexistent state," is so different from the usual materialistic ontology that one may doubt whether one is using a convenient terminology. On the other hand, if one considers the word *state* as describing some potentiality rather than a reality—one may even simply replace the term *state* by term *potentiality*—then the concept of "coexistent potentialities" is quite plausible, since one potentiality may involve or overlap other potentialities.

All these difficult definitions and distinctions can be avoided if one confines the language to the description of facts, i.e., experimental results. However, if one wishes to speak about the atomic particles themselves one must either use the mathematical scheme as the only supplement to natural language or one must combine it with a language that makes use of a modified logic or of no well-defined logic at all. In the experiments about atomic events we have to do with things and facts, with phenomena that are just as real as any phenomena in daily life. But the atoms or the elementary particles themselves are not as real; they form a world of potentialities or possibilities rather than one of things or facts.

Translator unknown

Otto Hahn

Reminiscences from the History of Natural Radioactivity

After graduating as an organic chemist and serving for two years as assistant at Marburg on Lahn under Theodor Zincke, I was given the prospect of what I regarded as an attractive appointment in the chemical industry, provided that in addition to my chemistry I could offer a better knowledge of English and possibly of French, so that they could send me abroad now and then. I therefore decided to go to England for a time and left for London armed with a short letter of recommendation from my Marburg principal to Sir William Ramsay. While improving my knowledge of English I also hoped to do some work in chemistry.

Sir William asked me if I would like to work on radium. When I said that I knew nothing about radium, he replied that it was an advantage to be able to approach the subject with a mind free from preconceptions. He handed me a cup containing 50 or 100 g of a salt of barium and said that the salt contained about 9 mg of radium which I was to separate from the barium by fractional crystallization and to use for preparing a number of salts of radium with the object of checking the atomic weight of the latter element. Ramsay, famed for his work on the rare gases, had only recently become acquainted with radium. In conjunction with F. Soddy he had proved by experiment that radium is "transmuted" into helium, Rutherford having previously inferred, from his work on the electric and magnetic deflection of alpha rays, that the alpha rays must be helium. It was Rutherford who had sent his co-worker Soddy to Ramsay in order to test and possibly confirm his inference. The famous work by Ramsay and Soddy was therefore the fruit of a suggestion by Rutherford.

I followed the method indicated by Mme Curie for fractionating the barium salts which had been handed to me. Very soon, however, I encountered inconsistencies which could not be disregarded. The lyes at the end of the process should have had practically no radioactivity. To my surprise, however, I found that their activity was still quite considerable and that the carrier of this activity developed not the long-lived radium-emanation of just on four days' half-life but the short-lived thorium-emanation of just about one minute half-life.

The final result of my work was therefore not the preparation, in a pure state, of presumably 9 mg of radium, but the discovery of a new "radio-element" which gave off the emanation of thorium, but was more strongly radioactive than the thorium we knew. I named the substance *radio-thorium*.

How did this substance come to be in the sample of radium? The explanation was that the sample was not extracted from a pure uranium-ore, but from an ore called thorianite, occurring in Ceylon and containing in addition to uranium a high percentage of thorium.

Strictly speaking, therefore, the discovery of "radio-thorium" was just a matter of luck . . . .

There was another investigation which I also carried out at the Ramsay Laboratory. This time I worked in conjunction with the late Otto Sackur, who unfortunately lost his life in the Haber Institute at the beginning of World War I in 1914. Debierne, who was working with the Curies, had found, among the hydroxides used in uranium pitch-blende processing, a new element to which he had given the name of *actinium*. This element was characterized by an extremely short-lived emanation with a half-life of only a few seconds. At the same time, the Brunswick Quinine-Factory was also engaged in preparing radium from pitchblende and it so happened that, independently of Debierne, Giesel had discovered an element which gave off a very short-lived emanation and to which he had given the name of *emanium*.

The chemical properties of Debierne's actinium and of Giesel's emanium, as originally described by the two discoverers, were different, so that two different elements seemed to be involved. Ramsay secured samples of the two substances and gave Sackur and me a little of each. We carried out an accurate determination of the half-lives and found them both to be 3.9 sec, thus definitely establishing that actinium and emanium were one and the same element. The name actinium was retained owing to the earlier publication of Debierne's investigation. It may be said, however, that Giesel had a better knowledge than Debierne of the properties—closely resembling those of lanthanum—of the new substance.

At the end of my stay in London in the summer of 1905, I was advised by Ramsay to give up the idea of going into industry and to continue with radium research. He followed this up by writing a letter to his friend Emil Fischer of Berlin who thereupon offered me a place at the Berlin Chemical Institute with the prospect of a lectureship later on. First of all, however, I made up my mind to get a more thorough grounding in this new field of study by spending another winter abroad working under Rutherford at Montreal in Canada; for Rutherford was already regarded as the leading authority on radium . . . .

As a kind of reference I had informed Rutherford that I had discovered a new radioactive element, radio-thorium, while working at the Ramsay Laboratory. My application was supported by Ramsay and a reply came inviting me to go to Montreal.

One fine day, in the autumn of 1905, I arrived in Montreal and called upon Professor Rutherford. At that very first interview he made me give him an account of my "radio-thorium." He was clearly somewhat skeptical. It did not take me long, however, to convince him that radio-thorium did really exist. A few weeks later he admitted to me that in the beginning he had not believed that I had got hold of anything new. He was evidently rather skeptical regarding work done on *radioactivity* at the Ramsay Laboratory . . . .

I continued my work in Montreal by making a more thorough investigation of the ranges of the alpha-rays of radio-thorium and of its transformation products. Rutherford cooperated with me in determining the magnetic deflection of the alpha rays of actinium (and of its transformation products) and I myself, when submitting actinium to a careful chemical investigation, discovered a substance which had up to that time escaped detection, namely, *radio-actinium* (half-life about nineteen days), a transition product intermediate between actinium and actinium X, a substance which had been discovered at the Rutherford Institute and in Germany by Giesel.

I may mention that Rutherford, who was no chemist, also had his doubts about radio-actinium; it did not take long, however, to bring about his conversion.

The atmosphere in the Rutherford Institute was most exhilarating. Rutherford had not yet become so world-famous as to attract too many pupils. Those who were with him at that time have all contributed largely toward the rapid development of research in radioactivity. There was McClung, who worked on beta radiation; H. Bronson, who carried out precision determinations of the half-lives of the transformation products of radium; A. S. Eve Rutherford's successor at Montreal—who was investigating gamma rays. Rutherford himself was chiefly occupied in searching for a definite clarification of the nature of alpha rays, of their deflection in magnetic and electric fields, of their absorption in their metal-foils. The only other foreigner there besides myself was Dr. Max Levin from Göttingen and he also was studying radioactivity . . . .

The apparatus we used in those days would appear very primitive today. We made our beta- and gamma-ray electroscope out of a largish tin can or other sheet-metal box, with a smaller tobacco or cigarette-box placed on top. The leaf-holder was insulated with sulfur because in those days we had no amber.

In his alpha ray experiments Rutherford used a rather ancient Töpler-pump for extracting the air. The result was that in many cases the deposit under examination underwent considerable disintegration before a good enough vacuum was obtained.

On the other hand, the field of study was so new that it was an easy matter, even with primitive means, to taste the joys of discovery.

In Montreal everybody, without a trace of jealousy, recognized Rutherford as the leader in scientific research. At one of the lectures held jointly with the chemists, for example, it might happen that at the end of a lecture on a subject in organic chemistry Rutherford would pass a remark and then, forgetting the matter under discussion, suddenly proceed with his usual enthusiasm to deliver a lecture on his latest experiments with his beloved gamma rays. Everything else was then forgotten.

Rutherford's enthusiasm and abounding energy infected us all and it was the rule, rather than the exception, to work on at the Institute after supper—at least for us foreigners who could not go on staying in Montreal as long as we wanted to . . . .

It was warmly appreciated by Rutherford that through Professor Giesel he was able to purchase from the Buchler Quinine Factory in Brunswick the radium salts he required; in the beginning, indeed, at an amazingly low price. He often said that without Giesel he would at the time never have been able to get hold of any radium. The price charged by Giesel in the beginning for radium bromide was about 10 to 12 marks per mg; a few years later the price had gone up to nearly 150 marks. Later on, when he was in England, Rutherford had half a gram of radium placed gratis at his disposal by the Vienna Academy of Sciences . . . .

The reader will remember the controversy over the names actinium-emanium. When I arrived in Montreal there was a controversy of the same kind going on, this time over the names *polonium* and *radio-tellurium*. Mme Curie had described the polonium as an element chemically closely related to bismuth. Marckwald in Germany was also investigating the active constituents of uranium minerals and had discovered a substance with properties very like those of tellurium. He had named the substance radio-tellurium. In the end it was found that the two substances were identical. The name radio-tellurium had therefore to be dropped, although polonium is in fact a higher homologue of tellurium. Marckwald did not immediately give way but after a time he also agreed that the name of radio-tellurium should be dropped. Writing to the *Physikalische Zeitschrift* on the matter, he closed his letter with the well-known quotation from Romeo and Juliet:

> What's in a name? That which we call a rose
> By any other name would smell as sweet.

When Rutherford read this he was highly delighted with what he called the "beautiful song of renunciation." He went about in the Institute reciting the quotation in his ringing tones and long afterwards, whenever the name of Marckwald was mentioned, the quotation was sure to be trotted out again.

This joyous, youthful naturalness was one of the qualities that rendered intercourse with Rutherford such a pleasure . . . .

In the summer of 1906 I left Montreal and, in accordance with previous arrangements, I joined the Emil Fischer Institute in Berlin at the beginning of the winter semester. I had turned down the offer made by the industrial firm and had definitely been "transmuted" from an organic into a radioactive chemist.

For experiments involving measurement they placed at my disposal what had formerly been a carpenter's shop, while for the regular chemical work I was received as a guest in the private laboratory of Professor Stock, head of the department at the Institute.

It was only natural that I should still be particularly interested in thorium and its transformation products. I got in touch with O. Knöfler and Co.'s thorium factory, which had been recommended to me by Sir William Ramsay, and the firm in question placed at my disposal all the chemicals and intermediate products I asked for, including, among other things, a series of practically pure thorium salts prepared at different dates. I tested their activity under conditions as identical as possible and to my delight I found a most interesting connection between the activities and the age of the samples. Newly prepared salts exhibited an activity equal to the activity of the same amount of thorium in the mineral. As the sample grew older, its activity declined, in a few years sinking to about half the value; one of the samples, however, a salt of substantially greater age, was again showing a higher activity. The explanation was that the radio-thorium remained with the thorium while the latter was being prepared. With its half-life of about two years its activity diminished—but not indefinitely, because a hitherto unknown intermediate product of greater longevity was gradually being formed out of the thorium, the result being that in some of the older samples the activity had again gone up. The unknown substance was not difficult to discover; it proved to be in the barium.

I named the new "element" *mesothorium*. Later on I saw clearly that the radium handed to me by Ramsay had also contained mesothorium and that the radiothorium discovered by me had first come into existence in the sample, having been formed out of the mesothorium. I could not separate the mesothorium from the radium and did not detect it.

It may be quite interesting to recall that in those days—1906 and 1907—chemists in Germany had not generally recognized and fully appreciated the important consequences of the atomic disintegration hypothesis, set up a few years before by Rutherford and Soddy, and the transformation of radium into helium, established experimentally by Ramsay and Soddy. Now in the spring of 1907 there was held in Hamburg a Bunsen Congress at which the main subject was radioactivity. Comprehensive treatment was given to the subject in lectures by Marckwald, G. Meyer, Levin, Engler and

Sieveking, among others, and also by me. I spoke on the atomic disintegration hypothesis and its consequences. There followed a lively discussion in which, for example, Professor Tammann even yet declared against the elementary nature of radium and tried to advance other explanations for the transformations of radium, the formation of helium, etc. I contradicted—possibly in rather a spirited manner—because after all I had, through Rutherford, attained a pretty good knowledge of the processes. In Germany, however, a young man should really have had more respect for a Geheimrat! During a break a friend of mine, Max Levin, advised me to exercise a little more discretion when arguing. He had just overhead one professor ask another who I was and the other answer: "Oh, he's one of those anglicized Berliners!"

We had never been expected to exercise discretion of that kind in democratic Canada.

Emil Fischer was also one of those who found it difficult to grasp the fact that it is also possible by radioactive methods of measurement to detect, and to recognize from their chemical properties, substances in quantities quite beyond the world of the weighable; as is the case, for example, with the active deposits of radium, thorium and actinium. At my inaugural lecture in the spring of 1907, Fischer declared that somehow he could not believe those things. For certain substances the most delicate test was afforded by the sense of smell and no more delicate test could be found than that!

This rather reserved attitude of normal chemists toward radioactivity was maintained for quite a time. They did not take things altogether seriously. A much more progressive spirit was shown by the physicists. I can still remember the great impression made on Nernst at the Bunsen Congress when F. Von Lerch, after mentioning the method he had devised of depositing Radium C (later on found to be an isotope of bismuth) on a nickel foil, proceeded to describe the extraordinary delicacy of radioactive measurements in the following terms: "If we divide up one mg of RaC among all the people living on this earth (about two billion), each person would receive a quantity of the substance sufficient to discharge five electroscopes in a fraction of a second."

Further progress was made in our work at the Institute. We found that mesothorium is separable into two substances, one consisting of mesothorium 1 with a half-life of 6.7 years and not emitting any detectable rays, and the other of mesothorium 2 with a half-life of 6.2 hours and emitting beta rays; we determined more accurately the chemical properties of mesothorium and we concentrated on separating mesothorium 1 from radium. It will be remembered that the monazite used for the production of thorium contains some uranium and therewith a little radium and this fact lead the Knöfler Thorium Factory to consider the feasibility of marketing high-activity mesothorium preparations, as substitutes for radium, which was so hard to obtain in German. The radium resulting as a sort of "by-product" could also be put to good use. The fresh samples of mesothorium contained, from the point of view of radiation, about twenty-five percent of radium. Owing to the formation of radio-thorium out of mesothorium 1 and 2, from now on referred to for short as *mesothorium*, the samples increase in strength for a year or two and then gradually decrease until after the lapse of many years only the radium is left. All my attempts to separate the two "elements" radium and mesothorium from each other resulted in failure. It proved just as impossible to separate the radio-thorium from the thorium. The chemical resemblance between the substances was clearly much greater than that, for example, between the rare earths; nobody had yet thought, however, of the possible existence of isotopes.

There was another case of surprising chemical resemblance which it will be of interest to consider rather carefully. Much attention was being given in those days to the question as to what was the direct parent substance of radium. It was known that radium occurred primarily only in uranium ores. It was also known that the half-life of radium was about two thousand years. Owing to the sensitivity with which radium could be detected from the emanation to which it gives rise, it could easily be calculated that the formation of radium in say 100 g of a pure radium-free uranium-salt would certainly be detectable after the lapse of a few weeks. The experiments carried out up to this time had not produced any result. Soddy, Boltwood and Strutt had carried out experimental measurements which showed that the formation of radium out of pure uranium must certainly be more than a thousand times slower than the assumption of direct formation would lead one to expect. The inevitable conclusion from this was that between the uranium and the radium there must be a very long-lived intermediate element that separates out of the uranium during the preparation of the uranium salt (just as in the earlier case of mesothorium already described). Nobody knew what this substance was and various hypotheses such, for example, as the genesis of radium out of actinium, were put forward only to be abolished.

At the time (1907) I was still engaged on mesothorium and its properties. During the course of this work I happened to observe the presence, in a fairly large amount of a pure thorium salt, of some small amounts of radium-emanation. This was remarkable because when the pure thorium was being prepared any radium that might have been present in the thorium mineral should have been wholly extracted. A number of samples varying in age were placed at my disposal by the firm and were carefully examined by me. I found only traces of radium-emanation in 100 g of a sample which had only just been prepared; in the other samples I found that the emanation present increased with the age of the sample, the increase being directly proportional to the age. I allowed some time to elapse and then reexamined the freshest sample and here again I found an increase. I found no increase, however, in the filtrates of the thorium precipitates. It was evident, then, that the radium parent substance for which we were looking was contained in the "pure" thorium salt, admittedly, of course, in very small quantity. The monazite sand from which the thorium had been extracted contains but very little uranium.

In order to obtain the unknown substance in greater concentration it was necessary to have actual uranium mineral to start with. Pitchblende might be the very thing. I therefore wrote to Vienna to find out if I could get a small amount of certain products which were obtainable at the Joachimsthal works run by Haitinger and Ulrich for processing pitchblende for radium. The products I wanted were the hydrates containing the thorium portion of the mineral.

I was too late, however. Owing to the summer holidays my letter did not receive very prompt attention and in a few weeks after I had sent it there appeared in *Nature* a communication by Boltwood stating that he had discovered the parent substance of radium. Its chemical properties, according to Boltwood, placed it next to thorium. He named the new "element" *ionium*. My work in detecting the newly christened ionium in the pure salt of thorium, following upon work in connection with mesothorium and radium on the one hand and thorium and radiothorium on the other hand, convinced me that the chemical resemblance between ionium and thorium must be extraordinary close. . . . I had not the courage, however, to conclude that in their chemical properties the elements referred to were absolutely identical.

It was left to Soddy several years later (1913) to draw from all these observations the important conclusion that there exist chemical elements with different radioactive properties and different atomic weights and nevertheless having the same chemical properties and occupying the same position in the Periodic System. To such elements Soddy gave the name of *isotopic* elements and he also applied the same conception to the ordinary chemical elements. This led to the early disappearance of the blemishes in the Periodic System and soon provided a feasible explanation of the fact that atomic weights are in many cases not whole numbers (e.g., the isotopes of chlorine). Experimental detection of "inactive" isotopes was first carried out in the gaseous element neon (Thomson, Aston 1913) and with the various kinds of lead of radioactive origin (Hönigschmid, Soddy 1914).

In the autumn of 1907 something happened which was to have considerable influence on my scientific development. The Viennese physicist Dr. Lise Meitner arrived in Berlin. She had come for the purpose of extending her theoretical studies, especially by attending the lectures of Professor Max Planck, and she also desired to do some experimental work. With regard to the latter there were various possibilities open to her. As she had done some work already in Vienna involving radioactivity, she decided to keep to that branch of research and came over to me. What was originally intended to be a short visit to Berlin resulted in a cooperation and a friendship which lasted for over thirty years, in fact until the conditions prevailing in the summer of 1938 brought an end (to the cooperation, not to the friendship!)

In those days women were not allowed to work at the Fischer Institute. When I put the matter to Emil Fischer, he granted permission to Miss Meitner to work with me in the carpenter's shop on the ground floor of the Institute, where the radioactive measurements were carried out; he requested her, however, not to enter the study rooms on the upper floor as that would be setting a precedent.

For a few years this agreement was duly observed. Later on, however, in addition to the Stock private laboratory it became possible to fit up another part of the ground-floor for chemical research and Miss Meitner was then able to take part in practical work of a purely chemical character such as, for example, the fractional crystallization of several hundred milligrams of mesothorium which we afterward displayed to Emperor Wilhelm II at the inauguration of the Kaiser Wilhelm Institute for Chemistry in the autumn of the year 1912.

At the end of 1907 I was the proud possessor of an almost complete collection of radioactive "elements." . . .

Having all these substances at our disposal, we decided that it would be useful to study their beta rays under identical conditions. So we put our decision into effect by undertaking in collaboration a series of investigations into the penetrating process of the rays by determining as accurately as possible their absorption in aluminum. The "half-value thicknesses" which we obtained for the rays in aluminum proved to be so characteristic for most of the decay-products that we were able to apply them in quite a number of cases as reliable touchstones in rapid analysis. We considered that we had established that under our experimental conditions the absorption of the beta rays from the individual elements proceeded in strict accordance with an exponential law and that this was a sign of their homogeneity; a crooked log absorption curve on the other hand, would indicate the presence of more than one element. One the basis of this hypothesis we did, in fact, find that a number of elements which had previously been regarded as nonradiating were really beta-radiating elements.

In order to obtain confirmation of our views regarding the homogeneity of the beta rays, we began in 1909, in conjunction with Otto Von Baeyer, an investigation of the magnetic deflection of the beta rays, just as Rutherford had done for the alpha particles of the radio-elements. The substance to be investigated was deposited on a fine wire so thinly as possible (in the case of active deposits the layer of substance was of infinitesimal thickness) and in a magnetic field those beta rays which had passed through a narrow slit were recorded on a photographic plate. The first sample investigated was the active deposit of thorium and on the plate just as we had expected, we found two and only two widely separated lines corresponding respectively to the penetrating rays of ThB (now ThC) and the softer rays of ThA (now ThB). Our assumption regarding the homogeneity of the beta-rays of the individual elements had apparently been confirmed.

Our jubilation did not last long, however, On testing in this way mesothorium 2, which we had taken to be a single element, we got quite a number of fine lines. Other substances submitted to the test provided similar results and later on, when we were able to get even stronger samples of the deposit of thorium we found that this substance also gave additional lines.

Our beta-ray hypothesis was therefore false. Like many another false hypothesis, however, ours gave a new trend to research—a trend which, in the course of time, found its fruition, especially later on in the work of Lise Meitner at Dahlem and of C. D. Ellis in England. A definite conception was formed of the difference between the band-spectra of primary beta rays and the fine line-spectra of secondary electrons released by the gamma rays from the electron-shell; and later on Lise Meitner was the first to establish the part played by gamma rays in the creation of line-spectra.

Other experimental work went on side by side with these investigations of the beta rays of all the important radio-elements. . . .

There was one investigation which deserves a special report because it provides a good example of how, in the case of radioactive measurements, minute deviations from what was expected—deviations which are regarded as of no interest owing to their minuteness—may, when submitted to careful scrutiny, lead to discoveries of considerable importance. In the years 1907 and 1908 several workers in the field of the "active deposit" of actinium had observed an extremely attenuated residual activity the origin and nature of which they were unable to elucidate. I carried out a systematic investigation of this activity and succeeded in establishing the fact that it was due to the barium-like actinium X. At first we could not explain how this nonvolatile alkali-metal could possibly get into the gaseous actinium-emanation, seeing that AcX precedes emanation in the decay series. Raising the temperature did not cause any increase in the minute, hardly detectable amount, but we did find that the yield from thin layers of the sample was greater than that from thick layers. Just as the active deposit accumulated on a negatively charged plate so the yield from the residual activity was also greater from a negatively charged plate than from an unelectrified plate and much greater than from a positively charged plate.

Finally we took layers, about equally thin, of radio-actinium, the parent substance of actinium X, and actinium X itself, and we compared one with the other. We found clear evidence of residual activity in the radio-actinium but none whatever in the actinium X. Evidently, therefore, it was the radio-actinium that caused the residual activity; but we could not find any hitherto unknown emanation between radio-actinium and actinium. I then discovered that the explanation lay in the alpha rays of radio-actinium which, like all the alpha rays of radioactive substances, are shot out of the active atom with considerable kinetic energy. The explanation was this: At the moment of its creation from the radio-actinium, the positively charged actinium X atom experiences a recoil due to the simultaneous emission of an alpha-particle. This recoil causes it to escape from the atomic structure, after which it travels to the negative electrode. In the case of radio-actinium the action does not in any way depend on the AcX content; the radio-actinium may be quite free from AcX. And so radioactive recoil, an effect which had been predicted years before by Rutherford, was discovered experimentally. Miss Meitner immediately suggested that we should in the same way test other alpha radiating transmutation products, especially the radioactive deposits, as these could easily be prepared in layers of infinitesimal thickness. It took us only a few days to detect short-lived transmutation-products in substantial amounts, including the hitherto unknown ThD, now called *thorium C′*, and also *actinium C′*, which we had shortly before discovered in another way.

The recoil method proved of great value in the preparation of various samples in a pure state and nowadays, above all in the case of artificially radioactive substances, plays an important role especially in the preparation of radioactive indicators (Szilard-Chalmers method).

We also went on with our chemical researches. Our investigation of the rays of mesothorium and of radiothorium had shown that both the beta and the gamma rays of these elements have penetrative powers equal to or even exceeding those of radium and, as we have already mentioned, the thorium factory of Knöfler & Co. had consequently started the manufacture of strong mesothorium preparations; checking and testing were regularly carried out in our "carpenter's shop." The final chemical operations were carried out by Miss Meitner and me in the annex to the "carpenter's shop."

These chemical separations carried out without a hood and without precautionary measures evidently caused us no harm, except for some slight damage to the fingers most exposed to the action of the rays. It must be borne in mind that the technical preparations contained about twenty-five percent of radium which came from the uranium-content of the monazite sand, so that during our work we were also continuously inhaling traces of radium-emanation.

In the year 1911 our mesothorium amounted to several hundred mg and its strength was equal to that of pure salt of radium. Just about that period there was a great demand for radium and in addition for mesothorium, which was being supplied by the firm to hospitals etc. at about half the price of radium. The firm of Auer had also taken up large-scale production of mesothorium and up to the outbreak of World War I had extracted considerable quantities of this "German radium." . . .

I still remember one or two amusing confusions caused by the name "mesothorium." The young ladies employed by the firm of Knöfler preferred to call it "little sunshine" because the salts, especially when strong and dry, shone beautifully in the dark (thermoluminescence added to the normal phosphorescence). One day I was requested by Emil Fischer to give some information about the mesothorium rays to a Berlin Charité Hospital professor who wanted to use them for irradiating tubercle cultures. The elderly Geheimrat received me very graciously and then began to describe the experiments he had already carried out with "semithorium." When I replied with all due modesty that the correct name was mesothorium he gave me a friendly tap on the shoulder and said: "Believe me, my young colleague, the substance is called semithorium!" Bethinking me of the bad impression I had made at the Bunsen Congress I was careful this time to correct his error with becoming modesty.

During World War I my colonel once introduced me to a higher officer with the words: "In civilian life Lieutenant Hahn is a professor and discovered mesothorium." The officer replied: "I believe Lieutenant Hahn is a chemist; what can he have to do with antediluvian animals?" . . .

After moving out of our radioactively contaminated quarters at the Chemical Institute into the recently erected Kaiser Wilhelm Institute for Chemistry (1913) it became possible for us to do experimental work with the weakly active elements potassium and rubidium. Many years later these investigations led to what was called the "strontium method" of determining geological age—a method that was elaborated when the precision mass-spectrograph of Professor Mattauch was at the disposal of the Kaiser Wilhelm Institute. In the case of geologically old minerals, the strontium method certainly has advantages over the hitherto usual lead and helium methods.

Shortly before World War I the most important substances in the three great radioactive decay-series, the uranium-radium, the actinium and the thorium series, had substantially been discovered and fitted into the decay-system. There was, however, one important substance still missing—the parent substance of the actinium series.

It had long been known that actinium must be genetically related to uranium, but its direct formation from uranium had never been established in spite of its comparatively short half-life of about fifteen years. This case was therefore very like that of radium before the discovery of ionium, or of radiothorium before the discovery of mesothorium.

The problem was, in fact, an even simpler one seeing that what are called the radioactive "displacement laws" has been known since 1913; from the Rutherford-Bohr model of the atom and from the works of Moseley it was known that there could not be more than 92 different elements. Atomic weights had given way to nuclear charge numbers or atomic numbers in the characterization of the elements. The "displacement rule" formulated by Soddy, Fleck and Fajans enabled one to deduce directly the chemical nature of the parent substance of actinium: Actinium with nuclear charge 89 could arise either out of an element 91 by emission of alpha particles (nuclear charge 2) or out of a radium isotope with nuclear charge 88 by emission of beta rays which would increase the positive charge by one unit. One short-lived representation of element 91 with a half-life of a few minutes was uranium X_2 to which its discoverer, Fajans had given the name *brevium*. But even the discoverer of this homologue of tantalum, eka-tantalum, had failed to discover the unknown substance although he had sought for it in the right place. Shortly before the World War I Miss Meitner and I had also tried to find the substance by the deposition of tantalum precipitate from solutions of pitchblende. We then tried to enrich the resulting weakly alpha-active preparations but our method did not at first lead to any definite results. Our work was interrupted for a few years by World War I, but in 1917 we met with some success. The substance did, in fact, prove to be a homologue of tantalum and a representative of element 91; we named it *protactinium*. We were easily able to trace the continual formation of actinium. As a spectrally pure element it was first successfully prepared by A. von Grosse at our Institute. Later on several hundred mg of the pure alpha-radiating element were produced at the Kaiser Wilhelm Institute. Its half-life being thirty-two-thousand years, it behaves practically like a stable element; it is present in uranium-ores to about the same extent by weight as radium, but owing to its great longevity its activity is only about a twentieth that of radium (also an alpha-radiating element).

I will now make brief mention of yet another substance—a substance whose importance lies in the fact that it is the first known example of "isomeric" isotopes, i.e., of those substances which are first produced in an "excited" state and then, with a definite half-life, pass over into the ground state of the atom. Stefan Meyer had already indicated the possibility of the existence of such "isotopes of higher order."

In this particular case I had designated the substance in question *uranium Z;* it had a half-life of 6.7 hours and was a protactinium isotope produced with a very low yield from uranium X_1; it is isomeric with the normal uranium X_2 which also arises directly out of uranium X_1. What started our search for the unknown substance was the detection of a very minute discrepancy in the first results obtained for a small quantity of uranium X contained in a protactinium fraction. The activity of the separated product amounted to only a few thousandths of the proper value for uranium X. By starting out with larger quantities of uranium we finally succeeded in extracting uranium Z in good intensity.

At first it was thought that uranium Z must be one link in a hitherto unknown uranium decay series which could easily have been overlooked owing to its very low intensity. We sought in vain, however, for a parent substance differing from ordinary UX and isotopic with uranium X, so the only explanation left was that uranium Z is the product of a weak secondary reaction of uranium X. Many years later quite a number of such "isomers" were found among the artificially radioactive elements; uranium Z was the first one.

These researches were carried out in the early twenties. In 1919 Rutherford had discovered the first transmutation of one element into another—nitrogen had been transmuted into oxygen by bombardment with alpha-particles.

And so a new "Age of Nuclear Research" had been heralded in! The age of natural radioactivity had given way to the age of artificial-radio elements. The history of this development belongs to the recent past and to the present, and my personal reminiscences of earlier days have thus reached their logical conclusion.

Translated by W. Gaade

Lise Meitner

The Atom

People were occupying themselves with the question of the structure of matter even at a time before one could speak of anything like systematic science. This question has grown out of philosophical reflections, out of the need to bring an ordering principle to the flux of phenomena. A type of atomic theory can be found as early as the twelfth century B.C.E., in early Hindu literature. Matter was looked upon as consisting of minute particles separate from one another by empty space and endowed with a powerful force binding them one to the other, an assumption that made it possible to explain the resistance to fragmentation put up by every solid body. The view held by Democritus and Leucippus, that these smallest of particles were indivisible (hence the name atom) and in rapid motion, represented a considerable advancement. The Greek philosophers even held the view that the various types of matter differed from one another only in the number and configuration of atoms, an assumption that seems to come very close the conceptions held today. Their conception of the atom, however, was founded only on philosophical reflections and did not contribute to any advances in experimental knowledge.

The Concepts of Element and Atom

The atomistic conception could bear no fruit for chemistry or physics until Robert Boyle (1627–91) and John Dalton (1766–1844) gave unequivocal definitions, on the basis of careful experimental investigations, to the concepts of element and atom. Boyle defined as elements (like lead, mercury, etc.) those types of matter that were not composed of and that could not be broken down into other types of matter, and observed that all decomposable types of matter represented chemical compounds of two of more elements.

Dalton demonstrated that when a chemical compound forms from two (or more) elements, a *definite* amount of the one element always combines with a *definite* amount of the other element. For example: a given amount, by weight, of hydrogen always combines with eight times the amount in oxygen, regardless of the proportion in which one brings these two elements together. Dalton concluded that each element consists of invisibly small, indivisible units; in short, of atoms, in which all the properties of the element are already present. Consequently there must be as many different types of atoms as there are elements. One or more atoms of one element can combine with one or more atoms of another element to form a chemical compound, the smallest unit of which is known as the molecule, which must be composed of at least two atoms. Two atoms of hydrogen and one atom of oxygen combine to form a molecule of water. Since, as previously mentioned, these elements combine in a weight ratio of 1:8, an atom of oxygen must be 16 times heavier than an atom of hydrogen.

Atomic Weight

The ratio of weight or mass of the atom of any one element to the weight or mass of the hydrogen atom is known as the atomic weight of the element in question. The atomic weight of oxygen is therefore 16. It is enough to know the atomic mass in grams for a single element to be able to specify on the basis of the atomic weights the masses of the atoms for all elements. Since atoms are invisibly small structures, their mass is unimaginably small as well. But this means nothing more than that a weighable amount of an element must contain an inordinately large number of atoms. Nowadays, we have a number of methods for determining this number. A gram of gold, for example, contains a number of atoms that, rounded off, is represented by the number 3 followed by 21 zeros (approx. 3 sextillion).

An approximation of the size of atoms can be reached in the following manner: let us consider a soap bubble whose radius we have measured, so that we know the surface area of the sphere formed by the soap bubble. When the soap bubble is burst, we can determine the weight of the soap solution and from this, the thickness of the bubble's soap skin. Such specifications have shown that some soap bubbles have thickness of less than one millionth of a millimeter. Since at least *one* molecule of soap must lie in the surface of the soap bubble, the molecules must have diameters of less than one millionth of a millimeter, and the atoms composing the molecules must be somewhat smaller.

The Periodic Table of Elements

There are ninety-two different elements, which can be arranged according to their chemical properties into a system known as *the periodic table of elements*. It begins with the lightest element, hydrogen, which is placed at the first position, and ends with the heaviest element, uranium, which is placed at the ninety-second position. Researchers have since succeeded in creating elements beyond uranium, up to the atomic number of 101, through irradiation with such highly dynamic particles as neutrons, protons, and so forth. All of these elements are unstable, however; they decay spontaneously, emitting thereby alpha or beta rays.

Each element consists of a particular type of atom. If the atom is indeed the final, indivisible unit of matter, then it is impossible to transmute one element into another. Consequently, the old dream of the alchemists can never be fulfilled. This, at any rate, was the model of the atom accepted by the majority of chemists of the nineteenth century, and the great advances in the field of chemistry seemed to justify this model completely.

Nevertheless, far-reaching ideas often follow their own, peculiar set of laws in the course of their development.

The periodic table of elements provided such powerful evidence of lawful regularities connecting various elements that it seemed fully incomprehensible to those who held the position that the individual types of atoms existed completely independently of one another. Consequently, the belief in a real existence of atoms was by no means universal, even though this belief had in the course of the nineteenth century been corroborated by a good number of sources, including that of physical research. One of the most ardent proponents of atomic theory was Ludwig Boltzmann, who, when I began my studies in 1902 at the University of Vienna, was lecturing in theoretical physics there. I have vivid memories of the enthusiasm with which he explained to us the meaning of the concept of the atom. And he spoke with an expression of grateful joy of the experimental proof that the discovery of the electron had furnished to atomic theory. He could not foresee that the discovery of radioactivity would lead to a complete revolutionizing of the concept of the atom.

Radioactivity and the Evolution of the Concept of the Atom

This new development takes up the discovery made by H. Becquerel in 1896, that substances containing uranium emit invisible rays capable of blackening a photographic plate, rays that turn gases that are not normally electrically conductive (air, for example) into electrical conductors; i.e., which split gas molecules into positively and negatively electrically charged atoms (ions), and so forth. The careful study of such phenomena, first by Pierre and Marie Curie in France, then by E. Rutherford and his school in England, his student Otto Hahn and many others in Germany and other countries, led to very surprising findings. An interplay of experimental and theoretical activities set in, which was to transform our entire model of the universe. It began with Mme. Curie's discovery that all uraniferous minerals contain a new element that emits radiation in much higher intensity than does uranium, and that Mme. Curie named for this reason radium. Its chemical properties place it at the 88th position of the periodic table. Furthermore, uranium was found to contain a whole series of other new elements, all endowed with the property of emitting rays; i.e., radioactivity. It was soon discovered that these rays fell into three different groups, which, since their true nature was at first unknown, were simply named after the first three letters of the Greek alphabet: alpha, beta, and gamma rays. Further experimentation showed that only the gamma rays resemble light rays and X rays. Alpha and beta rays are in reality material particles that fly out of the radioactive elements at extraordinarily high speeds (reaching at times nearly the propagation speed of light), and that because of this speed take on the character of rays. Beta rays are identical with the negatively charged electron or cathode rays that occur in electrical discharge tubes. Alpha rays are dipositive (doubly ionized) helium atoms, i.e., atoms of the element that occupies the second position of the periodic table.

The circumstance that alpha and beta rays are endowed as a result of their high speeds (more than 20,000 to 100,000 times greater than that of the fastest projectile) with extremely high energy, together with the extraordinary refinement of our measuring instruments, makes it possible to detect a single alpha or beta ray on the basis of its effects, to make it "visible," so to speak, in a similar manner to which the track made by a ski in newly fallen snow betrays the passing of a skier.

The observation that the newly discovered radioactive substances emit alpha or beta rays, or more correctly, alpha or beta particles, is identical with the assertion that these substances do not represent any stable elements. For if an element emits particles, it must undergo a change, and thus change into a different element. Radium, for example, a metal, decays by way of the emission of alpha particles to a gaseous element, the so-called radium emanation, which is in turn transmuted, again by way of the emission of alpha particles, into a new element, etc. In this way, uranium, which itself emits alpha particles, is transmuted by way of a series of intermediate products that are transmuted with simultaneous emission of alpha rays in some cases, beta rays in others, and which include radium, finally into the common, stable element of lead. In this process, each radioactive element is characterized by its own particular rate of decay. One-half of any given amount of radium is transmuted over a period of approximately 1,600 years into radium emanation, while one-half of any given amount of radium emanation decays after only 3.6 days into its resulting product.

Since any given element consists of homogeneous atoms, it follows from what has been said that the uranium atom is transmuted by way of a number of unstable intermediate atoms into a stable lead atom. This proves that the atom is not indivisible, that it must be composed of simpler parts. Strongly analogous conditions were found to apply to thorium as well.

The Age of the Earth

The establishment of this surprising fact became the starting point for the rapid development of atomic physics over the past forty years. Before we examine this development more closely, let us draw our attention for a moment to an interesting result of the continual transmutation of uranium to lead. If the uranium atom is transmuted into a lead atom at a speed that now has been precisely calculated, then the uranium atom represents for us a kind of clock capable of determining the minimum age of uranium-bearing rocks, and consequently, of the age of the earth, whereby "age of the earth" is taken to mean the interval of time beginning at the point when the earth's crust solidified. One can assume that from this point onward, certain minerals have not undergone any changes in the course of the earth's history. Nowadays, it is known that the question of whether minerals have undergone changes in the course of the earth's history is one that requires extremely careful consideration. The radioactivity of potassium and rubidium can now be used as well to determine the age of the earth. Such well-crystallized, uranium-bearing minerals will contain all the lead that has been created by the radioactive decay of uranium. We know that from 1 gram of uranium, 1/100 gram of lead is formed in about 70 million years. Thus, if one determines in a suitable uranium-bearing mineral the quantity of uranium it contains and the quantity of lead to which the uranium has given rise, one arrives at the interval of time it has taken for the lead to be created from the uranium, and consequently, the age of the rock in which the mineral was found. Such analyses have resulted in a maximum value of approximately 3 to 4 billion years for the age of the earth.

It may perhaps be worthy of note that such age determinations have attained significance for geology and paleontology as well. The geologist occupies himself with the history of the earth's crust, the transformations and dislocations that have gradually come about through sedimentary deposits from the oceans, volcanic eruptions, etc. Whereas in former times, determining the ages of the various geological periods had to be done almost exclusively by studying fossils, such determinations can now be augmented through the application of the uranium-lead clock for any rock strata that come into question. This method can also be applied to minerals that occur in sedimentary rock, whereby one arrives at a minimum age of the oceans; the greatest value arrived at by using this process has been 1.6 billion years.

The Rutherford-Bohr Model of the Atom

The realization that the atom is not immutable and therefore not indivisible naturally brought to the foreground the question of just what the ultimate, indivisible building blocks of matter are. If uranium gives rise by way of various intermediate stages to radium and ultimately lead, then the uranium atom must contain, among its building blocks, the elementary particles that compose all of these elements, including lead. The notion that the atoms of all elements consist of the same elementary particles and differ from one another only in the number and configuration of these particles, was not a new one. But it was the discovery of radioactivity and the subsequent experiments investigating the behavior of alpha particles when they pass through gases or solids with their characteristic high velocities that first gave scientists the opportunity to study the structure of the atom by way of experimentation. In alpha particles, one had a sort of ready-made atomic probe. One could study the interaction between alpha particles and the atoms of the materials they passed through, and from this interaction make inferences as to the constitution of the atoms. It has already been mentioned that we can make a single alpha particle "visible" through its effects, thanks to its great energy; we can follow it along its path through the matter, observe what happens when it collides with an atom of the material it is passing through, and how the effect of such a collision changes when one sends the alpha particle through different elements. The knowledge gleaned from experiments of this type led in the years 1911 to 1913 to the creation of the Rutherford-Bohr model of the atom.

Here, of course, the interrelations between matter and energy, having been common knowledge for quite some time, were taken into consideration as well.

The electrical charge itself is endowed with an "atomic" structure as well. There exists a minimum unit of electrical charge, whose size is independent of the positive or negative sign of the charge and which is never fallen short of. It therefore cannot be further divisible. Any given electrical charge is a whole multiple of this unit charge. If the unit charge is positive, then, except for in certain cases which shall not be mentioned here, it is never bound to a mass smaller than that of the lightest atom, the hydrogen atom. If the charge is negative, however, then the smallest mass that occurs as the carrier of the unit charge is only 1/1800 the mass of the hydrogen atom: a particle called the electron, whose size corresponds to a sphere with a radius fifty-thousand times smaller than that which we ascribe to the atom. The cathode rays that occur in discharge tubes are rapidly flying electrons. Positive and negative electricity particles and their mutual attraction must play a decisive role in the structure of the atom. On the other hand, ordinary matter is unelectrical, so atoms must normally be unelectrical as well; i.e., they must contain equal quantities of positively and negatively charged particles. The consideration of these circumstances as well as the results of the alpha-ray experiments mentioned above led to the following model of the structure of the atom.

Every atom consists of a positively charged nucleus, in which nearly the entire mass of the atom in question is concentrated. About this nucleus move a number of negative electrons, the same number as that of the positive charges carried by the nucleus. The number of the positive unit charges in the nucleus is equal to the position number of the element in question in the periodic table and is referred to as the atomic number of the element. The atom of hydrogen, which occupies the first position, consists accordingly of a nucleus with the positive charge of 1 and one electron orbiting the nucleus; helium, which occupies the second position, consists of a nucleus with the positive charge of 2 and two orbiting electrons, and so forth up to the heaviest element, uranium, which is placed at the ninety-second position of the periodic table, and which is accordingly composed of a nucleus with the positive charge of 92 and 92 outer electrons.

The alpha particle is thus a helium atom, flying at high velocity, which has been stripped of its two outer electrons: i.e., a helium nucleus. The size of the atom, as already mentioned at the beginning of this essay, has been estimated as corresponding to a sphere with a radius of a few hundred millionths of a centimeter.

The Size of the Nucleus

The experiments involving the collisions of alpha particles with the atoms of various substances demonstrated that the positively charged alpha particles were sharply deflected from their straight-lined paths by the repulsive forces of the positively charged nuclei of the atoms struck. It could be deduced from the sharpness of the deflection and the commonly known repulsive forces between like electrical charges that to bring about the sharp alpha particle deflections observed, the collision between the alpha particle and the nucleus had to take place at an extraordinarily small distance, a distance approximately ten-thousand times smaller than the radius of the atom. This, however, would not only be possible if the radius of the colliding *nucleus* were ten-thousand times smaller than the radius of the atom. Envisioned as a sphere, then, the nucleus has a spatial extension one-trillion-times smaller than the size of the atom. The size *ratio* of the nucleus to the atom corresponds approximately to that between a barely visible speck of dust and the interior of St. Stephen's Cathedral in Vienna. The size of the atom is determined by the distance of the external electron shell from the nucleus; the size of the electron itself in comparison to this distance is infinitesimal.

The Building Blocks of the Nucleus

Every element, as previously mentioned, is unequivocally determined in all of its properties by the magnitude of the positive charge of its nucleus. The nucleus of the simplest element, hydrogen, is the carrier of the positive unit charge. It thus represents one of the elementary particles of matter, known as the *proton*. The hydrogen nucleus contains one proton, that of helium contains two protons, as commensurate with the positive charge of its nucleus or its atomic number of 2, etc., up to uranium, whose nucleus contains 92 protons. Nuclei cannot be composed only of protons, however, for then their atomic weights would have to equal the number of their component protons. In reality, the atomic weights are much greater. Oxygen, for example, occupies the eighth position of the periodic table; the oxygen nucleus therefore contains 8 protons. Its atomic weight, however, as was demonstrated at the beginning of this essay, is not 8, but 16. Nuclei must therefore contain besides protons still other elementary particles which contribute considerably to their mass, but which leave their charge unchanged. Such particles are uncharged, or as it is commonly put, electrically neutral. Such particles have for this reason received the name *neutrons*. Researchers have split off neutrons from nuclei and have determined their mass, by way of the artificial transmutation of elements, which shall be spoken of later. The mass of the neutron has been found to nearly equal that of the hydrogen atom. Thus, the number of neutrons in a nucleus is equal to the difference between its atomic weight and the number of protons in this nucleus, which one of course knows from the position number of the element in question in the periodic table. From the atomic weight and the atomic number of an element we can immediately tell how many protons and neutrons compose its nucleus. The nucleus of ordinary hydrogen contains one proton and no neutron; that of helium, which occupies the second position of the periodic table and has an atomic weight of 4, must be composed of two protons and two neutrons; uranium, which occupies the ninety-second position and has an atomic weight of 238, must have a nucleus containing 92 protons and 146 = 238 minus 92 neutrons.

That such a large number of particles, squeezed together in the tiny space taken up by the nucleus, exist as a stable structure, demonstrates the extraordinarily powerful attractive forces at play between these particles. The electrons, which in comparison with the dimensions of the nucleus are very far away from it, are held within the atom in fixed states of equilibrium by the electrical attractive forces of the protons in the nucleus, and by the centrifugal forces brought about by the rapid motion of the electrons about the nucleus—forces much weaker than those at play within the nucleus.

Protons, neutrons, and electrons are the ultimate elementary building blocks of matter. The discovery of the meson, whose mass lies between that of the electron and that of the proton, and the discovery of the hyperon have since demonstrated just how complicated the actual situation really is. All of these new particles are unstable; they decay spontaneously into lighter particles.

Isotopes

A stable nucleus can contain a maximum of ninety-two protons; beyond uranium, no stable elements exist. Is there an analogous simple limit to the possible number of *neutrons* in the nucleus? This number, together with the number of protons present, determines the atomic weight of an element. The chemists of the nineteenth century subscribed without exception to the notion that each element had a definite atomic weight by which it was unambiguously characterized. In light of the modern conception of the atom, this implies that a given number of protons can only form a stable nucleus with *one* determinate number of neutrons. It has since been shown that this is not the case. Nuclei that contain a definite number of protons, which therefore belong to one definite element, have a number of neutrons that varies between definite limits, and consequently a correspondingly varying atomic weight. Besides ordinary hydrogen, for example, the nucleus of which is composed of only one proton, there exists the so-called heavy hydrogen, whose nucleus consists of one proton and one neutron, and whose atomic weight is consequently almost twice that of ordinary hydrogen. Water always contains a small percentage (0.02 percent) of "heavy" water, whose molecules are composed of "heavy" hydrogen. (It is perhaps worth mentioning that heavy water may have played an important role in the construction of the atomic bomb.) Most elements are mixtures of atom types differing somewhat in weight, which are known as isotopic atom types, because they (belonging as they do to the same element) are categorized in the same place in the periodic table.

The existence of isotopic atom types proves that thè atomic weight does not have the significance previously ascribed to it; it is not a characteristic constant of the *element.* It is a constant of the atomic *nucleus,* a constant that determines a highly significant value; namely, the work or the energy we would have to expend if we wanted to break up an atomic nucleus into its component parts, or the other way around, the energy we would obtain if a nucleus were to assemble itself from protons and neutrons. This process occurs continually in the interior of the sun (and other fixed stars) and gives rise to the conservation of solar energy, to which all life on earth owes it existence. In principle, it forms the basis for the construction of the hydrogen bomb as well.

Equivalence of Mass and Energy

In order to make this comprehensible, it must be remembered that mass—as Einstein has shown—is only a special form of energy, which can just as well be transformed into thermal energy or electrical energy, as is possible with mechanical energy (or work), for example. The reverse holds as well, of course: if we increase the energy of a body, by supplying it with thermal energy, for example—i.e., by raising its temperature—we increase thereby its mass as well. The only reason we cannot generally prove this is the mass represents such an enormous reservoir of energy. A mass of 1/1000 of a unit of atomic weight (and as such, one thousand times smaller than the mass of a hydrogen atom) represents an energy of approximately one million electron volts; that is, the energy an electron receives when it undergoes a voltage difference of one million volts. Since the mass of the hydrogen atom in grams is represented by a number that does not produce a digit other than zero until the twenty-fourth decimal place, it should be easy to understand why we cannot produce any *measurable* change in the mass of a macroscopic body by increasing or reducing its energy. The kinetic energy of the fastest projectiles increases their mass by a factor of only approximately one trillionth of their value. This, of course, is impossible to detect. But for masses as small as those of atoms, the changes in mass caused by changes in energy are quite easily detectable.

Let us consider for a moment the nucleus of the heavy hydrogen atom. It is the simplest nucleus that is composed of protons and neutrons; it consists of *one* proton and *one* neutron. Our knowledge of the mass of the two particles is very precise. If the mass were a constant, the mass of the heavy hydrogen nucleus would have to be equal to the sum of the masses of the proton and the neutron. In reality, it is smaller by an amount that, measured in electrical terms, corresponds to an energy of approximately two million volts. This energy was apparently emitted when the heavy hydrogen nucleus formed out of one proton and one neutron billions of years ago. And this is the exact amount of energy we must expend if we want to split up this nucleus into its two constituent parts, which we can in fact do. The reverse of this process, the formation of a heavy hydrogen nucleus from one proton and one neutron, can also be brought about artificially. We then obtain (in the form of gamma radiation) an energy of approximately two million volts. That which has been demonstrated here, using the particular example of the heavy hydrogen nucleus, holds for the atomic nuclei of all stable elements; the mass of an atom's nucleus is always somewhat smaller than the sum of the masses of the protons and neutrons that constitute it. This difference in mass, or mass defect, as it is known, can be readily deduced from the pertinent atomic weight and converted to amounts of energy by means of the relation given above. It represents the binding energy of the nucleus in question.

The amounts of energy stored in atomic nuclei are millions of times greater than those we can obtain by means of the most dynamic chemical processes. Chemical processes take place only in the outer electron shell of the atom. When two hydrogen atoms and one oxygen atom combine to form a molecule of water, the nuclei of these atoms remain completely unchanged; all that changes is the configuration of the outer electrons. And since the distances of the electrons from each other and from the nucleus are very great with respect to the dimensions of the nucleus, changes in the configuration of electrons entail only relatively insignificant changes in energy—at any rate insignificant compared with the energies that come into play in the nuclei of atoms. All electrical, magnetic, and optical processes as well are limited to occurrences in the electron shell of the atom; the nuclei are affected to no degree whatsoever. This is why all attempts to transmute one element into another by chemical means or by drawing upon ordinary physical processes were doomed to failure.

Artificial Transmutations

The transmutation of elements requires the transmutation of the atomic nuclei. When uranium decomposes, by way of radium, to lead, such transmutations take place continually and spontaneously. Radioactivity is a property of the atom's *nucleus*. Nowadays, we are thoroughly acquainted with the energies related in the course of this process. When a gram of radium decays completely to lead, the kinetic energy present in the alpha and beta rays emitted is enough to bring 25 tons of water to a boil. Let us compare this to one of the most dynamic chemical processes known, the formation of water by way of the combustion of hydrogen and oxygen. When a gram of water is formed in this way, enough thermal energy is released to bring 38 grams of water to a boil; this is almost one million times less than with the transmutation of radium to lead. Since, due to the slow decay of radium, it takes many thousands of years for this great energy to develop, this process is unsuitable for technical application; yet it demonstrates nevertheless the energies to be derived from nuclear processes as well as the energies that would have to be expended to bring about an artificial transmutation of the atomic nucleus. These energies are approximately one million times greater than those that can be brought about through chemical processes. For this reason, chemical processes cannot be employed for the transmutation of elements. On the other hand, the alpha particles of naturally radioactive substances are endowed with energies of several million volts. Indeed, Rutherford brought about the first artificial atom transmutations in 1919 by irradiating various substances, such as aluminum and nitrogen, with alpha rays—i.e., with highly dynamic helium nuclei. These helium nuclei, when they come into proximity to a nitrogen nucleus, are generally deflected from their trajectory, whereupon they fly off in another direction, a process that can be compared with the collision of two billiard balls. In isolated cases, however, the helium nucleus can head straight for the nitrogen nucleus and come so close to it that the two nuclei react with one another, in the same way that colliding atoms react chemically with one another and form a chemical compound. In this case, the helium nucleus enters the nitrogen nucleus, and a proton is split off in the process. The original nitrogen nucleus is transmuted into an oxygen nucleus, as one can easily imagine. The nitrogen nucleus has the (positive) charge of 7. When it absorbs a helium nucleus and emits a proton, its charge is increased by one unit, to 8, and a nucleus with a charge of 8 is an oxygen nucleus. This process renders itself observable in the following manner: the proton flies out of the nitrogen nucleus with great energy and thus, just like a single alpha ray, by virtue of its ionizing effects, becomes "visible." We can consequently confirm the transmutation of a single atom into a new atom.

Artificially Produced Radioactive Nuclei

The oxygen that originates from nitrogen is usually stable oxygen. It happens, however, in the course of such nuclear reactions, that a new nucleus is formed that is not stable, but radioactive. It is transmuted through the emission of rays into a stable nucleus of higher or lower atomic number. Let us consider as an example the nuclear reaction that occurs when alpha particles are induced to strike aluminum, a process often referred to as the bombardment of aluminum with alpha particles. In isolated cases, the aluminum nucleus absorbs an incoming helium nucleus and emits one neutron. Since the helium nucleus has a charge of 2 and the emitted neutron has no charge, the new nucleus formed from the aluminum nucleus must have a charge greater by two units. Aluminum has a nuclear charge of 13; the new nucleus must therefore have a charge of 15. The fifteenth position in the periodic table is taken up by the element phosphorus. Through the bombardment with alpha rays, aluminum has been transmuted into phosphorus. This phosphorus, however, contains in its nucleus one neutron less than ordinary phosphorus; it is an isotope of phosphorus, a radioactive isotope, which by way of the emission of radiation is transmuted into stable silicon. As a result of the radioactivity of this artificially formed phosphorus, one can detect not only the neutron flying off with great energy, but the resulting phosphorus as well. It is endowed with all of the chemical properties of ordinary stable phosphorus. One can therefore separate it from aluminum using the chemical methods characteristically used with phosphorus, and thereby prove that it is in fact an isotope of phosphorus. And although only inconceivably small amounts of radioactive phosphorus can be created by means of such a nuclear reaction, the emission of radiation makes it possible to detect it with certainty, because every single emitted ray can be observed. The radioactivity of this artificially produced phosphorus isotope was discovered by Frédéric and Irène Joliot-Curie in 1934; this amounted to the discovery of artificial radioactivity.

Nuclear Reactions by Means of Fast Protons and Neutrons

Since atomic nuclei are composed of protons and neutrons, these particles will naturally react with atomic nuclei as soon as they are close enough to the nuclei; for this to come about, they must be endowed with considerable energies. Alpha rays as projectiles capable of penetrating other nuclei and thus reacting with them are provided to us by the natural conversion products of the uranium and thorium [actinide] series. These radiation sources are relatively weak. In the last twelve years, we have succeeded, with the help of large-scale high-voltage equipment, in creating highly dynamic protons, alpha rays, and neutrons; ones of incomparably higher intensity than those that come about by means of natural alpha radiation. This has made it possible to create radioactive isotopes of all elements. In this way, we can create gold from mercury, for example, but this artificially created gold is an unstable gold isotope that transmutes over the course of a few days, accompanied by the emission of radiation, back into mercury.

It is characteristic of all of these nuclear reactions that the newly created nucleus differs by only one or two units in its nuclear charge from the original nucleus, which has entered into a state of interaction with the incoming neutrons, protons, or helium nuclei. Any newly created elements will therefore always be close neighbors of the original element in the periodic table. To trigger these nuclear processes, we must always expend energy in the form of the kinetic energy of the "projectiles" reacting with the nuclei. This is obvious, for the nucleus we are transmuting is initially a stable nucleus, and a structure is considered stable when work or energy must be expended to bring about its transmutation. The transmutation process itself can take place either in such a way that the energy released after the completed transmutation is greater than the energy originally brought into the process, in which case we have gained energy; or this energy is less, in which case we have lost energy.

Balance of Energy in Nuclear Reactions

In any case, due to the law of the conservation of total energy, the energy gained or lost must be accounted for by the energy reservoir represented by the masses of nuclei that take part in the transmutation process. Let us consider the two special cases referred to previously. The transmutation of a nitrogen nucleus into an oxygen nucleus entails an energy loss of 1.3 million volts. The atomic weight of the nitrogen nucleus plus the atomic weight of the helium nucleus reacting with it is less than the sum of the atomic weights of the resulting oxygen nucleus and the emitted proton by an amount that corresponds exactly to the energy lost. Here, then, the added kinetic energy has been transformed into mass.

In the case of the transmutation of aluminum, by way of radioactive phosphorus, into silicon, there is an energy gain of more than two million volts that results from the masses of the nuclei reacting with one another (aluminum and helium). The balances of energy in these artificial transmutation processes have provided us with one of the most elegant experimental confirmations of the equivalence of mass and energy.

Although many of these artificial transmutations of elements entail energy gains millions of times greater than those brought about by the most dynamic chemical reactions (adjusting for equal amounts), technical utilization of these nuclear transmutations is not possible, for even under the most favorable conditions only minute amounts are transmuted.

Harnessing the intraatomic energies on a technical scale did not enter the realm of possibility until late 1938, when a totally new artificial transmutation process involving the heaviest elements, uranium and thorium, was discovered.

Uranium Fission

The importance of this discovery will certainly justify saying a few words about the road that led to it.

The neutron had proven itself a particularly suitable "reagent" for the transmutation of elements; it is to Fermi that we owe our knowledge of this. Since the neutron has no electrical charge, it can be brought into very close proximity to the nucleus without being repulsed by the latter's positive charge. Out of sixty elements tested by Fermi and his colleagues, forty were found to be transmutable into other elements by way of bombardment with neutrons. The newly formed element always had an atomic number at most two units lower or one unit higher than that of the original element. Consequently, when uranium was irradiated with neutrons, the expected result was either one of the two lower elements thorium and protactinium, or else the next higher element, an element that would have to have an atomic number of 93, one which does not exist as a stable element.

After Fermi had made a number of experiments along these lines, Hahn and Meitner, and later, Hahn, Meitner, and Strassmann continued the investigations on a broader basis. A good number of radioactive substances were found; for all of them it was positively demonstrated that they could not be identical with one of the two elements preceding uranium. All that remained was the assumption that they were elements higher than uranium, and were dubbed accordingly "transuranic" elements. Further investigations, however, led researchers to the realization that they were dealing with an entirely novel process. Hahn and Strassmann found that bombarding uranium with neutrons resulted in an element as low as barium, which has the atomic number 56. *This could only be explained by a fission of uranium into two approximately equal-sized components.* Frisch and Meitner demonstrated, drawing thereby on the conceptual models developed by Bohr to illustrate the structure of the atomic nucleus, that such fission processes are to be expected with the heaviest nuclei, and that a fission of this type would have to entail the generation of nearly 200 million volts of energy. In the uranium nucleus, which contains 92 protons and 146 neutrons, the repulsive forces that prevail between the positively charged protons are just barely compensated for by the attractive forces that hold together the building blocks of the nucleus. If a neutron penetrates this nucleus, the energy of the nucleus is increased and its equilibrium is disturbed to such an extent that it breaks into two parts, i.e., two lower nuclei. Since the two fragments are highly charged (together they must have a charge of 92), they repel each other violently and fly apart with energies that combined amount to nearly 200 million volts. This kinetic energy is again supplied by the energy reservoir of the masses; the sum of the masses of the two fragments is smaller by the equivalent amount than the mass of the uranium nucleus after it absorbed the neutron. Frisch was the first to demonstrate by experimentation that the lower nuclei created by the fission of uranium were indeed endowed with the energies calculated here; his findings were later confirmed by a number of other experimenters.

Uranium fission accordingly represents an artificially induced transmutation process that generates approximately a hundred times more energy than the ordinary nuclear processes. There is, however, another circumstance that lends this fission process particular significance. The uranium nucleus contains besides the 92 protons 146 neutrons, and when the absorbed neutron is counted, 147 neutrons. The nuclei of the lower elements into which the uranium nucleus breaks apart possess together fewer neutrons; a surplus of neutrons is therefore present, and a number of these neutrons are expelled when the uranium nucleus breaks up. These extra neutrons can split new uranium nuclei, whereby more neutrons are released; the fission process multiplies itself and takes on the character of a "chain reaction," which, if it proceeds at a rapid pace, amounts to an explosion. In this way, exceedingly large quantities of uranium can be split, resulting in the generation of extremely high levels of energy. This represents an energy source of unfathomed power, a source fed by the energy reservoir of mass.

Conclusion

It is unfortunate that this discovery happened to have been made during wartime. Defense requirements on the one side, the desire for aggression on the other, have concentrated the efforts of competent scientists on the goal of putting the newly discovered source of energy in the service of war, an effort that has led to the construction of the first atomic bombs.

The terrible weapon of destruction that has come into the hands of men will hopefully serve as a warning to everyone to put every effort into making sure that the development of this immense source of energy will contribute to the betterment of mankind and not to its doom.

Science will gradually show the way to harness the enormous intraatomic energies for peaceful industries in the spirit of ideal cooperation, the spirit in which the true scientists of the world have always felt themselves bound each to each.

Translated by Daniel Theisen

The Status of Women in the Professions

In trying to tell you about the history of professions for women, I shall deal mainly with the problem of academically trained women because this is likely to interest you most, and is certainly the aspect most familiar to me. Let me start, however, with a few remarks about women's work in general.

The cooperation of women in such fields as agriculture and home economics is surely very old. Even today, there are some primitive peoples about whose patterns of culture we are well informed by the books of two outstanding American women, Ruth Benedict and Margaret Mead, who assign greatly varying tasks to their women. I am mentioning those books, not only because of their great importance for the science of man, but also because they show so clearly how much in a group of people the development of cultural problems is affected by accepted customs and the common way of life of the group. In the same way the gradual development of the professional and legal equality of women can only be properly understood if one remembers how many accepted customs had to be overcome in the struggle for the emancipation of women.

It has often been said that the Bible has contributed to the discrimination against women by the role it assigned to Eve in Paradise. It is Eve who bears the chief blame for the sin against God's commandment, not Adam. On the other hand, the Old Testament mentions highly respected woman prophets and judges, and in the New Testament we find many examples of noble behavior and self-sacrificing devotion among women. As to witch hunts (the last of which, as far as I can tell, seem to have taken place in 1782 in Glarus, Switzerland) it is very debatable whether they were connected with the fact that, particularly in the Puritan-Protestant religion, women were considered the embodiment of evil. Men, too, have been burnt as witches, while, on the other hand, in Catholic countries the mother superior of a convent had the rank of a bishop.

The question about the position of women—before the onset of the *Frauenbewegung*—cannot be answered properly without considering sociological, sexual-psychological, and many other aspects of our Western culture. Certainly, women did not live a life of leisure in ancient times. Most things needed for daily life were made in the home, and much of it was women's work. This is not only true of agriculture, both for sale and home consumption, but also applies to such domestic occupations as spinning and weaving, sewing and cooking. This work in the home was not based on professional training, although spinning, weaving, etc. were skills expected from every young girl. But already in the Middle Ages there existed certain industries, such as silk manufacture in Italy and southern France, which were organized on factory lines and where women and children were employed preferentially, in particular for certain kinds of work like the spooling of the silk. Of course, that too was "unskilled" work.

It was the French Revolution that created the feminist movement in its modern sense, when the demand for equality of men and women was first publicly formulated and discussed. But the Industrial Revolution in England too was of influence here, mainly between 1750 and 1832. The rise of industrialism was not accompanied by changes in the current political system, but the earlier puritanical revolution and the changes after 1688 had a profound influence on economic thought. Later, the idea of evolution gave further support to the ambitions of women by counteracting the tendency to cling to traditional ways. There was a growing desire for new things and a belief that they were possible.

The supporters of equality for women naturally demanded in the first place the establishment of technical schools for training women for crafts and trades, for home economics and agriculture, and, of course, they also demanded suitable schools for preparing women for a university career. In Germany, the first agricultural school for women was opened in 1920, but in Prussia only men were allowed to teach in those schools!

The professional training of women encountered great opposition in nearly all the professions. It was a hard struggle which in each country was paid in its own way; but the motives for the opposition were essentially the same everywhere, and the influence and aftereffects of old habits and traditions can be clearly seen. As an example, let me quote some of the famous plays by Molière like "Les Précieuses," "Les Femmes Savantes," "L'Ecole des Femmes," and others.

Molière's ideas were used in Germany, against higher education for women, as late as the twenties! Molière's attitude is well known to have been conditioned by a literary group who used to meet in the palais of a French marquise, whose female members, among them the well-known writer Mlle. de Scuderi, called themselves "les précieuses," a term of distinction which Molière turned into a term of ridicule. But to explain that attitude, I must say something about those questions concerning education which were much debated at the time. It was the time when people tried, particularly in England and France, to reconcile the demands of humanism and realism in rationalism. Not the acquisition of knowledge, but the education and cultivation of the mind were regarded as essential. In France, this gave rise to the aristocratic ideal of the "honnête homme," who acquires vision and freedom of mind by a variety of studies but refrains from any practical occupation or service. The English equivalent was the gentleman, represented as an education ideal, particularly by John Locke. The précieuses, ridiculed by Molière, presumably aimed at a similar goal.

As against this aristocratic idea of education, the great Czech educator and theologian Comenius presented a very different attitude: he demanded general education for all. It is perhaps interesting to hear one of his arguments, as he put it: "If someone asks what is to be the outcome if craftsmen, peasants, porters and even the womenfolk become scholars, then answer: When this general education of the young is properly provided, then in future none will lack good material for thinking, wishing, ambition or work."

Almost at the same time as Molière's plays there appeared the English translation of a paper written by a woman in Latin; it was called "The Learned Maid; or, Whether a Maid May Be a Scholar?" The English translator, a school teacher named Clemens Barkdale, added a lengthy comment, saying among other things, "that maids may and ought to be excited and encouraged by the best and strongest reason, by the testimonies of wise men, to the embracing of this kind of life." Barkdale probably felt that way because he realized that the destruction of the convent schools in England had deprived the girls of a place of education for which no replacement had yet been produced. The game was always the same. There were sharp adversaries and passionate advocates of the emancipation and higher education of women, and both were found among men as well as women. The literature that grew up around this is understandably of great variety, since so many questions are tied up with it: political and economic conditions, cultural and moral attitudes and institutions, in brief, everything that belongs to the pattern of culture of a society. And the value of the more recent writings for and against women's emancipation varies as much as their motivation.

The struggle for the establishment of secondary schools for girls and for their admission to universities took place mainly in middle-class circles. A number of periodicals were dedicated to the problem and aims of the feminist movement, and older pamphlets were translated afresh, such as "Vindication of the Rights of Woman" by Mary Wollstonecraft.

I am, of course, most familiar with the corresponding literature of Austria, Germany, and Sweden. In the desire to find arguments in favor of the equality of women with men, people studied the education of women in old times, centuries back. Of course, there were well organized women's organizations to represent women's rights in all civilized countries. In Germany, we must mention in the first place Helene Lange, who started her struggle for a new kind of school education for girls in 1887, with a petition to the Prussian Ministry of Culture, in which also the admission of women to universities was demanded and argued for. She caused an enormous sensation but had at first no success. She devoted, however, all her time and all her strength to her aim, and twenty-one years later, in 1908, she achieved together with the reform of girls' schools also the admission of women to German universities. In Austria, it was Marianne Hainisch, and in Sweden Fredrika Bremer, who did much for the modern education of girls. Marianne Hanisch did this in connection with the Vienna Society for Expanding Women's Education; that society issued in 1927 a celebration volume *Dreißig Jahre Frauenstudium,* giving statistical material on the advances during thirty years.

Fredrika Bremer fought chiefly in her novels for the equality of women; nevertheless, she is still honored and indeed venerated as the leader of the feminist movement in Sweden. In Stockholm, she has a monument; a large women's association is named after her, and her personality has been the subject of many studies by present-day Swedish (male) authors. She was really much ahead of her time, traveled as a single woman as far as Greece and America, and has found a very charming appreciation by the famous Swedish writer Selma Lagerlöf.

When we look for male supporters of the higher education of women and of their professional equality with men, then it is remarkable how few men of general reputation we find. Perhaps we should mention the well-known German writer, Graf Hermann Keyserling, who, in his book *America, the Rise of a New World,* mentions the great influence of middle-class women in America, and considers it, without reservation, as favorable. Also the famous theologian Adolf von Harnack, father of Mrs. von Zahn-Harnack, who was very active in the German feminist movement, supported the striving for education among women, and opposed the prejudice that women teachers should be inferior to men. This was also the view of Friedrich Althoff, the well-known organizer of the Prussian universities. However, Harnack would have liked to see the professional training of women limited essentially to the unmarried ones.

On the other hand, you find a considerable number of very respectable names among those men who—from the most varied viewpoints—have made strong objections to the higher education of women and to their admission to various professions. Those attacks against women's emancipation were directed partly against their training for certain professions, partly in principle against any kind of higher education for women, ambitions that got lumped together as "emancipation of women" or "feminism." I won't say much about some extreme writings, as for example a book that appeared in Germany in 1910 under the title *Are Women Human?* with the Latin subtitle *Mulieres homines non sunt.* More serious and obstructive were books by respected scientists, as the book by the famous German physiologist, Paul Möbius, *The Physiological Feeblemindedness of Woman,* whose twelfth unaltered edition appeared as late as 1922. Or the pamphlet of the reputable Austrian medical doctor Max von Gruber on *Girls' Education and Racial Hygiene,* published in 1916, which claimed that the deliberate aim of the feminist movement was the destruction of the family.

The same attitude is represented by the American A. Smith, as shown by the title of his book, *Women's Higher Education and Racial Suicide,* which appeared in New York in 1905 in *Popular Science Monthly* and which attempted to prove that mental emancipation of women is a serious menace to the existence of the human race.

In this list of adversaries we should also mention the famous philosopher Eduard von Hartmann who, in his "Contributions to the Feminist Question," declared in 1922 that there was a sexual differentiation of morality whereby women had a lack of conscious morality. There was even sharp opposition against female physicians on the part of famous medical men, such as the Viennese professor Eduard Albert. Almost as much opposition against the higher education of girls came from various women's circles.

Women have achieved equality in different countries at different times, and differently in its different aspects. It is by no means the case that progressive countries showed their progressiveness equally in all professional fields. For instance, Switzerland, for many years the Mecca for women who wanted to study, has to this day no vote for women and has recently again voted against it, on February 1, 1959.

There are, of course, exceptions, such as the Russian Sonja Kowalewska, who obtained a professorship for mathematics in Stockholm, in the 1880s, or Dorothea von Schlözer, who became a doctor of philosophy in Göttingen as early as the beginning of the nineteenth century.

In some respects the United States was far ahead of other countries because it admitted women as parsons as early as 1851. In Sweden, on the other hand, the possibility of admitting women theologians as priests was recently discussed thoroughly, and then declined by the leading bishops, though accepted by the government. In Germany, the problem was discussed in 1927, in a paper "What Shall We Do With Our Women Theologians?" from the viewpoint of the Protestant churches; the author, Paul Ebert, came to the conclusion that women should be admitted to auxiliary posts, but not to service on the pulpit or at the altar. Even so, the question was studied thirty years earlier in Germany than in Sweden. On the other hand, the legal regulation for the admission of women to the university was already settled in Sweden in 1873, but in Germany only in 1908. Amusingly, the main difficulty in Sweden—and in England too—was that the regulation before 1873 referred specifically to men; the whole problem ultimately was to replace the word "men" by the word "persons," in order to make the admission of women to higher schools possible. But when this was done, it also gave women the possibility to acquire the right to lecture; in Germany, this did not happen until after the first World War. Even in 1918, when the great mathematician Hilbert, in Göttingen, tried to obtain the faculty's permission for his talented woman assistant to apply for "the venia legendi" (which would have made her a member of the faculty), he met with such indignation that he answered with the famous remark: "But, gentlemen, a faculty is not a swimming pool!" Nevertheless, Dr. Emmy Nöther was not allowed to become a lecturer at that time. In Austria, women were at first admitted as students to the philosophical faculties only in 1897. In 1901, the medical faculties followed suit, and only in 1910 the faculties of law.

You probably know better than I how things went in America. I happen to know that the centenary of the Female Medical College of Pennsylvania was celebrated in 1950 in Philadelphia by the Medical Women's International Association.

The leading role which the United States has played in establishing good training possibilities for women has often been stressed abroad, and particularly in Germany. In one of the German books on the American educational system you read: "In no other field have the Americans done such excellent work as in the education of women." In a 1959 issue of the Smith College alumnae quarterly, it is mentioned that New Englanders pioneered education in America, having provided the first secondary school and the first women's college.

Looking back, I have the impression that the problems of professional women in general, and particularly of academic women, have found fairly satisfactory solutions in the last 80 to 100 years. Not all that can be desired has been achieved. In principle, nearly all-male professions have become accessible to women; in practice, things often look different.

In England, it was only a few years ago that the right of female teachers to receive the same pay for the same work as their male colleagues was recognized, and the actual process of equalization has been spread over seven years. On the other hand, there are in England a number of excellent women scientists who are recognized as such, and are fellows of the Royal Society, such as the biologist Charlotte Auerbach, the mathematician Mary Cartwright (principal of Girton College, Cambridge), and the crystallographer Dame Kathleen Lonsdale (Dame is an honorary title, equivalent to Sir). All these are well-known outside England. Dame Caroline Haslett, an engineer, was sent to Sweden during the last war in order to study important electrotechnical problems. This makes a pleasant contrast to the struggle of English women teachers for equal pay.

There is much I could tell from my own experience, both of instances of help and assistance and also of discouraging and sometimes comical prejudices. For example, between 1910 and 1915, I had written several review articles on physical subjects for the semipopular magazine *Naturwissenschaftliche Rundschau.* As usual, I had signed them with my family name, without the first name. One day, the publisher received a letter in which one of the editors of *Brockhaus* (a well-known German encyclopedia) asked for my address, because he wanted an article on radio-activity for his encyclopedia. But when the answer revealed my sex, the editor of *Brockhaus* wrote back almost indignantly that "he would not think of printing an article written by a woman!" (This, after reading, and apparently liking, some of my previous articles!) Even Max Planck, to whom both as a human and as a scientist I owe so much, considered it at first very peculiar that I was thinking of doing scientific work. I had obtained my doctor's degree at the University of Vienna, and had published several papers in scientific journals; in 1907, I went to Berlin for further studies and presented myself to Planck, in order to attend his lectures. He was very friendly, but clearly astonished; he said, "You have a doctor's degree, what more do you want?" When I replied that I wanted to understand physics more thoroughly, he said a few friendly words, but did not pursue the point. But five years later he offered me a job as assistant lecturer at his Institute of Theoretical Physics at the University of Berlin; this, in Prussia, was a complete innovation. Not only did this give me a chance to work under such a wonderful man and eminent scientist as Planck; it was also the entrance to my scientific career. It was the passport to scientific activity in the eyes of most scientists and a great help in overcoming many current prejudices against academic women. The great organic chemist Emil Fischer was at first reluctant to allow me to work in his laboratory with Otto Hahn, and made it a condition that I must not go into the classrooms where Hahn and many other students did their experimental work; consequently, I could not study radiochemistry for the first few years. But in later years he gave me much support, and I owe it largely to him that I was eventually entrusted with equipping and directing the physical-radioactive section of the Kaiser-Wilhelm-Institute for Chemistry in Berlin-Dahlem.

But my own experiences are just those of an individual and are of little value in getting a clear picture of the general conditions. Unique achievements like those of the scientists Marie Curie or Irène Joliot-Curie, of Selma Lagerlöf, of Florence Nightingale can silence the current prejudice in the individual case, but the prejudice still persists. It is directed mainly against women in middle-class occupations, and particularly in high-ranking posts. Nobody seems to have protested against women as factory workers. But I don't know of any woman who has a leading position in heavy industry. I would not know whether this is because of the lack of women aspiring to such positions or because industrial firms are reluctant to have women in leading positions. But there seems to be no doubt that women often have great difficulty in reaching high positions in the educational system. In Germany, the women's associations have made official complaint about this; they point out that the school authorities consider themselves generous if they appoint even one woman into school administration. The Austrian Association of Academic Women has carefully studied the question of women's equality in positions with a high salary, e.g., higher teaching posts, and has formulated a number of demands that largely coincide with those made by the corresponding committees of UNESCO. The International Federation of University Women is represented in UNESCO, and in addition some of its members attend UNESCO meetings as representatives of their respective governments. In November and December, 1956, there was in New Delhi a General Conference of UNESCO, which cooperated with the Status-of-Women Commission on general questions of education and teaching; of the eighty member states, seventy-five were represented, mostly by their ministers of education or by educationists. One of the main points was the study of the conditions prevalent in the teaching profession. I am glad to say that great stress was also placed on the importance of educating people toward international understanding.

It must, however, be admitted that some objections against women's professional work, objections which fifty years ago were rightly branded as prejudices, must now be considered more seriously because of the great social and economic changes which have happened in the more advanced countries. For instance, in the early years of the feminist movement, the objection was often made, and in a very exaggerated form, that the education of women would destroy the family. In that form the objection was surely to be rejected. Eduard von Hartmann, the philosopher I mentioned before, wrote a paper "The Survival of the Family," in which he considered the finishing school as the great menace to the family, and wished to limit the education of girls to the level of the primary school. One should think that such views are nonexistent today. But, surprisingly, some Swedish priests in their refusal to admit women theologians to priesthood have uttered similar opinions about the higher school education of girls and about their study at universities; and that in 1958! For that there can be no argument, and no excuse.

More difficult is the problem of professional women with children. Here the increasing disappearance of domestic service has created a real problem. Some women are sufficiently healthy and well-balanced to cope with the double task of profession and family, without detriment to either, and without damage to themselves. I have encountered a good many such women in Sweden, and also in Germany; one of them was Mrs. von Zahn-Harnack. But many are not able to do that. The great difficulty of solving this problem in the right way might be demonstrated by saying something about the problem of women teachers in Germany.

In Germany, a woman teacher must quit when she marries. Now, as you know, in Germany—as in all countries—there is a great shortage of teachers for all kinds of schools. So the question is under discussion whether one should not employ married women teachers. However, full-time teaching under present conditions—large classes and long duty hours—is a strenuous occupation, in particular if in addition one has to look after a family. And, of course, a good teacher ought to keep herself informed, not only on her special subject but also on pedagogical problems, and should contribute to their solution. All this can become too heavy a load, and that is true for any professional woman with a family, whether she is a teacher, doctor, or scientist. I do not say it is necessarily too much, but it *can* be too much.

In some countries, including Sweden, it has been proposed that half-time posts be created for married women; but some women's organizations have opposed this plan, with the probably justified argument that this part-time employment would stamp women as inferior employees and would handicap them greatly in the possibility of promotion.

Undoubtedly, women can see no ideal solution to their problem: profession and family. But for what human problems do ideal solutions exist? The husband can assist by helping in the house, and in many young households he does; maybe it is not the complete answer.

We can no longer doubt the value and indeed necessity of woman's intellectual education, for herself, for the family, and for mankind. Let me conclude with the words of Matthew Vassar, founder of Vasser College, spoken in 1865:

"A woman having received from her Creator the same intellectual constitution as a man, should have the same rights as man to intellectual culture and development."

Translator unknown

Kurt Gödel

About the Relationship between Relativity Theory and Idealistic Philosophy

One of the most interesting aspects of relativity theory for the philosophical-minded consists in the fact that it gave new and surprising insights into the nature of time, of that mysterious and seemingly self-contradictory being which, on the other hand, seems to form the basis of the world's and our own existence. The very starting-point of special relativity theory consists in the discovery of a new and very astonishing property of time, namely the relativity of simultaneity, which to a large extent implies that of succession. The assertion that the events *A* and *B* are simultaneous (and, for a large class of pairs of events, also the assertion that *A* happened before *B)* loses its objective meaning, insofar as another observer, with the same claim to correctness, can assert that *A* and *B* are not simultaneous (or that *B* happened before *A)*.

Following up the consequences of this strange state of affairs one is led to conclusions about the nature of time which are very far reaching indeed. In short, it seems that one obtains an unequivocal proof for the view of those philosophers who, like Parmenides, Kant, and the modern idealists, deny the objectivity of change and consider change as an illusion or an appearance due to our special mode of perception. The argument runs as follows: change becomes possible only through the lapse of time. The existence of an objective lapse of time, however, means (or, at least, is equivalent to the fact) that reality consists of an infinity of layers of the "now" which come into existence successively. But, if simultaneity is something relative in the sense just explained, reality cannot be split up into such layers in an objectively determined way. Each observer has his own set of "nows" and none of these various systems of layers can claim the prerogative of representing the objective lapse of time.

This inference has been pointed out by some, although by surprisingly few, philosophical writers, but it has not remained unchallenged. And actually to the argument in the form just presented it can be objected that the complete equivalence of all observers moving with different (but uniform) velocities, which is the essential point in it, subsists only in the abstract space–time scheme of special relativity theory and in certain empty words of general relativity theory. The existence of matter, however, as well as the particular kind of curvature of space–time produced by it, largely destroy the equivalence of different observers and distinguish some of them conspicuously from the rest, namely those which follow in their motion the mean motion of matter. Now in all cosmological solutions of the gravitational equations (i.e., in all possible universes) known at present the local times of all *these* observers fit together into one world-time, so that apparently it becomes possible to consider this time as the "true" one, which lapses objectively, whereas the discrepancies of the measuring results of other observers from this time may be conceived as due to the influence which a motion relative to the mean state of motion of matter has on the measuring process and physical processes in general.

From this state of affairs, in view of the fact that some of the known cosmological solutions seem to represent our world correctly, James Jeans has concluded that there is no reason to abandon the intuitive idea of an absolute time lapsing objectively. I do not think that the situation justifies this conclusion and am basing my opinion chiefly on the following facts and considerations.

There exist cosmological solutions of another kind than those known at present, to which the aforementioned procedure of defining an absolute time is not applicable, because the local times of the special observers used above cannot be fitted together into one world–time. Nor can any other procedure which would accomplish this purpose exist for them, i.e., these worlds possess such properties of symmetry, that for each possible concept of simultaneity and succession there exist others which cannot be distinguished from it by any intrinsic properties, but only by reference to individual objects, such as, for example, a particular galactic system.

Consequently, the inference drawn above as to the non-objectivity of change doubtless applies at least in these worlds. Moreover it turns out that temporal conditions in these universes show other surprising features, strengthening further the idealistic viewpoint. Namely, by making a round trip on a rocket ship in a sufficiently wide curve, it is possible in these worlds to travel into any region of the past, present, and future, and back again, exactly as it is possible in other worlds to travel to distant parts of space.

This state of affairs seems to imply an absurdity. For it enables one, for example, to travel into the near past of those places where he has himself lived. There he would find a person who would be himself at some earlier period of his life. Now he could do something to this person which, by his memory, he knows has not happened to him. This and similar contradictions, however, in order to prove the impossibility of the worlds under consideration, presuppose the actual feasibility of the journey into one's own past. But the velocities which would be necessary in order to complete the voyage in a reasonable length of time are far beyond everything that can be expected ever to become a practical possibility. Therefore it cannot be excluded a priori, on the ground of the argument given, that the space–time structure of the real world is of the type described.

As to the conclusions which could be drawn from the state of affairs explained for the question being considered in this paper, the decisive point is this: that for *every* possible definition of a world–time one could travel into regions of the universe which are passed according to that definition. This again shows that to assume an objective lapse of time would lose every justification in these worlds. For, in whatever way one may assume time to be lapsing, there will always exist possible observers to whose experienced lapse of time no objective lapse corresponds (in particular also possible observers whose whole existence objectively would be simultaneous). But, if the experience of the lapse of time can exist without an objective lapse of time, no reason can be given why an objective lapse of time should be assumed at all.

It might, however, be asked: of what use is it if such conditions prevail in certain *possible* worlds? Does that mean anything for the question interesting us whether in *our* world there exists an objective lapse of time? I think it does. For, (1) our world, it is true, can hardly be represented by the particular kind of rotating solutions referred to above (because these solutions are static and, therefore, yield no red-shift for distant objects); there exist however also *expanding* rotating solutions. In such universes an absolute time also might fail to exist, and it is not impossible that our world is a universe of this kind. (2) The mere compatibility with the laws of nature of worlds in which there is no distinguished absolute time, and, therefore, no objective lapse of time can exist, throws some light on the meaning of time also in those worlds in which an absolute time *can* be defined. For, if someone asserts that this absolute time is lapsing, he accepts as a consequence that, whether or not an objective lapse of time exists (i.e., whether or not a time in the ordinary sense of the word exists), depends on the particular way in which matter and its motion are arranged in the world. This is not a straightforward contradiction; nevertheless, a philosophical view leading to such consequences can hardly be considered as satisfactory.

Translator unknown

LIFE SCIENCES: BIOCHEMISTRY, ECOLOGY, ETHOLOGY

Adolf Butenandt

Life as an Object of Chemical Research

The question, "what is life?," has been answered by rational humankind in very different ways—depending on whether an answer was attempted from a mythological, theological, philosophical, or scientific viewpoint.

In our topic "Life as an Object of Chemical Research," it is naturally not the original, ambiguous concept of "life" that is being referred to, the concept with which humans attempt to interpret their own, particular, exceptional form of existence as compared to that of all other organisms. Rather, we are speaking of "life" as defined by natural science. It may seem superfluous to emphasize this, but we shall do so nevertheless to elucidate our topic, to delineate its limits, and to promulgate at the outset of these observations our chosen epistemological model. This model shall predetermine the segment of reality accessible to our apprehension by determining the methodology to be used by us in the analysis of any given phenomena we might encounter. Particularly the analysis of the phenomenon of life leads us to the realization that even the methodology employed by the natural sciences—like all methodology—affords access to only a limited aspect of reality, not to the whole of reality, since "the totality of nonspatial occurrence, the sphere in which human, intellectual, spiritual, and historical life are realized, is removed from the jurisdiction of this methodology." (T. L i t t).

Despite this limitation of our point of view, it is not easy to give a scientific definition of life. We must without a doubt proceed from the experience that in the scientifically apprehensible world, life "as such" does not exist, only living organisms. This means that all scientifically analyzable phenomena of life occur within material systems characterized by a high level of organization and by an individualized nature; we encounter such systems on this earth in the form of "organisms," ranging from the single-celled protozoans to the highly evolved multicellular organisms of the animal and plant kingdoms. With this circumstance, however, the search for a scientific definition of "life" becomes a problem capable of being formulated even more clearly: "Which properties must individual, material, ordered systems exhibit for us to be able to classify them as 'living'?"

Individuality and material arranged in an ordered system do not in and of themselves make an organism: atoms, molecules, and crystals all fulfill these conditions, but we do not regard them as living, not even if one considers that even today, a Japanese can carry on a true conversation with a stone in his garden! At first glance, it does not seem so difficult to point to the properties exhibited by organisms but lacking in these anorganic ordered systems, but upon closer inspection, it becomes evident that it is not that easy to point to the simplest form of organization that can be rightfully regarded as living. Our day and age has been witness to a difference of opinion on the question of the structure of the simplest form of life, the question of the border between animate and inanimate nature.

With his book *Microscopic Investigations of the Similarities in Structure and Growth between Animals and Plants* (Louvain, 1839), Theodor Schwann paved the way for the cell theory that regards to this day living cells, encapsulated cytoplasmic regions containing for the most part nuclei, as the elementary living individuals, as the simplest bearers of life. Only recently, however, Paul Bordet has written in Brussels, not far from Louvain, in an article about the science pavilion at the 1958 World's Fair: many things "are forcing us to revise fundamentally the concept of the smallest unit of life; this concept appears no longer bound to the cell as an indivisible whole."

What are the reasons for this attempt to dethrone the cell theory, and are these reasons valid? In that which follows, an attempt shall be made to demonstrate that from the point of view of the biochemist, the cell must still be regarded as the smallest unit of life, and that any doubts as to the validity of this notion have grown only from false interpretation of recent biochemical findings.

Let us first recall the properties—apart from its individuality, its status as an ordered system, and its marked form—which cause a cell to appear animate. There are essentially three:

(1) Living cells exhibit a continual m e t a b o l i s m ; i.e., a constant change arising from internal causes. In physical-chemical terms, we can classify them as "open systems" in a "steady state"; that is, systems that maintain through continual assimilation and emission of substances a state of exchange with their environment. Over certain periods of time, cells can maintain a "steady state," as can cell communities, i.e., higher organisms. In such a state, the cell's size, structure, and supply of substances appear to remain constant and the metabolism appears to limit itself to the combustion of nutrients within this plexus; the breakdown of nutrients provides the energy needed for the maintenance of the structure and for all other conceivable manifestations of life. Modern-day biochemistry teaches us, however, that even the cell's steady state in substance, supply, and structure contains very few truly static elements; that it is more properly conceived of as an almost totally dynamic event: a living cell is constantly breaking down its own structures, continually drawing structural and formal elements into its catabolic metabolism, and synthesizing aliquot structural elements anew. The cell itself is "material in a constant state of turnover." That it retains throughout this dynamic activity its external form and its visible inner structure by virtue of what appears to be an interactive r e g u l a t i o n of all processes—so that its state appears nearly static—is one of life's great chemical mysteries, one which should prevent us from daring to make superficial comparisons between a living system and an energy-consuming, work-generating machine!

(2) The second property of the living cell can be regarded for our purposes as comprising the phenomena of g r o w t h , d e v e l o p m e n t , and r e p r o d u c t i o n . Chemically, we can trace these phenomena back to the cell's ability to increase its specific supply of material; if I may make a marginal observation, to duplicate this material supply exactly, and in the process of an ordered cell division to distribute it between two new individual cells, both of which then go on to develop anew their characteristic

structures. The developmental phases a cell passes through and the specific structures it is able to form are determined by the origin of the cell. Fundamental conditions for a specific course of development are passed on from the mother cell to the daughter cell; this process is known as hereditary transmission. The "fundamental conditions" so transmitted are tied to certain substances known as "hereditary factors" or "genes," the sum of which is defined as the genotype of a cell. The material constancy of the genotype gives rise to the constancy of traits in succeeding generations; the ability of the genotype to change to a certain extent according to predetermined laws, to "mutate," brings with it the possibility of the development of new traits and developmental phases.

(3) The third characteristic property of a living cell is its irritability, the ability to respond to certain external stimuli with certain manifestations of life, with meaningful "reactions." An example, deliberately chosen for its simplicity, of a response to a stimulus can be found in typical locomotion phenomena.

Cell theory defines as the smallest unit of life an ordered system in which the following properties are present and subject to a regulative force: metabolism, transmutability (combining the phenomena of growth, development, and reproduction), and irritability.

The development of experimental biology in our century can be aptly characterized by the increasing success with which chemical methods, in the analysis of vital processes, have been employed to isolate smaller material regions, partial component structures of a material nature, from the total structure of living cells, in a form in which such structures are able to perform outside of the cell, in vitro, all the functions they carry out purposefully in the intact, living cell.

Let us examine more closely a number of such functional units isolated from living cells, regard them as typical examples of the development, referred to above, of our science of biochemistry, and inquire of their significance to the entire plexus of life phenomena.

Let us begin with examples from the realm of metabolism. A metabolic process employed systematically by people since time immemorial to provide for certain essentials of life is that of alcoholic fermentation; that is, the decomposition of sugar by microorganisms, certain strains of yeasts, to yield alcohol and carbon dioxide. This process, referred to by Pliny as *fermentatio,* is carried out by the yeast cell to generate energy for its own life. Since the energy content (the so-called free energy) of the end products (alcohol and carbon dioxide) is less than the energy content of the starting material (sugar), the process of alcoholic fermentation makes energy available for the vital processes of the cell. Of course, none of this was of much interest to the people who tended to their fermenting vats. They were—and still are—interested primarily in the end product of fermentation, alcohol, as an ingredient in intoxicating beverages, and only few beer lovers and connoisseurs of a fine wine know that alcoholic fermentation has assumed for biochemistry the character of a model reaction to explain the dynamics of metabolic processes, or that a dispute concerning the scientific analysis of the fermentation process was carried out in the second half of the last century between Munich and Paris!

Justus von Liebig, summoned to Munich at the height of his fame in 1852, founder of our great schools of chemistry, was honored at this year's ceremony celebrating the 800th anniversary of our city as one of the minds who made cultural history here in the nineteenth century. In the inquiry into the nature of alcoholic fermentation, he upheld the position that the yeast does in fact take part in the fermentation process, but only by way of a "dead portion" that can be released upon its decomposition. He based the defense of his theory, later referred to as the "mechanical theory of fermentation," on the ideas of the great Scandinavian, the Swede Berzelius, who had given a particularly novel impulse to biology with his pioneering work in the field of catalysis. A catalyst is understood as a chemical substance capable of inciting, by virtue of its presence in mere trace quantities, inert compounds to a chemical conversion of measurable speed. The catalyst apparently takes no part whatsoever in the chemical reaction; according to Berzelius, it operates by virtue of its "mere presence." We now know that the catalyst does enter into the reaction, that it forms intermediate compounds with the coreactants, whose inactivity is reduced in this very bond with the catalyst, and that the resulting chemical conversion takes place in such a way that the catalyst is liberated unchanged. Berzelius expressed the brilliant notion that the chemical reactions occurring in the metabolism of living cells were made possible by the presence of catalysts of living substance, of "biocatalysts." Today, this idea is universally accepted, now that we are thoroughly familiar with the structure and the effects of hundreds of such biocatalysts that have been isolated from cells. They are known as "ferments" or "enzymes," since the analysis of fermentation (Latin: *fermentatio*) by yeast (Greek: *zyme*) helped considerably to solve their mystery. L i e b i g defended, in modern idiom, with his "mechanical theory of fermentation" the now proven conception that fermentation is a process not linked to living yeast cells, but rather one that can also take place in the test tube (in the absence of living cells) with the help of biocatalysts—material, molecular structural units of the smallest size—isolated from the cells.

In Paris, L o u i s P a s t e u r sharply contradicted this opinion; according to him, the chemical process of fermentation is bound to a vital activity *(essentiellement un phénomène correlatif d'un acte vital);* "it begins and ends with this process; alcoholic fermentation never occurs without the simultaneous formation, development, and multiplication of yeast or continued life of mature yeast." The state of experimental research at that time provided P a s t e u r with solid evidence for his "vitalistic theory of fermentation"; many prominent experts agreed with him, but the most lucid minds sided with L i e b i g . No less a person than W ö h l e r in Göttingen had published anonymously years before in Liebig's "Annals of Chemistry" a highly entertaining "Tentative Letter of Notification," in which he ridiculed in a curious fashion the vitalistic theory, comparing the brewer's yeast with sugar-eating infusoria, which store the alcohol within themselves in vesicles that when filled presumably take on the form of champagne bottles. . . .

Fortunately, this type of publication is not the valid method of settling scientific disputes; only experimentation counts here! Perhaps, in this year of Munich's jubilee, we may be proud not only that Munich's own L i e b i g eventually carried the day in this dispute, but also that the decisive experiment was carried out in Munich as well, in 1897—twenty-four years after L i e b i g ' s , two years after P a s t e u r ' s death—by a son of the city at that.

E d u a r d B u c h n e r , working in laboratories at the old Physiological Institute of our university, pulverized yeast together with kieselguhr and quartz sand (in a mortar that until its destruction in a bombing attack during the last war kept as a precious relic) and was able to extract under high pressure a liquid indubitably free of living cells and capable of bringing about the normal fermentation of sugar. "It has been proven that to initiate the process of fermentation, no such apparatus as complex as that represented by the yeast cell is required. A dissolved substance, no doubt a protein, must be seen as the perpetrator of the fermentative effect; this substance shall be known as zymase" (E. Buchner). This prodigious step into new territory was honored with a Nobel Prize in 1907.

With Buchner's discovery of noncellular fermentation, the last remnant of the theory of *vis vitalis,* the mysterious vital force purported to be at work behind the chemical processes of cells, was done away with once and for all. Let us recall for a moment that until 1828, the synthesis of every single organic-chemical substance in nature was attributed to this force. Wöhler's successful attempts to synthesize urea in 1828, however, demonstrated that it was possible to reconstruct in the laboratory the component substances and fuels of organisms; this discovery ushered in a long chain of successes for organic chemistry, leading to the realization that the chemist can in principle synthesize with his laboratory methods every substance found in organisms—what a brilliant role have Munich's laboratories played in the further development of such findings! We can think of Adolf von Baeyer, Richard Willstätter, Hans Fischer; we think of Heinrich Wieland, who graced us yet with his presence last year on the occasion of his eightieth birthday.

At the end of the last century, it was common knowledge that the substances of the living world could be synthesized in the laboratory, but it was also recognized that the methods used to do so were fundamentally different from those encountered in the living cell. High temperatures and pressures were necessary, as was the use of highly active reactants, none of which are characteristic of physiological occurrences. It is therefore understandable that the theory of vis vitalis retreated to the field of the dynamics of reactions, until it was driven away from here as well at the turn of the century by Buchner.

The discovery of noncellular fermentation paved the way for the comprehensive study and understanding of the process by which sugar is converted to alcohol and carbon dioxide. This has required a vast amount of work, right up to the present day. We may regard it as a brilliant feat of biochemical research that we have now arrived at a most comprehensive knowledge of the dynamics and the biological significance of alcoholic fermentation. The glucose molecule is led through a complex sequence of reactions, by way of at least twelve derivative products, and a different enzyme is supplied for every single chemical reaction phase. Buchner's zymase has proven to be a highly complex mixture of many fermentation enzymes. Researchers have succeeded in making pure preparations of each intermediate product of the fermentation process and every enzyme that enters into this process; they have been able to isolate each individual phase of the reaction and reunite these phases to come up with the original reaction in its entirety. What is more, scientists are able to bring about these reactions in vitro in such a physiologically correct manner that even the energy the cell gains from the fermentation process, and for the sake of which the cell "came up with" the process in the first place, can be apprehended in the same output and in the same form as if the process had taken place in vivo. This demonstrated that the energy to be generated through biochemical processes is always initially stored in the cell in the form of a certain, so-called energy-rich compound. This compound—we shall dispense with an explanation and simply refer to it as ATP—is synthesized in the course of all energy-generating reactions when a carrier molecule links up with anorganic phosphoric acid and the resulting conglomerate "loads up" the energy to be generated. When the energy-laden ATP is split back into its components, its stored energy can be regained and utilized by the cell for chemical, mechanical, or caloric work.

The sum of these findings concerning the dynamics and the nature of this one fermentative reaction have made this a classic model for the fundamental occurrence that takes place in the course of cellular metabolism.

Biochemistry has since arrived at equally detailed findings concerning the dynamics of numerous other metabolic processes of living cells. Whether we trace the fates of sugars, fats, or proteins, whether we trace their breakdown or their synthesis in the chemism of living matter, we always encounter the same principle: some starting material A undergoes numerous transformations, passing through the intermediate stages B, C, D, E . . . , proceeding through individual reaction phases to arrive at the desired end product, and each individual reaction phase is made possible and regulated by a specific enzyme acting as a biocatalyst. If a reaction leads to the generation of energy, this energy is stored in the form of the previously mentioned, energy-laden compound ATP, which we can regard as a kind of chemical "storage battery"; a chemical reaction that requires energy (i.e., the synthesis of new structural elements) fulfills its energy needs from the cell's ATP supply, thus taking place by way of the splitting of ATP molecules back into their original components. What is important for our purposes is above all the fact that one can isolate the individual enzymes from the cell as chemical substances with the character of proteins, and that these molecular protein structures can carry out their metabolic feats outside of the cell as well. Let us choose, from the plethora of examples we could consider in this connection, one with particular significance to our inquiry.

The cell can generate far greater amounts of energy from the breakdown of nutrients with the help of oxygen, from their combustion to water and carbon dioxide, than it can from a fermentation process that takes place without the involvement of oxygen. The process by which oxygen is taken from the air to carry out these combustion processes and the resulting carbon dioxide is given off is known as r e s p i r a t i o n, or simply b r e a t h i n g. Every cell requiring oxygen respirates. We need only recall how instinctively we associate the concept of respiration with that of life! It has now become possible to isolate from the cytoplasm, by means of modern, low-temperature cell fractionation methods, structural elements so small as to lie at the limit of microscopic visibility and whose morphological structure has been revealed to us by the electron microscope. These structures are tubular in shape and are known as mitochondria. Isolated mitochondria respirate! In the test tube, they take up oxygen and use it in the process of combustion to break down nutritive substrates supplied under the proper cellular-physiological conditions, to water and carbon dioxide. That the isolated mitochondria fulfill their physiological function quite unscathed, is made particularly evident by their ability to store, in the form of energy-laden ATP, the high amounts of energy released by the combustion of the substrates. It has been discovered that the total respiration of a living cell and the oxidative breakdown of nutritive substrates bound up with this respiration is carried out only by the mitochondria structures in the cytoplasm; these structures consist of enzymes united in a purposeful manner, the enzymes of biological oxidation.

The isolation of fermentation enzymes and the analysis of their function in vitro has always been regarded as a purely chemical affair, which—as mentioned previously—has been used to disprove the theory of a vital force. Surprisingly, after mitochondria (cellular component structures that respire in vitro) had been isolated, voices were raised that asked whether mitochondria were not perhaps living structures, whether we would not have to revise our conception of the cell as the smallest living unit. After all, can dead structures breathe?

To pose such a question means not to have fully considered the implications of the chemical data produced thus far and to find oneself laboring under a misconception stemming from the subconscious association of "living" and "breathing." While the mitochondria represent structural units of a higher plane than those of individual isolated fermentation enzymes, they are still nothing more than a number of enzymes efficiently combined to form a functional unit, and the combustion of sugar derivatives and oxygen to water and carbon dioxide is fundamentally a chemical process no more or less complicated than the conversion of sugar to alcohol and carbon dioxide. This is demonstrated with particular clarity by the fact that the biochemist can progressively subdivide the mitochondria and thereby progressively restrict their functionality. To put it in a somewhat simplified form, one may say that it is fundamentally possible to extract from the mitochondria the water-forming system and to separate it from the carbon dioxide–forming system, or to separate the respiratory enzyme system from the energy-absorbing ATP-forming system. Ultimately, the mitochondria are capable of being divided up into all of their individual enzymes. We can conclude that mitochondria do not constitute a new site for a vital force, nor is it possible to characterize them as organisms. At any rate, though, the analysis of the mitochondria opens up for us an initial channel for determining the meaning of the structure for the function and investigating the efficient interplay of biocatalysts; more on this later.

We shall now leave the field of metabolism and turn to the exciting findings arrived at by biochemistry concerning the various types of v i r u s e s . The term *virus* is used to designate microscopically invisible pathogens much smaller than bacteria; unlike bacteria, they cannot be bred on an artificial, inanimate cultural medium. They reproduce only within living cells, which "fall ill" as a result of this infestation. Many dreaded infectious diseases that befall humans, animals, and plants are caused by viruses, such as measles, smallpox, polio, mumps, and influenza among humans, cattle plague, swine plague, fowl plague, canine distemper, foot-and-mouth disease among domestic animals; leaf roll, leaf curl, yellows, and mosaic diseases among plants. Bacteria, too, have their viral diseases, brought about by *bacteriophages.*

Biochemists have developed methods for the pure preparation of viruses and discovered that many viruses are actually chemical substances, which in pure form often develop spectacular crystal formations. The first preparation of a crystallized virus, the causative of the tobacco mosaic virus, was made by Stanley in 1935; the most recent preparation in a long series was one of the crystallized polio virus, made by Schwerdt and Schaffer in 1955. The chemical analysis of pure viruses has shown that some of them are relatively simple structures: very large chemical molecules consisting only of proteins and nucleic acids. The latter are long, chain-shaped compounds composed of a large number of similarly constructed links. Each link *(nucleotide)* consists of phosphoric acid, sugar, and an organic base. Nucleic acid was first isolated from cell nuclei; hence its name.

What an apparently irreconcilable contradiction: chemical substances, crystallizable and with definable molecular weights, indistinguishable in vitro from other polymolecular substances of a similar type, fully analyzable with chemical and physical methods and capable in principle of being characterized with chemical formulae—yet able to reproduce in living cells! The question arises, perhaps more justifiably so here than with the previously mentioned examples, of whether viruses are organisms of the most primitive sort, or even links between lifeless and living matter. The dispute between Liebig and Pasteur repeats itself in our day on another level of material structures! Many biologists today indeed regard viruses as living organisms of the most primitive degree of organization, and even one of our leading biologists, Max Hartmann, places himself in this group when he declares that "viruses must now be regarded as the simplest manifestation of living systems."

Biochemists can on no account join this group; rather, their discovery of crystallized viruses and determination of the viruses' constitution represent a fortunate encounter with additional isolated component structures of the living cell—this time it is not enzymes that set off certain metabolic reactions, but rather chemical structures capable of fulfilling another partial function of animate organization, a function from the realm of growth, developmental, and reproductive phenomena.

This conclusion appears at first perhaps bolder than the assumption that viruses are living organisms more primitive than simple cells. This is not the case, however, for it is thought that simple viruses possess all of the properties that have been necessarily attributed to the hereditary factors within living cells, but which have not yet been successfully isolated. Let us compare the properties of both.

Hereditary factors (genes) are components of the genotype. Since the genotype of each cell reduplicates itself before the cell undergoes division, so that it can be passed on in full to the daughter cells, a duplication, an "identical reproduction" of all hereditary factors must precede the cell division. This means that hereditary factors can reproduce in living cells. We made an identical assertion for viruses.

Biochemists have come to realize that hereditary factors consist chemically of nucleic acids, whose molecules have the form of long chains. Each chain has thousands of individual links (nucleotides), but only four different types of link exist. The order in which these links occur determines how a gene will chemically react; i.e., what its function within the cell will be. The nucleic acid of the gene is bound to protein at the gene's locus. All viruses contain—as mentioned earlier—nucleic acid as an integrating component; the specificity of a virus, like that of a gene, is without a doubt determined by the type of its nucleic acid; the respective viral nucleic acid determines the functional range of the pathogen. The nucleic acid in the virus as well is bound to protein.

The reproductive capacity of nucleic acid from cell nuclei can be explained in the same way as the reproductive capacity of nucleic acid from viruses in living cells; namely, on the basis of their molecular structure. Each nucleic acid chain can function as a type of matrix, by attracting individual links from the surrounding environment and linking them together to form a complementary molecular chain. The repetition of this process with the new matrix leads to an identical reproduction of the original chain.

The genotype of a cell determines which substances the cell is able to create and to employ in the building up of its structures; the genotype determines the total range of chemical reactions that can take place within a cell. Since the range of possible chemical reactions is determined by the types of enzymes a cell contains, one can apodictically conclude that the sum of the hereditary factors united in the genotype determines the allocation of enzymes to a cell. Indeed, biochemical studies of the hereditary factors' mechanisms of action have shown that genes are responsible for the formation of active, specific enzymes in the cell. The loss of a hereditary factor leads to the loss of the corresponding specific enzyme activity and thus to the absence of a certain reaction, the one dependant upon this very enzyme. Since an enzyme is a protein with a specific structure, the knowledge we gain from these findings brings us to the highly significant realization that the information for the structure of a protein, its "code system," is contained within the structure of a nucleic acid chain.

The same applies to the nucleic acids of a virus particle. With some virus types, for example with the coli phage and the tobacco mosaic virus, it has been convincingly demonstrated that to infect a host cell with the virus, not even the entire virus particle is necessary, only its nucleic acid. This alone contains the information about the whole virus particle, and communicates this information, in a manner of speaking, to the host cell. The host cell, following the command of the viral nucleic acid, reprograms its own entire metabolism to fabricate new virus particles; not only their nucleic acid, but their protein as well, the nature of which was completely unknown to the host cell, since it had only been invaded by a nucleic acid. It cannot be more conclusively demonstrated that the nucleic acids of hereditary factors and viruses carry within their molecular structure the entire information for the structure of specific proteins and force their commands in the same manner on the living cells, assuming thereby a role in the shaping of biological characteristics.

All of these findings afford a deep insight into the phenomenon of growth; they explain how specific structures are duplicated and how, ultimately, like gives rise to like. Yet at the same time, we can acquaint ourselves with the laws that account for exceptions to the rule "like gives rise to like," for hereditary factors and viruses also share the trait of being able to change, to "mutate," and to reproduce themselves in this altered form. Mutation is understood as a small change in the structure of the nucleic acid, a change that can occur as a kind of "minting error" in the course of the nucleic acid's duplication according to the matrix principle; the mutation is perhaps brought about by the incorporation of particular links or by a different sequence of links that form the chain. Having attained the ability to make preparations of nucleic acids from viruses, experimental researchers have nearly reached the point where they can chemically transform nucleic acids in vitro, and make in this way preparations of "mutated nucleic acids." It can be expected that such mutated nucleic acids will provide a living cell with information different from that provided by the normal initial form: the cell will produce mutated viruses!

We recognize the full validity of the parallel between virus and gene, and we deduce: viruses are, in their function and their structure, isolated particles of genotype structures; perhaps they came about through extreme retrogression culminating in their present status as remnants of genotype structure. On no account are they animate creatures. When the nucleic acid of a virus enters a suitable host cell, this nucleic acid augments, as it were, the normal nucleic acid supply of the living cell with a new, additional link. The subsequently occurring events are triggered by the total information now present, information originating in part from the genotype, in part from the viral nucleic acid. New virus particles result from the ensuing chain reaction. Whether this process comes to a standstill, and a certain number of newly formed viruses come to reside permanently, as quiet "parasites," in the host cell, which for its part goes on living normally, or whether the cell exhausts itself in the continuous production of viruses and eventually dies, depends on the material systems reacting with one another. Nature provides numerous examples of both occurrences.

To round out this representation, in which the viruses were paralleled with parts of the genotype structure, let us point out that scientists are conducting increasingly successful experiments in which portions of the genetic structure (in the form of nucleic acids) of microorganisms are isolated and introduced into other living microorganisms. In numerous cases, this method has been successfully used to "augment" the existing genotype of the host cells and thereby endow these cells with new, additional properties that continue to exist alongside those already present, which persist into succeeding generations, and which thus become "hereditary." In this way, certain membrane-free, "unencapsulated" microorganisms (pneumococci types) can be transformed into capsule-forming strains by providing them in their nutritive medium with the nucleic acid from the appropriate capsule-forming types. By having foreign nucleic acid from capsule-forming organisms incorporated into its own supply, a cell gains the ability to synthesize a complex membrane, one composed of polymolecular sugars, and sheath itself in this membrane. The cell "knew" nothing of the structure of this membrane beforehand; the newly assimilated nucleic acid gave it the information it needed to synthesize new enzymes and build up new substances for the process of capsule formation. The parallel with the phenomena which follow a viral infection is obvious. Human nature leads us to designate as a "disease" the case in which the cell perishes from the production of viruses, while we regard as benevolent the case in which the cell is transformed into another, one with new properties. Seen from a biological perspective, however, there is no reason to give preference to one phenomenon over the other.

Enzymes, mitochondria, viruses, genes—partial component structures of living matter, of increasing complexity—perform as such only partial functions in the life of a cell. They themselves cannot be designated as living.

Let us take another look at the analysis of stimulus phenomena; more specifically, at motile processes triggered by stimuli. Such processes can also be analyzed as chemical reactions occurring in defined partial structures of the cell.

About one hundred years ago, it was discovered (Kühne, 1868) that large quantities of a viscous protein known as myosin could be extracted with the help of saline solutions from striated animal muscle tissue. Myosin forms long fiber molecules that can be seen with the electron microscope and that can be combined to form macroscopically visible fibers (H. H. Weber, 1934).

Myosin can be broken down into two components, a lighter fraction and a heavier, highly viscous one known as "actomyosin." The Hungarian biochemist Szent-Györgyi discovered in 1941 that actomyosin threads in a dilute saline (potassium chloride) solution quickly contract—just like a muscle fiber in vivo—after the mere addition of ATP, the previously mentioned energy reserve substance of all cells. Szent-Györgyi himself has this to say about the experiment: "Watching myosin contract, and watching one of the most ancient and mysterious manifestations of life, movement, take place for the first time in vitro with components isolated from the contractile system was the most thrilling experience of my scientific career."

It is indeed thrilling! The subsequent history of this discovery was to become even more exciting: H. H. Weber and Hoffman–Berling succeeded in isolating even more completely the fundamental chemical structures upon which movement in all organisms appeared to be contingent. Whole contractile cells, muscle fibers, or even single cilli and flagella, the structures used by protozoans or sperm cells for locomotion, can be extracted with an aqueous solution of glycerin; in this way, all substances and structures not belonging to the chemical locomotor material are removed. The remaining inanimate "locomotor models," which are insoluble in glycerin, exhibit in the presence of certain salts (magnesium ions), after the addition of ATP as an energy-supplying substance, motion sequences that in no way differ from the corresponding processes in living systems.

When a creeping amoeba is electrically or mechanically stimulated, it stops moving forward and rolls itself into a ball. This contraction is in principle identical to that of a muscle cell. This can be demonstrated directly by isolating the contractile structures in the manner previously described; i.e., by transforming the cells by way of extraction with glycerin into corresponding "locomotor models." These locomotor models contract when ATP is added, just as do the muscle models, and roll themselves into balls, just as do living organisms.

Many experiments have shown that cellular and muscular contractile processes are in principle the same. An isolated muscle model contracts and relaxes again, solely under the influence of natural substances to which it is subjected. Locomotor models obtained from flagella (for example, from the spermatic filaments of a species of tropical grasshopper) are made to beat and whip rhythmically by the addition of ATP. All of these processes have been captured on film, and no viewer can detect any difference between the movements depicted in such films and the movements of living organisms. Nevertheless, what we are dealing with here are only isolated structures, composed of protein molecules and embodying in their structure the mystery of form change. The molecular threads can contract by employing the chemical energy contained in ATP, and can revert from this contraction back to their extended form. By isolating these processes from the living cell, we can study their chemism and express it in chemical equations, which would at the same time provide us with information about the amount of energy required and the amount of energy available to meet this requirement.

Again we are faced with the question: can structures that demonstrate visible rhythmic movement in the test tube be inanimate? They are indeed. . . .

* * *

We could offer a number of additional examples, but we shall let the matter rest with those that have already been brought forth. These examples demonstrate that the progress of biochemistry has been marked by a steady increase in the ability to isolate partial component structures of living matter and to study their function outside of the living cell. No matter how completely any of these partial systems may perform the same task in vitro as they do within the plexus of life, none of them can be regarded as animate. Yet what can we learn from the study of these partial functions?

The examples chosen represent fundamental chemical processes that are in principle the same as those taking place throughout the entire organic world. There is but o n e life, o n e living matter—it is founded on the application of a few fundamental principles that, modified to accommodate the individual case at hand, await rediscovery in all objects of the animate world. Yet the simplest form in which all fundamental principles characteristic of life are united in a concerted effort is that of the cell. The cell exhibits the dynamic and energy-generating process of metabolism, the ability to reproduce identically its specific structures, and movement. It contains all of these—and other—partial phenomena combined with one another in a coherent, efficient manner. The question posed at the beginning, whether in the analysis of vital processes chemistry would be able to dethrone cell theory, must be answered, I believe, with a clear no.

Still, this question gives rise to yet another. Is the living cell, as the simplest form of the living, o n l y a combination of isolated, functional, partial structures or is it m o r e than this; is "the whole more than the sum of its parts?" The biochemist can at first work only analytically; he is convinced that only by understanding the parts can he arrive at the meaning of the whole. Here lies the root for justifying the study, in painstaking and often highly specialized work, of small excerpts from the highly complex whole. L i e b i g was profoundly convinced of the wisdom of this method when he wrote to B e r z e l i u s : "I hope that I have succeeded in instilling in others the profound conviction that chemistry alone is capable of shedding light upon the vital processes." Without a doubt, though, each specific quantum of knowledge acquires meaning only when we are able to incorporate it into a whole. It causes us unending concern that our specific knowledge is constantly increasing while we are losing our capacity to grasp the meaning concealed within the whole.

Just as a chemical compound represents more and possesses different properties than the sum of the elements it comprises; just as the chemical structure of polymolecular substances represents more and possesses different properties than the sum of the chemical compounds it comprises, a living cell is most certainly more than the mere coexistence of functionally specialized partial structures! Having analyzed these partial structures, we are faced with the task of understanding their incorporation into a higher structural order and learning to recognize which n e w additional functions and capabilities result from the system of entire cell structures, tissue structures, and organismic structures.

We are fortunate enough to be able to witness already the beginning of a new line of research, one that strives to uncover the meaning and the significance of highly organized structures for the vital processes. Work in this direction is only just beginning; will this line of inquiry one day lead us to the knowledge of why all individual processes in a living cell take place for the benefit of the whole, why their interplay is r e g u l a t e d ?

If a living system wants to "stay alive," each partial process, regardless of its nature, within the system can take place only as long as and to the extent that it serves the entire system. Accordingly, the cell arranges all of its chemical processes into cycles; the entire chemism of the living cell can be described in simple terms as such a cycle: the nucleic acids of the genotype produce specific proteins, that in turn, as enzymes, regulate chemical reactions whose end products serve in part as the raw materials for the synthesis of enzymes and nucleic acids. Thus is each process dependant upon others. The rate of breakdown and synthesis of substances; i.e., the metabolic volume of the entire cycle, conforms to the needs of the whole—every disturbance, be it an excess or a deficit, leads to imbalances that perilously disrupt the cycle and can bring about death. Without a system of b i o l o g i c a l r e g u l a t i o n which covers every process, the whole cannot function; without such regulation, the living state of the cell cannot be maintained in the face of constant disturbances from the environment. This amounts to a new, highly significant phenomenon, the analysis of which has led our physiologist, R i c h a r d W a g n e r , who has made significant contributions to the line of inquiry known as "cybernetics," to the conclusion: "Where the first regulatory mechanism was, there was the first form of life."

We do not know the way in which the cell has come to exist, in the course of the earth's development, as a biologically, holistically regulated interaction of many partial functions. Even if we allow for long periods of time for its gradual emergence on earth, the birth of the first cell will continue to strike anyone capable only of causal, analytical thought as an extremely improbable event, in spite of everything we have been able to bring to light about certain aspects of the cell's nature.

In closing, we should like to suggest in all modesty that only the scientist who nurtures and develops in himself and in the students entrusted to him a l l the qualities of character that distinguish the human being from the animal; who combines the thirst for knowledge characteristic of the scientists referred to in this essay with modesty and love for all of God's creatures on this earth, with respect for the ultimate mysteries unfathomable by our intellect; only such a scientist will be able to truly fulfill the task with which he has been charged. Only such a scientist, innerly enriched by his work, will fathom the ultimate meaning revealed to us in the "inherited, living, developing form."

Translated by Daniel Theisen

Robert Koch

On Bacteriological Research

When I was accorded the honor of delivering a lecture before the International Congress of Medicine, I found myself in the position of having to choose between two sciences as the source for the topic of this lecture; namely, that of hygiene or that of bacteriology; the latter being one to which in earlier years I was able to devote myself almost exclusively.

I have decided in favor of the latter, for I assume that bacteriology still commands the most general interest, and so I will try to give to you a brief account of the current state of bacteriological research, or at least of some of its more important branches. I must admit that I will not be able to offer anything new to those already familiar with bacteriology. So as not to appear empty-handed before this portion of my audience, however, I intend to weave into my presentation a number of facts that have resulted from my continuing study of tuberculosis and that have not yet been made public.

Bacteriology, insofar as it concerns us physicians, is a very young science. Only fifteen years ago, little more was known than that in cases of anthrax and recurrent fever, peculiar foreign bodies appeared in the blood, and that in cases of wound infection diseases, the so-called vibrios were present. A proof that these things were the causes of those diseases was not yet given, and with the exception of a few scientists who were considered visionaries, such findings were interpreted more as curiosities than as causative pathogens. One could hardly help but think otherwise, since it had not even been proven that the things in question were independent entities specific to these diseases. In putrescent fluids, but particularly in the blood of asphyxiated animals, bacteria had been found that were indistinguishable from anthrax bacilli. A few scientists did not want to regard them as living creatures at all, but saw them as crystalloid structures. Bacteria identical to recurrent fever spirilli were said to occur in swamp water and dental mucus, and bacteria very similar to the micrococci of wound infection diseases were reported to have been found in healthy blood and in healthy tissues.

Neither were the experimental and optical aids available at that time any guarantee of progress, and this would have remained the situation for quite a while if new research methods had not presented themselves at just that time—methods that brought about an entirely new situation overnight and opened up new inroads to further penetration of this dark region. With the help of improved lens systems and their proper application, aided by the use of aniline dyes, scientists succeeded in rendering clearly visible the smallest bacteria and in differentiating them morphologically from other microorganisms. At the same time, the use of nutrient substrates, which could be delivered in solid or liquid form, as the situation required, made it possible to separate the individual germs and obtain pure cultures, from which the characteristic properties of each individual species could be determined with absolute certainty. It was soon evident what these new aids were capable of accomplishing. A number of new, well-characterized species of pathogenic microorganisms were discovered, and what is particularly significant, the causal connection between these species and the accompanying diseases was established. Since the pathogens thus discovered all belonged to the group of the bacteria, this had to give the impression that the infectious diseases proper were caused by definite and discrete species of bacteria, which consequently gave rise to the justified hope that in the not too distant future, the pertinent pathogens would be found for all infectious diseases.

This expectation remained unfulfilled, however, and the further development of bacteriological research has in other respects as well taken an unexpected course. If I may keep at first to the positive results of bacteriological research, then I shall accentuate the following points of these results.

It is now considered an established fact that bacteria, like the higher organisms of the plant kingdom, form definite species—ones, however, which are admittedly difficult to distinguish from one another at times. The opinion, stubbornly adhered to up until a few years ago and held even today by a few scientists, that bacteria are transmutable in a manner differing from all other living creatures, and are capable of taking on at times a certain set of morphological or biological properties, at other times a set differing completely from these, and that at most, a few species are to be assumed to exist; or that bacteria are not independent organisms at all, but rather belong to the same developmental stage as the molds, or, as some will have it, the lower algae; or, a conception that even further attacks their independence, that they have descended from animal cells, from blood corpuscles, for example—all of these notions are untenable in the face of the observations that have been made in great number, which without exception uphold the notion that these entities, too, fall into well-characterized species. If we keep in mind that a number of infectious diseases caused by bacteria, such as leprosy and phthisis, have been described with their unmistakable properties by the earliest medical writers, we can go so far as to conclude that pathogenic bacteria have more the tendency to retain their properties over long periods of time than the tendency, as is usually assumed in light of the changeable nature of many an epidemic disease, to transmute quickly. Within certain limits, deviations from the usual type can admittedly occur within a species of bacteria, particularly with pathogenic bacteria. But bacteria are no different even in this respect from the higher plants, among which a variety of transmutations can be observed, transmutations that can generally be traced to external influences and that move us at most to speak of different varieties, but that still allow us to acknowledge the existence of the species as such.

It sometimes happens that under unfavorable nutritional conditions, a species of bacteria produces stunted forms; that certain properties that may strike us or that may be interesting from a medical standpoint but are of little importance for the overall life of the plant—for example, the formation of a pigment, the ability to grow in a living animal body, or to produce certain toxins—that such properties can temporarily or, as far as we know, permanently disappear. Such phenomena, however, are nothing but fluctuations between certain limits that never move far enough away from the central point of the species-type that the transition to a new or another already known species would have to be assumed, such as the anthrax bacillus being transformed into the hay bacillus, for example.

But because of the small size of the bacteria and the resulting lack of ubiquitous distinguishing morphological characteristics that could aid systematization, such as we have at our disposal with the higher plants, we cannot simply look for isolated characteristics in our attempt to classify the species, since from the start we cannot be sure if such characteristics represent essential or accidental properties of the species in question. Rather, we must conscientiously take note of as many properties as possible, as insignificant as they may seem at the moment, morphological and biological properties alike. It is only on the basis of this overall picture that we can attempt to determine the species. One cannot be meticulous enough in this respect, and many a misunderstanding, many a contradiction in the field of bacteriology can be traced back to the circumstance, which unfortunately prevails to this day, that this rule is insufficiently observed.

The typhoid bacillus provides a very characteristic example of the difficulty faced when trying to determine a species. If one encounters this bacillus in the mesenteric gland, the spleen, or the liver of a deceased typhoid patient, then no doubt will ever arise that it is indeed a genuine typhoid bacillus, since in these places, no other bacteria have ever been found that could be mistaken for it. But the situation changes completely when one tries to detect the presence of the typhoid bacillus in the intestinal contents, the ground, the water, or in airborne dust. In such places are found numerous bacteria very similar to it, which only a very experienced bacteriologist can differentiate from the typhoid bacilli with absolute certainty, since no unmistakable and constant characteristics have yet been found for the latter. The numerous, recent claims that typhoid bacilli have been detected in the ground, in tap water, and in foodstuffs can for this reason be met only with justified skepticism. The situation with diphtheria bacteria is a similar one. But as luck would have it, a number of other important pathogenic bacteria, such as tubercle bacilli and cholera bacilli, were found from the start to be endowed with such unmistakable characteristics that they can be reliably identified as such under all, even the most difficult conditions. The great advantages that have resulted from the unequivocal diagnosis of the pathogens in these cases must assume for us the character of an urgent admonition to keep up the search for similar unmistakable characteristics in typhoid, diphtheria, and other important pathogenic bacteria, in spite of the futility of our past efforts. Only then will it be possible to pursue these pathogens as well on their obscure and tortuous paths outside of the body and thus to secure a firm foundation for a rational prophylaxis.

The tubercle bacilli gave me a lesson, however, on the care with which one must judge the distinguishing characteristics used to differentiate the bacteria, even with familiar species. This species of bacteria, as we all know, is characterized so unmistakably by its behavioral response to dyes, by its vegetation in pure cultures, and by its pathogenic properties, and so unmistakably by each one of these traits, that confusing it with other bacteria appears quite impossible. And yet even in this case one should not rely on any one of the given characteristics in the attempt to identify the species, but should follow the tried and tested rule of always considering all the characteristics one has at one's disposal and only declaring the bacteria's identity to be positively established when all such characteristics are accounted for. When I carried out my first experiments on the tubercle bacilli, I took it upon myself to proceed in strict accordance with this rule; tubercle bacilli from the most diverse sources were accordingly tested not only for their reactions to dyes, but for their vegetative conditions in pure cultures and for their pathogenic properties. With respect to tuberculosis in chickens, however, this was not possible, since I was not able at the time to procure fresh material from which I could have bred pure cultures. But since all other species of tuberculosis had produced identical bacilli and the chicken tuberculosis bacilli corresponded completely with them in appearance and in their behavioral response to aniline dyes, I believed in spite of this gap remaining in the study that I could declare the species to be identical. I later procured from a number of different sources pure cultures that had supposedly been bred from tubercle bacilli, but that differed from these in a number of respects; in particular, inoculation attempts made with these bacilli by experienced and thoroughly reliable researchers on animals led to irregular results that even now are looked upon as unresolved contradictions. I initially believed I was dealing with mutations, such as can be observed not infrequently with pathogenic bacteria when they are bred in pure cultures outside of the body—i.e., under more or less unfavorable conditions—for longer periods of time. But to solve the riddle, the attempt was made to induce the ordinary tubercle bacilli, by subjecting them to the most diverse influences, to transmute into the previously mentioned putative variety. They were cultured over a period of many months at such high temperatures that only a stunted growth resulted; in other series of experiments, the cultures were repeatedly subjected to even higher temperatures for such a long time that they were brought as close as possible to death. I subjected the cultures in an analogous manner to chemicals, light, and desiccation; they were bred for many generations in combination with other bacteria and inoculated in continuous series into animals with low susceptibility. But despite all of these manipulations, only insignificant changes in the properties could be brought about, changes that fell far short of those that occur in other pathogenic bacteria under the same conditions. This gives rise to the impression that the tubercle bacilli in particular retain their properties with great tenacity. This, in turn, tallies with the circumstance that pure cultures of these bacteria, bred continuously by me in petri dishes for more than nine years now, which accordingly have not seen the inside of a living body for the space of this time, have apart from a slight decrease in virulence managed to keep themselves free of all change. After all attempts to explain the connection had failed, the clarification was brought about by accident. One year ago, it happened that I was given a number of live chickens that were suffering from tuberculosis, and I took this opportunity to make up for what had previously been impossible—to establish cultures directly from the diseased organs of these animals. As the cultures grew, I saw to my surprise that they were identical in appearance, and shared all other properties as well, with the "mystery culture" that resembled the true tubercle bacilli. I found out afterwards that the mystery cultures had been obtained from chicken tuberculosis, but had been regarded, under the assumption that all forms of tuberculosis were identical, as true tubercle bacilli. I find my observations to have been confirmed in studies of chicken tuberculosis carried out and recently published by Professor Maffucci. I am quite prepared to regard the chicken tuberculosis bacilli as a separate species, but one very closely related to the true tubercle bacilli, and the obvious question presents itself—one of great significance for medical practice—namely, whether the chicken tuberculosis bacilli are pathogenic for humans as well. The question, however, cannot be answered until this species of bacilli is encountered in a human in the course of continued studies, or until its absence can be confirmed by a sufficiently long series of cases. Testing with dye reagents cannot remain the only method used to accomplish this task, of course, as it has in the past; the culture method will have to be used in every single case.

Thus have all recent findings demonstrated conclusively that one must proceed as carefully as possible when distinguishing between the different species of bacteria, and that the borders between the different species are better drawn too narrowly than too widely.

In another important matter of principle as well, the situation has been clarified and simplified considerably in comparison to earlier times, namely, in respect to the establishment of a causal connection between pathogenic bacteria and their respective infectious diseases.

While a few great minds had proposed early on the notion that microorganisms had to be the cause of infectious diseases, general acceptance of such notions was not forthcoming, and the first discoveries made in this field were received with considerable skepticism. This made it all the more imperative to furnish irrefutable proof, particularly in the initial cases, that the microorganisms found in conjunction with an infectious disease were in fact the cause of this disease. At that time, one could still justifiably object that the simultaneous presence of the illness and the microorganisms might be a chance occurrence, that the latter consequently did not play the role of pernicious parasites, but of harmless ones that found only in diseased organs the conditions necessary for their existence, conditions that the healthy body lacked. Some did in fact acknowledge the pathological properties of bacteria, yet deemed it possible that they had only in the course of the disease changed from other harmless, incidentally or normally present microorganisms into pathogenic bacteria. If, however, it could be proven that (a) the parasite was found to be present in every single case of the disease in question, under circumstances that corresponded to the pathological changes and the clinical course of the disease; (b) that it occurred in connection with no other disease as an incidental and nonpathogenic parasite; and (c) that it was capable of producing anew the disease after having been totally isolated from the body and recultivated sufficiently often in pure culture, then it could no longer be seen as incidental to the disease. In this case, the only conceivable relationship between the parasite and the disease would be that the parasite were the cause of the disease.

This proof in its entirety turned out to be applicable to a number of infectious diseases, to anthrax, tuberculosis, erysipelas, tetanus, and many animal diseases; in fact, to nearly all diseases communicable to animals. But what is more, in all cases of infectious diseases in which the regular and exclusive presence of bacteria has been positively established, such bacteria have never exhibited the behavior of incidental parasites, but rather that of the bacteria already conclusively diagnosed as pathogenic. We can therefore justifiably assert that even if only the first two demands of our argumentation are met—i.e., if the regular and exclusive presence of parasites is established—then the causal connection between the parasite and the disease is thereby irrefutably established. Proceeding from this assumption, a number of diseases with which laboratory animals have not yet been successfully infected and which therefore would not meet the third requirement of the aforementioned proof, would nevertheless have to be regarded as parasitic. Such diseases include abdominal typhus, diphtheria, leprosy, relapsing fever, and asiatic cholera. In this connection, I would like to give particular emphasis to cholera, since people have been extraordinarily loath to regard it as a parasitic disease. Absolutely no efforts have been spared to rob the cholera bacteria of their specific character, yet they have withstood triumphantly all attacks, and it can now be considered a firmly grounded and universally confirmed fact that they constitute the cause of cholera.

Apart from these general, yet fundamentally significant questions, bacteriological research has gained a firm foothold in many branches of science and has made clear the interrelations between pathogenic bacteria and infectious diseases. It would be going too far, however, to want to examine such interrelations too closely; let it suffice to say that we are only now in a position to be able to form proper conceptions of how contagious matter behaves outside the body: in the water, in the ground, and in the air; conceptions considerably divergent from the earlier ones, from those derived from uncertain hypotheses. Only now are we able to procure for ourselves reliable information on the extent to which pathogens are to be seen as true parasites; i.e., whether they are dependant solely on the human or animal organism, or whether they are parasites that can find the conditions necessary for their existence outside the body as well and that function only occasionally as pathogens. These are conditions of incisive significance for the prophylactic measures against a number of diseases, particularly against tuberculosis. Furthermore, the manner in which pathogens invade the body has for a number of pathogenic bacteria been determined to a degree sufficiently exact to enable us to arrive at more accurate conceptions of these processes as well. Our knowledge of the behavior of pathogenic bacteria within the body is also becoming more complete, and many a pathological process that in earlier times could only afford us puzzlement is rendered thereby more comprehensible. This includes the high incidence of more than one infectious disease occurring in combination, whereby one is seen as the primary, the other as the secondary disease.

The latter lends the actual disease an aberrant, particularly difficult character, or else follows it as a sequela. Such are conditions observed chiefly in cases of smallpox, scarlet fever, diphtheria, cholera, and in cases of typhus and tuberculosis as well. Also worthy of mention are the results brought forth by the experiments investigating the metabolic products of bacteria, since a number of such products bring about characteristic toxic effects and may well exert influence on the symptoms of infectious diseases, and perhaps even cause the most important of these symptoms. Of particular interest in this respect are the recently discovered toxic proteins, the so-called toxalbumins, which can be extracted from cultures of anthrax, diphtheria, and tetanus bacteria.

A related question, that of the nature of immunity, is being worked upon with ardent diligence; its solution will only be brought about with the assistance of bacteriology. While research in this direction has not yet been conclusive, it is becoming more and more evident that the notion that prevailed for a time, of a purely cellular process, a sort of battle between the invading parasites and the phagocytes acting in defense of the body, is losing more and more ground and that here, too, it is most likely chemical processes that play the main role.

In this relatively short time, bacteriological research has furnished a plethora of material pertaining to the biological aspects of bacteria, and a good deal of this material has its significance for the medical side of bacteriology as well. An example of this would be the phenomenon of static condition, which in the case of some bacteria, such as the anthrax and tetanus bacilli, occurs in the form of spores and is characterized by a level of resistance, unparalleled in the biological world, to high temperatures and the effects of chemical agents. The numerous investigations into the influence exerted by heat, cold, desiccation, chemical substances, light, etc., on the nonsporiferous pathogenic bacteria have furnished a good deal of data capable of being utilized prophylactically.

Of these factors, I find light one of the most important. For the past few years, it has been known that direct sunlight is capable of killing bacteria rather quickly. I can confirm this for tubercle bacilli, which depending on the thickness of the layer in which they are exposed to the sunlight, are killed in a time ranging from a few minutes to several hours. I think it particularly noteworthy, however, that diffused daylight brings about the same effect, even if it takes a correspondingly longer time to do so. The cultures of tubercle bacilli die, when placed close to the window, in five to seven days.

That bacteria are only able to breed under moist conditions, i.e., in the presence of water or some other suitable liquid, and that they are unable to pass under their own power from moist surfaces into the air, is not without significance for the etiology of infectious diseases. Consequently, pathogenic bacteria can only take to the air in the form of dust and borne by dust particles, and only such bacteria as remain viable for longer periods of time in the desiccated state can be carried away by currents of air. But they are never capable of actually breeding in the air, as was assumed for pathogens in earlier conceptions.

In all of the areas we have discussed until now, bacteriological research has fulfilled completely, in some cases even exceeded, what it had seemed to promise at the time of its initial development. In other areas, however, it has not met the expectations to which it gave rise. Despite staining methods that are continually being perfected and despite the use of lens systems of ever greater angular aperture, we have not, for example, been able to learn any more about the inner structure of bacteria than we had learned using the original methods. It is only in recent times that new staining methods have been developed that seem capable of providing further data on the structure of bacteria; this will depend on whether an inner part, probably a nucleus, can be successfully distinguished from the outer plasma membrane and whether the organs of locomotion, the cilia, which apparently grow out of the plasma layer, can be rendered visible with a degree of clarity hitherto unattainable.

In several points, however—the very points where it was least expected—bacteriological research has left us completely in the lurch, namely, in the investigation of a number of infectious diseases, which because of their pronounced infectiousness would appear to be particularly vulnerable to the probing tools of research.

This applies primarily to the entire group of exanthematous infectious diseases, i.e., measles, scarlet fever, smallpox, exanthematous typhus. Not for a single one of these has the least bit of evidence been found as to what the nature of their pathogens might be. Even the vaccine, which is readily available and which can be tested so easily on a laboratory animal, has withstood all efforts to determine the nature of its actual agent. The same holds for rabies as well.

Nor do we know anything about the pathogens for influenza, whooping cough, trachoma, yellow fever, cattle plague, pneumonic plague, or many other diseases we know to be infectious. With most of these diseases, there has been no lack of skill or perseverance in the employment of all the aids we have at our disposal, and the only way we can interpret the negative results of the efforts of so many researchers is by concluding that the research methods that have until now proven useful in so many cases no longer suffice for these tasks. I am tempted to believe that the pathogens of the diseases mentioned are not bacteria at all, but organized pathogens that belong to different groups of microorganisms altogether. This belief is all the more justified when one considers that in the blood of some animals, as well as in that of humans who have contracted malaria, peculiar parasites have been discovered that belong to the most primitive phylum of the animal kingdom, that of the protozoans. To be sure, scientists have not gotten beyond simply demonstrating the existence of these strange and highly significant parasites, and will probably not make any further progress until they have succeeded in breeding these protozoans using methods similar to those used with bacteria, in artificial culture media or under other conditions, as naturally as possible, outside the body, and in studying their living conditions and life cycles. Should this problem be solved, and we have no reason to doubt that it will, then the study of pathogenic protozoa and related microorganisms will develop into a line of inquiry ancillary to bacteriological research, one which will hopefully plumb the depths of the etiologically yet unfathomed infectious diseases mentioned.

There is one question that I have not yet touched upon, even though it is the very question asked most often of bacteriologists—asked, I might add, not without a certain tone of reproach: "What is the use of all the toilsome effort that has been spent studying bacteria?" Actually, the question should not be posed in this way at all, for true science follows its course unencumbered by the question of whether or not its work provides some immediate utility. Yet I cannot consider the question completely unjustified in this case, since of those involved in bacteriological research, very few indeed will have completely disregarded practical goals in the course of their work.

The practical returns that bacteriological research has already produced are by no means as meager as the askers of this question would have it.

Let us look at what has been accomplished just in the field of disinfection. This is the very field that previously was characterized by such a lack of fruitful leads, by such stumbling about in utter darkness. Great sums of money were often enough wasted on useless disinfections, not to mention the indirect harm that results additionally from unsuccessful hygienic measures. Now we are in possession of reliable criteria for testing the efficacy of disinfectants, and while there is still a good deal left to be accomplished in this field, we can nevertheless maintain that the disinfectants in use today, insofar as they have been judged effective by such tests, really do serve their purpose.

One of these practical successes has been the use of bacteriological methods to control the effectiveness of water filtration, since such methods have proven themselves irreplaceable in the accomplishment of this task. Related to this are the data provided by bacteriological research on the filtration properties of the ground and the important conclusions that have been drawn from these data for the exploitation of ground water as a source of fresh water and for the proper construction of wells. In the same manner as it is applied to water, bacteriological research can be applied to the quality control of milk, particularly insofar as this milk is used for the nourishment of children, and to the analysis of other foods and personal articles suspected of being infected. The analysis of the air in sewers and the resulting revision of widespread notions as to the noxiousness of sewer air, the analysis of the air in classrooms, the detection of pathogenic bacteria in foodstuffs, in the ground, etc.—all represent an undeniably close intermeshing of theory and practice. Further examples of practical successes I would like to mention are the diagnoses, made possible through the help of bacteriology, of isolated cases of asiatic cholera and the initial stages of pulmonary tuberculosis; the former having importance for the prophylaxis of cholera, the latter for the early treatment of tuberculosis.

All of these advantages, however, are ones that can be utilized only indirectly in the battle against bacteria. Agents that act directly, i.e., therapeutic agents, can still hardly be compared with such indirect agents. The only example that can be given in this context are the successful results obtained by P a s t e u r and others with the vaccinations against rabies, anthrax, rauschbrand (symptomatic anthrax), and swine erysipelas. And particularly in the case of the rabies vaccination, the only one suitable for use with humans, one could object that the cause of rabies is not yet known and is most likely not even bacterial, and that the discovery of this vaccination can therefore not be credited to bacteriology. Still, this discovery grew out of bacteriological soil, and would most likely not have been made without the foregoing discoveries of vaccinations against pathogenic bacteria.

Although bacteriological research has such insignificant results to show for its untiring efforts, particularly in this direction, I do not believe that this shall remain the case. On the contrary, I am convinced that bacteriology will one day reattain the great significance it once had for therapeutic applications. I must admit, however, that I have no great hopes of therapeutic success for diseases with short incubation periods and rapid progression. With such diseases, as with cholera, for example, the greatest emphasis will always have to be placed on prophylaxis. I am thinking of diseases, rather, that do not progress too rapidly, because such diseases are far more susceptible to therapeutic intervention. And there exists hardly a disease, in part for this reason, in part on account of its significance over and above all other infectious diseases, that presents as great a challenge to bacteriological research as does tuberculosis.

Prompted by such considerations, I began very soon after the discovery of the tubercle bacilli to search for agents that could be used therapeutically against tuberculosis, and have continued these experiments unremittingly until now—interrupted, to be sure, on many occasions by professional concerns. I stand by no means alone in my conviction that there must be remedies against tuberculosis.

In one of his most recent works, B i l l r o t h expressed himself quite emphatically to the same effect, and it is common knowledge that the same goal is aspired to by numerous scientists. Only it seems to me that the latter as a rule have not been following the right course, insofar as they have begun their studies by experimenting with human subjects. This I hold responsible for the circumstance that all the discoveries that have resulted from this line of experimentation, from benzoated caustic soda to the hot-air method, have turned out to be illusory. One should initially experiment not on humans, but on the parasites themselves in pure culture; even when agents capable of arresting the development of the tubercle bacilli in cultures have been found, one should not immediately begin experimenting on humans, but should experiment first on animals, to see whether the observations made in the test tube hold for the living animal body as well. Only when the animal experiment has proven successful should one go on to experiment on humans.

Following these rules, I have tested over the course of time a great number of substances for their influence on tubercle bacteria bred in pure culture, with the result that a good number of substances are able, even in very low dosages, to impair the growth of these bacteria. An agent, of course, need not do any more than this. It is not necessary, as is commonly and erroneously assumed, for bacteria to be killed within the body. It is enough to hinder their growth, their multiplication, to render them harmless to the body.

The following, to name only the most important examples, are agents that have been found to impair growth: a number of volatile oils; among the aromatic compounds, beta-naphthylamine, paratoluidine, xylidine; a number of the so-called coal-tar dyes, namely fuchsine, gentian violet (methylrosaniline chloride), methylene blue, quinoline yellow, aniline yellow, auramine; among the metals, mercury in vapor form, silver and gold compounds. The cyanogen-gold compounds, because their effects exceeded those of all other substances, left a particularly striking impression; even in a dilution of 1 : 2,000,000 they were able to impede the growth of tubercle bacilli.

None of these substances has the least effect, however, when used in experiments on tubercular animals.

This lack of success has not hindered my search for development-retarding agents, and I have finally encountered substances that are capable of arresting the growth of tubercle bacilli not only in the test tube, but in the animal body as well. All studies involving tuberculosis, as anyone who has ever carried out experiments with this disease has sufficiently experienced, take an inordinate amount of patience. Accordingly, my experiments with these substances are not yet finished, even though I have been carrying them out for over a year. All that I can impart, therefore, is that when guinea pigs, with their well-known susceptibility to tuberculosis, are subjected to the effects of one of these substances, they no longer react to an inoculation with tuberculosis virus, and in the case of guinea pigs already quite ill with general tuberculosis, the disease can be brought to a complete standstill without the body exhibiting any adverse side effects from the agent.

I should like to draw, for the time being, but one conclusion from these experiments: namely, that the possibility of destroying pathogenic bacteria in the body without any adverse effects to the latter, a possibility that has until now been justifiably doubted, can now be considered confirmed.

Should, however, any of the further hopes to which these experiments give rise be fulfilled, and should scientists ever succeed in conquering within the human body, initially in a bacterial infectious disease, the microscopically small but until that time predominant enemy, then very soon, other diseases will likewise be conquered; of this I am certain. A promising field of activity shall therewith be opened, with tasks worthy of constituting the objects of the noblest sort of international competition. My one and only reason for going against my usual habit and communicating the results of unfinished experiments was to provide even now the impetus for further experimentation.

And so allow me to close my lecture with the wish that the nations might compete with one another in this field of activity, in the war against the tiniest, but most dangerous enemy of humanity, and that in this struggle for the well-being of the entire human race, the nations might continually outstrip one another in their successes.

Translated by Daniel Theisen

Jakob von Uexküll

A Stroll through the Worlds of Animals and Men

This little monograph does not claim to point the way to a new science. Perhaps it should be called a stroll into unfamiliar worlds; worlds strange to us but known to other creatures, manifold and varied as the animals themselves. The best time to set out on such an adventure is on a sunny day. The place, a flower-strewn meadow, humming with insects, fluttering with butterflies. Here we may glimpse the worlds of the lowly dwellers of the meadow. To do so, we must first blow, in fancy, a soap bubble around each creature to represent its own world, filled with the perceptions which it alone knows. When we ourselves then step into one of these bubbles, the familiar meadow is transformed. Many of its colorful features disappear, others no longer belong together but appear in new relationships. A new world comes into being. Through the bubble we see the world of the burrowing worm, of the butterfly, or of the field mouse; the world as it appears to the animals themselves, not as it appears to us. This we may call the *phenomenal world* or the *self-world* of the animal.

To some, these worlds are invisible. Many a zoologist and physiologist, clinging to the doctrine that all living beings are mere machines, denies their existence and thus boards up the gates to other worlds so that no single ray of light shines forth from all the radiance that is shed over them. But let us who are not committed to the machine theory consider the nature of machines. All our useful devices, our machines, only implement our acts. There are tools that help our senses, spectacles, telescopes, microphones, which we may call *perceptual tools*. There are also tools used to effect our purposes, the machines of our factories and of transportation, lathes and motor cars. These we may call *effector tools*.

Now we might assume that an animal is nothing but a collection of perceptual and effector tools, connected by an integrating apparatus which, though still a mechanism, is yet fit to carry on the life functions. This is indeed the position of all mechanistic theorists, whether their analogies are in terms of rigid mechanics or more plastic dynamics. They brand animals as mere objects. The proponents of such theories forget that from the first, they have overlooked the most important thing, the *subject* which uses the tools, perceives and functions with their aid.

The mechanists have pieced together the sensory and motor organs of animals, like so many parts of a machine, ignoring their real functions of perceiving and acting, and have even gone on to mechanize man himself. According to the behaviorists, man's own sensations and will are mere appearance, to be considered, if at all, only as disturbing static. But we who still hold that our sense organs serve our perceptions, and our motor organs our actions, see in animals as well not only the mechanical structure, but also the operator, who is built into their organs, as we are into our bodies. We no longer regard animals as mere machines, but as subjects whose essential activity consists of perceiving and acting. We thus unlock the gates that lead to other realms, for all that a subject perceives becomes his perceptual world and all that he does, his effector world. Perceptual and effector worlds together form a closed unit, the *Umwelt*. These different worlds, which are as manifold as the animals themselves, present to all nature lovers new lands of such wealth and beauty that a walk through them is well worth while, even though they unfold not to the physical but only to the spiritual eye. So, reader, join us as we ramble through these worlds of wonder.

Anyone who lives in the country and roams through woods and brush with his dog surely made the acquaintance of a tiny insect which, hanging from the branches of bushes, lurks for its prey, be it man or animal, ready to hurl itself at its victim and gorge itself with his blood until it swells to the size of a pea. The tick, though not dangerous, is still an unpleasant guest of mammals, including men. Recent publications have clarified many details of its life story so that we are able to trace an almost complete picture of it.

From the egg there issues forth a small animal, not yet fully developed, for it lacks a pair of legs and sex organs. In this state it is already capable of attacking cold-blooded animals, such as lizards, whom it waylays as it sits on the tip of a blade of grass. After shedding its skin several times, it acquires the missing organs, mates, and starts its hunt for warm-blooded animals.

After mating, the female climbs to the tip of a twig on some bush. There she clings at such a height that she can drop upon small mammals that may run under her, or be brushed off by larger animals.

The eyeless tick is directed to this watchtower by a general photosensitivity of her skin. The approaching prey is revealed to the blind and deaf highway woman by her sense of smell. The order of butyric acid, that emanates from the skin glands of all mammals, acts on the tick as a signal to leave her watchtower and hurl herself downwards. If, in so doing, she lands on something warm—a fine sense of temperature betrays this to her—she has reached her prey, the warm-blooded creature. It only remains for her to find a hairless spot. There she burrows deep into the skin of her prey, and slowly pumps herself full of warm blood.

Experiments with artificial membranes and fluids other than blood have proved that the tick lacks all sense of taste. Once the membrane is perforated, she will drink any fluid of the right temperature.

If after the stimulus of butyric acid has functioned, the tick falls upon something cold, she has missed her prey and must again climb to her watchtower.

The tick's abundant blood repast is also her last meal. Now there is nothing left for her to do but drop to earth, lay her eggs and die.

The tick's life history provides support for the validity of the biological versus the heretofore customary physiological approach. To the physiologist, every living creature is an object that exists in his human world. He investigates the organs of living things and the way they work together, as a technician would examine a strange machine. The biologist, on the other hand, takes into account each individual as a subject, living in a world of its own, of which it is the center. It cannot, therefore, be compared to a machine, but only to the engineer who operates the machine. If we ask whether the tick is a machine or an operator, a mere object or a subject, the physiologist will reply that he finds receptors, that is, sense organs, and effectors, that is, organs of action, connected by an integrating device in the central nervous system. He finds no trace of an operator.

To this the biologist will reply, "You mistake the character of the organism completely. No single part of the tick's body has the nature of a machine; everywhere operators are at work." The physiologist will continue, undeterred, "We can show that all the actions of the tick are reflex* in character and the reflex arc is the foundation of all animal machines. It begins with a receptor, which admits only certain influences such as butyric acid and warmth, and screens out all others. It ends with a muscle which moves an effector, a leg or proboscis. The sensory cells that initiate the nervous excitation and the motor cells that elicit the motor impulse serve only as connecting links to transmit the entirely physical waves of excitation (produced in the nerves by the receptor upon external stimulation) to the muscles of the effectors. The entire reflex arc works by transfer of motion, as does any machine. No subjective factor, no engineer or engineers appear anywhere in this process."

"On the contrary," the biologist will counter, "we meet the operator everywhere, not merely machine parts. For all the cells of the reflex arc are concerned, not with the transfer of motion, but with the transfer of the *stimulus*. And the stimulus must be 'perceived' by a subject; it does not occur in objects." Any machine part, such as the clapper of a bell, produces its effect only if it is swung back and forth in a certain manner. To all other agents, such as cold, heat, acids, alkalies, electric currents, it responds as would any other piece of metal. The action of living organs is fundamentally different from this. Since the time of Johannes Müller we know that a muscle responds to all external agents in one and the same way—by contraction. It transforms all external interference into the same effective stimulus, and responds to it with the same impulse, resulting in contraction. Johannes Müller showed also that all external influences affecting the optic nerve, whether ether waves, pressure, or electric currents, elicit a sensa-

---

*Reflex originally means the intercepting and reflecting of a light ray by a mirror. Transferred to living creatures, the reflex is conceived as the reception of an external stimulus by a receptor and the stimulus-elicited response by the effectors. In the process the stimulus is converted into nervous excitation, which has to pass through several stations on its way from the receptor to the effector. The course thus described is referred to as a reflex arc.

tion of light. Our visual sensory cells produce the same perception whatever the source of stimulation. From this we may conclude that each living cell is an engineer who perceives and acts, and has *perceptual* or *receptor* signs (*Merkzeichen*) and impulses or *effector signs* (*Wirkzeichen*) which are specific to it. The manifold perceiving and acting of the whole animal may thus be reduced to the cooperation of all the tiny cells, each of which commands only one receptor sign and one effector sign.

In order to achieve an orderly collaboration, the organism uses the brain cells (these, too, are elementary mechanics) and groups half of them as "receptor cells" in the stimulus-receiving part of the brain, or "perceptive organ," into smaller or larger clusters. These clusters correspond to groups of external stimuli, which approach the animal in the form of questions. The other half of the brain cells is used by the organism as "effector cells" or impulse cells, and is grouped into clusters with which it controls the movements of the effectors. These impart the subject's answers to the outer world. The clusters of receptor cells fill the "receptor organs" (*Merkorgan*) of the brain, and the clusters of effector cells make up the contents of its "effector organs" (*Wirkorgan*).

The individual cells of the perceptor organ, whatever their activity, remain as spatially separate units. The units of information which they separately convey would also remain isolated, if it were not possible for them to be fused into new units which are independent of the spatial characters of the receptor organ. This possibility does, in fact, exist. The receptor signs of a group of receptor cells are combined outside the receptor organ, indeed outside the animal, into units that become the properties of external objects. This projection of sensory impressions is a self-evident fact. All our human sensations, which represent our specific receptor signs, unite into perceptual cues (*Merkmal*) which constitute the attributes of external objects and serve as the real basis of our actions. The sensation "blue" becomes the "blueness" of the sky; the sensation "green," the "greenness" of the lawn. These are the cues by which we recognize the objects: blue, the sky; green, the lawn.

A similar process takes place in the effector organ. The isolated effector cells are organized into well-articulated groups according to their effector signs or impulses. The isolated impulses are coordinated into units, and these self-contained motor impulses or rhythmical impulse melodies act upon the muscles subordinated to them. And the limbs or other organs activated by the separate muscles imprint upon the external objects their effector cue or functional significance (*Wirkmal*).

Figuratively speaking, every animal grasps its object with two arms of a forceps, receptor, and effector. With the one it invests the object with a receptor cue or perceptual meaning, with the other, an effector cue or operational meaning. But since all of the traits of an object are structurally interconnected, the traits given operational meaning must affect those bearing perceptual meaning through the object, and so change the object itself. This is best expressed briefly as: *The effector cue or meaning extinguishes the receptor cue or meaning.*

Beside the selection of stimuli which the receptors let through, and the arrangement of muscles which enables the effectors to function in certain ways, the most decisive factor for the course of any action is the number and arrangement of receptor cells which, with the aid of their receptor signs, furnish the objects of the *Umwelt* with receptor cues, and the number and arrangement of effector cells which, by means of their effector signs, supply the same objects with effector cues.

The object participates in the action only to the extent that it must possess certain qualities that can serve as perceptual cue-bearers on the one hand and as functional cue-bearers on the other; and these must be linked by a connecting counterstructure. . . .

If we further consider that a subject is related to the same or to different objects by several functional cycles, we shall gain insight into the first principle of *Umwelt* theory: all animals, from the simplest to the most complex, are fitted into their unique worlds with equal completeness. A simple world corresponds to a simple animal, a well-articulated world to a complex one.

And now let us set into the schema of the functional cycle, the tick as subject, and the mammal as her object. It shows at a glance that three functional cycles follow each other in well-planned succession. The skin glands of the mammal are the bearers of perceptual meaning in the first cycle, since the stimulus of butyric acid releases specific receptor signs in the tick's receptor organ, and these receptor signs are projected outside as an olfactory cue. By induction (the nature of which we do not know) the processes that take place in the receptor organ initiate corresponding impulses in the effector organ, and these impulses induce the tick to let go with her legs and drop. The tick, falling on the hairs of the mammal, projects the effector cue of shock onto them. This in turn releases a tactile cue, which extinguishes the olfactory stimulus of the butyric acid. The new receptor cue elicits running about, until it in turn is replaced by the sensation of heat, which starts the boring response.

We are admittedly confronted here with three successive reflexes. Each is elicited by objectively demonstrable physical or chemical stimuli. But anyone who is content with this statement and assumes that it solves the problem proves only that he has not grasped the basic question. We are not concerned with the chemical stimulus of butyric acid, any more than with the mechanical stimulus (released by the hairs), or the temperature stimulus of the skin. We are concerned solely with the fact that, out of hundreds of stimuli radiating from the qualities of the mammal's body, only three become the bearers of receptor cues for the tick. Why just these three and no others?

What we are dealing with is not an exchange of forces between two objects, but the relations between a living subject and its object. These occur on an altogether different plane, namely, between the receptor sign of the subject and the stimulus from the object.

The tick hangs motionless on the tip of a branch in a forest clearing. Her position gives her the chance to drop on a passing mammal. Out of the whole environment, no stimulus affects her until a mammal approaches, whose blood she needs before she can bear her young.

And now something quite wonderful happens. Of all the influences that emanate from the mammal's body, only three become stimuli, and those in a definite sequence. Out of the vast world which surrounds the tick, three stimuli shine forth from the dark like beacons, and serve as guides to lead her unerringly to her goal. To accomplish this, the tick, besides her body with its receptors and effectors, has been given three receptor signs, which she can use as sign stimuli. And these perceptual cues prescribe the course of her actions so rigidly that she is only able to produce corresponding specific effector cues.

The whole rich world around the tick shrinks and changes into a scanty framework consisting, in essence, of three receptor cues and three effector cues—her *Umwelt*. But the very poverty of this world guarantees the unfailing certainty of her actions, and security is more important than wealth.

From the example of the tick we can deduce the basic structural traits of the *Umwelt,* which are valid for all animals. However, the tick possesses another most remarkable faculty, which affords a further insight into these worlds.

The lucky coincidence which brings a mammal under the twig on which the tick sits obviously occurs very rarely. Nor does the large number of ticks caught in the bushes balance this drawback sufficiently to insure survival of the species. To heighten the probability of a prey coming her way, the tick's ability to live long without food must be added. And this faculty she possesses to an unusual degree. At the Zoological Institute in Rostock, ticks who had been starving for eighteen years have been kept alive. A tick can wait eighteen years. That is something which we humans cannot do. Our time is made up of a series of moments, or briefest time units, within which the world shows no change. For the duration of a moment, the world stands still. Man's moment lasts one-eighteenth of a second. We shall see later that the length of a moment varies in different animals. But whatever number we wish to adopt for the tick, the ability to endure a never-changing world for eighteen years is beyond the realm of possibility. We shall therefore assume that during her period of waiting the tick is in a sleep-like state, of the sort that interrupts time for hours in our case, too. Only in the tick's world, time, instead of standing still for mere hours, stops for many years at a time, and does not begin to function again until the signal of butyric acid arouses her to renewed activity.

What have we gained by realizing this? Something extremely significant. Time, which frames all happening, seems to us to be the only objectively stable thing in contrast to the colorful change of its contents, and now we see that the subject sways the time of his own world. Instead of saying, as heretofore, that without time, there can be no living subject, we shall now have to say that without a living subject, there can be no time.

Translated by Claire H. Schiller

Konrad Lorenz

Habit, Ritual, and Magic

Redirection of the attack is evolution's most ingenious expedient for guiding aggression into harmless channels, and it is not the only one, for rarely do the great constructors, selection and mutation, rely on a *single* method. It is in the nature of their blind trial and error, or to be more exact, trial and success, that they often hit upon *several* possible ways of dealing with the same problem, and use them all to make its solution doubly and triply sure. This applies particularly to the various physiological mechanisms of behavior whose function it is to prevent the injuring and killing of members of the same species. As a prerequisite for the understanding of these mechanisms it is necessary for us to familiarize ourselves with a still mysterious, phylogenetic phenomenon laying down inviolable laws which the social behavior of many higher animals obeys much in the same way as the behavior of civilized man obeys his most sacred customs.

Shortly before World War I when my teacher and friend, Sir Julian Huxley, was engaged in his pioneer studies on the courtship behavior of the Great Crested Grebe, he discovered the remarkable fact that certain movement patterns lose, in the course of phylogeny, their original specific function and become purely "symbolic" ceremonies. He called his process ritualization and used this term without quotation marks; in other words, he equated the cultural processes leading to the development of human rites with the phylogenetic processes giving rise to such remarkable "ceremonies" in animals. From a purely functional point of view this equation is justified, even bearing in mind the difference between the cultural and phylogenetic processes. I shall try to show how the astonishing analogies between the phylogenetic and cultural rites find their explanation in the similarity of their functions.

A good example of how a rite originates phylogentically, how it acquires a meaning, and how this becomes altered in the course of further development, can be found by studying a certain ceremony of females of the duck species. This ceremony is called "inciting." As in many birds with a similar family life, the females of this species are smaller but no less aggressive than the males. Thus in quarrels between two couples it often happens that the duck, impelled by anger, advances too near the enemy couple, then gets "frightened by her own courage," turns around, and hurries back to her own strong, protective drake. Beside him, she gathers new courage and begins to threaten the neighbors again, without however leaving the safe proximity of her mate.

In its original form, this succession of behavior patterns is variable according to the varying force of the conflicting drives by which the duck is impelled. The successive dominance of aggression, fear, protection-seeking, and renewed aggressiveness can clearly be read in the expression movements and, above all, in the different positions of the duck. In our European Common Shelduck for example, the whole process, with the exception of a certain head movement coupled with a special vocal utterance, contains no ritually fixed component parts. The duck runs, as every bird of this species does when attacking, with long, lowered neck toward her opponent and immediately afterward with raised head back to her mate. She often takes refuge behind the drake, describing a semicircle around him so that finally, when she starts threatening again, she is standing beside him, with her head pointing straight forward toward the enemy couple. But if she is not in a particularly frightened mood when fleeing, she merely runs to her drake and stops in front of him. Now her breast faces the drake, so if she wants to threaten her enemy she must stretch her head and neck backward over her shoulder. If she happens to stand sideways before or behind the drake, she stretches her neck at right angles to her body axis. Thus the angle between the long axis of her body and her outstretched neck depends entirely upon her position in relation to that of her drake and that of the enemy; she shows no special preference for any of these positions of movement patterns.

In the nearly related East European–Asiatic Ruddy Sheldrake, the motor pattern of "inciting" is a small step further ritualized. In this species the duck may "still," on some occasions, stand beside her drake, threatening forward, or she may run around him, describing every kind of angle between the long axis of her body and the threatening direction of her neck; but in the majority of cases she stands with her breast to the drake, threatening backward over her shoulder. I once saw the female of an isolated couple of this species carrying out the movements of inciting without any eliciting object, and she threatened backward over her shoulder just as though she could see the nonexistent enemy in this direction.

In surface-feeding ducks, including our Mallard, the ancestor of the domestic duck, threatening backward over the shoulder has become the only possible, obligatory motor coordination. Before beginning to incite, the duck always stands with her breast as close as possible to the drake, or if he is moving she runs or swims closely after him. The head movement, directed backward over the shoulder, still contains the original orientation responses which produce, in the Ruddy Sheldrake, a motor pattern identical in its phenotype, that is, in its outer appearance, but composed of independently variable elements. This is best seen when the duck begins to perform the movement in a mild state of excitation and gradually works herself into a fury. If the enemy is standing directly in front of her, she may first threaten directly forward, but in direct proportion to her rising excitement, an irresistible force seems to pull her head backward over her shoulder. Yet an orientation reaction is still at work, striving to direct her threatening toward the enemy; this can literally be read in her eyes, which remain resolutely fixed on the object of her anger, although the new, ritually fixed movement is pulling her head in another direction. If she could speak, she would say, "I want to threaten that odious, strange drake but my head is being pulled in another direction." The existence of two conflicting directional tendencies can be demonstrated objectively: if the enemy bird is standing in front of the duck the deflection of her head backward over the shoulder is least, and it increases in direct proportion to the size of the angle between the long axis of the duck and the position of the enemy. If he is standing directly behind her, that is at an angle of one-hundred-eighty degrees, she almost touches her tail with her beak.

This conflict behavior observed in most female dabbling ducks has only one explanation, which must be correct however remarkable it may at first seem; in addition to those factors which originally produced the movements described, and which are easy to understand, there has evolved, in the course of phylogeny, a further, new one. In the Common Shelduck, the flight toward the drake and the attack on the enemy suffice to explain the behavior of the duck; in the Mallard, the same impulses are obviously still at work, but the behavior pattern determined by them is superseded by an independent new motor coordination. Analysis of the whole process is made extremely difficult by the fact that the new fixed motor pattern, which has arisen by "ritualization," is a hereditarily fixed copy of a behavior pattern originally induced by several other motives. The original behavior differs from case to case according to the varying force of each separate, independently variable impulse; the newly arisen, fixed motor coordination represents only one stereotyped average case. This has now become "schematized" in a manner strongly reminiscent of symbols in human cultural history. In the Mallard, the original variability of the positions in which drake and enemy may be situated is schematically programmed so that the drake must stand in front of the duck and the enemy behind her. The retreat toward the drake, originally motivated by escape drive, and the aggressive advance on the enemy are welded into one fixed, ceremonial to-and-fro movement whose rhythmical repetition increases its effectiveness as a signal. The newly arisen fixed motor pattern does not suddenly become preponderant but exists first beside the unritualized model over which it predominates only slightly. . . .

The above example of inciting in the Mallard is typical of most cases of phylogenetic ritualization: a new instinctive motor pattern arises whose form copies that of a behavior pattern which is variable and which is caused by several independent motivations. . . .

The example of inciting may further serve to illustrate the peculiarity of rite formation. In diving ducks, the inciting of the females is ritualized in a somewhat different and more complicated way: in the Crested Pochard, not only the enemy-threatening movement but also the protection-seeking movement is ritualized, that is established by a fixed motor pattern which has evolved *ad hoc.* The female Crested Pochard alternates rhythmically between a backward thrusting of her head over her shoulder and a pronounced turning of the head toward her drake, each time moving her chin up and down, a set of movements corresponding to a mimically exaggerated fleeing movement.

In the White Eye, the female advances threateningly some distance toward the enemy and then swims quickly back to her drake, making repeated chin-lifting movements which are here scarcely distinguishable from the movements of taking off. In the Goldeneye, inciting is almost entirely independent of the presence of a member of her species representing the enemy. The duck swims behind her drake and performs, in rhythmic regularity, extensive neck and head movements, alternately to the right backward and to the left backward. These would hardly be recognized as threatening movements if the phylogenetic intermediate steps were not known.

Just as the form of these movements, in the course of their progressive ritualization, has become different from those of the nonritualized prototype, so also has their meaning. The inciting of the Common Shelduck is "still" exactly like the ordinary threatening of the species and its effect on the drake is in no way different from that which, in species lacking a special inciting ceremony, the threatening of one member of a group has on another: the latter may be infected by the anger of the companion and join in the attack. In the somewhat stronger and more aggressive Ruddy Sheldrake and particularly in the Egyptian Goose, this originally mildly stimulating effect of inciting is many times stronger. In these birds, inciting really deserves its name, for the males react like fierce dogs which only await their master's signal to release their fury. In these species, the function of inciting is intimately connected with that of territorial defense. Heinroth found that the males could agree in a communal enclosure if all the females were removed.

In dabbling and in diving ducks, it is relatively seldom that the drake responds to the inciting of his duck by attacking the "enemy"; in this case the quotation marks are merited. In an unpaired Mallard, for example, inciting simply implies an invitation to pair, though *not* to mate: the precopulatory ceremony looks quite different and is called pumping. Inciting is the invitation to permanent pair formation. If the drake is inclined to accept the proposal, he lifts his chin, turns his head slightly away from the duck, and says very quickly, "Rabrab, rabrab," or, especially when he is in the water, he answers with a certain likewise ritualized ceremony: drinking and sham preening. Both these ceremonies mean that the drake Mallard is answering, "I will!" The utterance "Rabrab" contains an element of aggression; the turning away of the head with lifted chin is a typical gesture of appeasement. If he is very excited, the drake may actually make a small demonstration attack on another drake which chances to be standing near. In the second ceremony, drinking and sham preening, this never happens. Inciting on the one hand, and drinking and sham preening on the other, mutually elicit each other, and the couple can persist in them for a long time. Though drinking and sham preening have arisen from a gesture of embarrassment in whose original form aggression was present, this is no longer contained in the ritualized movement seen in dabbling ducks. In these birds, the ceremony acts as a pure appeasement gesture. In Crested Pochards and other diving ducks, I have never known the inciting of the duck to rouse the drake to serious attack.

Thus while the message of inciting in Ruddy Shelduck and Egyptian Geese could be expressed in the words "Drive him off, thrash him!," in diving ducks it simply means, "I love you." In several groups, midway between these two extremes, as for example in the Gadwall and the Widgeon, an intermediate meaning may be found: "You are my hero. I rely on you." Naturally the signal function of these symbols fluctuates even within the same species according to the situation, but the gradual phylogenetic change of meaning of the symbol has undoubtedly progressed in the direction indicated. . . .

In several species of so-called Empid Flies (in German very appropriately called *Tanzfliegen*—Dancing Flies), closely related to the fly-eating Asalid Flies, a rite has developed as pretty as it is expedient. In this rite the male presents the female, immediately before copulation, with a slaughtered insect of suitable size. While she is engaged in eating it, he can mate her without fear of being eaten by her himself, a risk apparently threatening the suitors of fly-eating flies, particularly as the male is smaller than the female. Without any doubt, this menace exerted the selection pressure that has caused the evolution of this remarkable behavior. However, the ceremony has also been preserved in a species, the Hyperborean Empis, in which the female no longer eats flies except at her marriage feast. In a North American species, the male spins a pretty white balloon that attracts the female visually; it contains a few small insects which she eats during copulation. Similar conditions can be observed in the Southern Empid, Hilara maura, whose males spin little waving veils in which food is sometimes, but not always, interwoven. But in Hilara sartor, the Tailor Fly, found in Alpine regions and deserving more than all its relations the name of dancing fly, the males no longer catch flies but spin a lovely little veil, spanned during flight between the middle and hind legs, to which optical stimulus the female reacts. In the revised edition of Brehm's

Tierleben, Heymons describes the collective courtship dance of these flies: "Hundreds of these little veil-carriers whirl through the air in their courtship dance, their tiny veils, about 2 mm. in size, glistening like opals in the sun."

In discussing the inciting ceremony of female ducks, I have tried to show how the origin of a new hereditary coordination plays an essential part in the formation of a new rite, and how in this way an autonomous and essentially fixed sequence of movements, a new instinctive motor pattern, arises. The example of the dancing flies is perhaps relevant to show us the other, equally important side of ritualization, namely the newly arising reaction with which the member of the species to whom the message is addressed answers it. In those dancing fly species in which the females are presented with a purely symbolic veil or balloon without edible contents, they obviously react to this idol just as well as or better than their ancestors did to the material gift of edible prey. And so there arises not only an instinctive movement which was not there before and which has a definite signal function in the one member of the species, the "actor," but also an innate understanding of it by the other, the "reactor." What appears to us, on superficial examination, as one ceremony, often consists of a whole number of behavior elements eliciting each other mutually.

The newly arisen motor coordination of the ritualized behavior pattern bears the character of an independent instinctive movement; the eliciting situation, too, which in such cases is largely determined by the answering behavior of the addressee, acquires all the properties of the drive-relieving end situation, aspired to for its own sake. In other words, the chain of actions that originally served other objective and subjective ends, becomes an end in itself as soon as it has become an autonomic rite. It would be misleading to call the ritualized movement pattern of inciting in the Mallard, or even in most diving ducks, the "expression" of love, or of affinity to the mate. The independent instinctive movement is not a by-product, not an "epiphenomenon" of the bond holding the two animals together, it is itself the bond. The constant repetition of these ceremonies which hold the pair together gives a good measure of the strength of the autonomous drive which sets them in motion. If a bird loses its mate, it loses the only object on which it can discharge this drive, and the way it seeks the lost partner bears all the characteristics of so-called appetitive behavior, that is the purposeful struggle to reach that relieving end situation wherein a dammed instinct can be assuaged.

What I have here tried to show is the inestimably important fact that by the process of phylogenetic ritualization a new and completely autonomous instant may evolve which is, in principle, just as independent as any of the so-called "great" drives such as hunger, sex, fear, or aggression, and which—like these—has its seat in the great parliament of instincts. This again is important for our theme, because it is particularly the drives that have arisen by ritualization which are so often called upon, in this parliament, to oppose aggression, to divert it into harmless channels, and to inhibit those of its actions that are injurious to the survival of the species. . . .

Those other rites, which evolve in the course of human civilization, are not hereditarily fixed but are transmitted by tradition and must be learned afresh by every individual. In spite of this difference, the parallel goes so far that it is quite justifiable to omit the quotation marks, as Huxley did. At the same time these functional analogies show what different causal mechanisms the great constructors use to achieve almost identical effects.

Among animals, symbols are not transmitted by tradition from generation to generation, and it is here, if one wishes, that one may draw the border line between "the animal" and man. In animals, individually acquired experience is sometimes transmitted by teaching and learning, from elder to younger individuals, though such true tradition is only seen in those forms whose high capacity for learning is combined with a higher development of their social life. True tradition has been demonstrated in jackdaws, greylag geese, and rats. But knowledge thus transmitted is limited to very simple things, such as pathfinding, recognition of certain foods and of enemies of the species, and—in rats—knowledge of the danger of poisons. However, no means of communication, no learned rituals are ever handed down by tradition in animals. In other words, animals have no culture.

One indispensable element which simple animal traditions have in common with the highest cultural traditions of man is habit. Indubitably it is habit which, in its tenacious hold on the already acquired, plays a similar part in culture as heredity does in the phylogenetic origin of rites. Once an unforgettable experience brought home to me how similar the basic function of habit can be in such dissimilar processes as the simple formation of path habits in a goose and the cultural development of sacred rites in Man. At the time, I was making observations on a young greylag goose which I had reared from the egg and which had transferred to me, by that remarkable process called imprinting, all the behavior patterns that she would normally have shown to her parents. In her earliest childhood, Martina had acquired a fixed habit: when she was about a week old I decided to let her walk upstairs to my bedroom instead of carrying her up, as until then had been my custom. Greylag geese resent being touched, and it frightens them, so it is better to spare them this indignity if possible. In our house in Altenberg the bottom part of the staircase, viewed from the front door, stands out into the middle of the right-hand side of the hall. It ascends by a right-angled turn to the left, leading up to the gallery on the first floor. Opposite the front door is a very large window. As Martina, following obediently at my heels, walked into the hall, the unaccustomed situation suddenly filled her with terror and she strove, as frightened birds always do, toward the light. She ran from the door straight toward the window, passing me where I now stood on the bottom stair. At the window, she waited a few moments to calm down, then, obedient once more, she came to me on the step and followed me up to my bedroom. This procedure was repeated in the same way the next evening, except that this time her detour to the window was a little shorter and she did not remain there so long. In the following days there were further developments: her pause at the window was discontinued and she no longer gave the impression of being frightened. The detour acquired more and more the character of a habit, and it was funny to see how she ran resolutely to the window and, having arrived there, turned without pausing and ran just as resolutely back to the stairs, which she then mounted. The habitual detour to the window became shorter and shorter, the 180 degree turn became an acute angle, and after a year there remained of the whole path habit only a right-angled turn where the goose, instead of mounting the bottom stair at its right-hand end, nearest the door, ran along the stair to its left and mounted it at right angles.

One evening I forgot to let Martina in at the right time, and when I finally remembered her it was already dusk. I ran to the front door, and as I opened it she thrust herself hurriedly and anxiously through, ran between my legs into the hall and, contrary to her usual custom, in front of me to the stairs. Then she did something even more unusual: she deviated from her habitual path and chose the shortest way, skipping her usual right-angle turn and mounting the stairs on the right-hand side, "cutting" the turn of the stairs and starting to climb up. Upon this, something shattering happened: arrived at the fifth step, she suddenly stopped, made a long neck, in geese a sign of fear, and spread her wings as for flight. Then she uttered a warning cry and very nearly took off. Now she hesitated a moment, turned around, ran hurriedly down the five steps and set forth resolutely, like someone on a very important mission, on her original path to the window and back. This time she mounted the steps according to her former custom from the left side. On the fifth step she stopped again, looked around, shook herself and greeted, behavior mechanisms regularly seen in greylags when anxious tension has given place to relief. I hardly believed my eyes. To me there is no doubt about the interpretation of this occurrence: the habit had become a custom which the goose could not break without being stricken by fear. . . .

To the pedagogue, the psychologist, the ethnologist, and the psychiatrist, the above-described behavior pattern will seem strangely familiar. Anyone who has children of his own, or has learned how to be a tolerably useful aunt or uncle, knows from experience how tenaciously little children cling to every detail of the accustomed, and how they become quite desperate if a storyteller diverges in the very least from the text of a familiar fairy tale. And anyone capable of self-observation will concede that even in civilized adults habit, once formed, has a greater power than we generally admit. I once suddenly realized that when driving a car in Vienna I regularly used two different routes when approaching and when leaving a certain place in the city, and this was at a time when no one-way streets compelled me to do so. Rebelling against the creature of habit in myself, I tried using my customary return route for the outward journey, and vice versa. The astonishing result of this experiment was an undeniable feeling of anxiety so unpleasant that when I came to return I reverted to the habitual route.

My description will call to the mind of the ethnologist the magic and witchcraft of many primitive peoples; that these are very much alive today even in civilized people can be seen by the fact that most of us still perform undignified little "sorceries" such as "touching wood" or throwing spilled salt over our shoulder.

My examples of animal behavior will remind the psychiatrist and the psychoanalyst of the compulsive repetition of some acts, a symptom of certain types of neurosis. In a mild form, the same phenomenon can be observed in many children. I remember clearly that, as a child, I had persuaded myself that something terrible would happen if I stepped on one of the lines, instead of into the squares of the paving stones in front of the Vienna Town Hall. A. A. Milne gives an excellent impression of this same fancy of a child in his poem "Lines and Squares."

All these phenomena are related. They have a common root in a behavior mechanism whose species-preserving function is obvious: for a living being lacking insight into the relation between causes and effects it must be extremely useful to cling to a behavior pattern which has once or many times proved to achieve its aim, and to have done so without danger. If one does not know which details of the whole performance are essential for its success as well as for its safety, it is best to cling to them all with slavish exactitude. The principle, "You never know what might happen if you don't," is fully expressed in such superstitions.

Even when a human being is aware of the purely fortuitous origin of a certain habit and knows that breaking it does not portend danger, nevertheless an undeniable anxiety impels him to observe it, and gradually the ingrained behavior becomes a custom. So far, the situation is the same in animals as in man. However, a new and significant note is struck from the moment when the human being no longer acquires the habit for himself but learns it from his parents by cultural transmission. First, he no longer knows the reasons for the origin of the particular behavior prescription. The pious Jew or Moslem abhors pork without being conscious that it was insight into the danger of trichinosis which probably caused his lawmakers to impose the prohibition. Second, the revered father-figure of the lawmaker, remote in time as in mythology, undergoes an apotheosis, making all his laws seem godly and their infringement a sin.

The North American Indians have evolved an appeasement ceremony which stirred my imagination in the days when I still played Red Indians: it is the ritual of smoking the pipe of peace, the calumet of friendship. Later, when I knew more about the phylogenetic origin of innate rites, about their aggression-inhibiting action, and above all, about the amazing analogies between the phylogenetic and the cultural origin of symbols, I suddenly visualized the scene that must have taken place when, for the first time, two enemy Indians became friends by smoking a pipe together.

Spotted Wolf and Piebald Eagle, chiefs of neighboring tribes, both old and experienced and rather tired of war, have agreed to make an unusual experiment: they want to settle the question of hunting rights on the island in Little Beaver River, which separates the hunting grounds of their tribes, by peaceful talks instead of by war. This attempt is, in the beginning, rather embarrassing, because the wish to negotiate might be misinterpreted as cowardice. Thus when they finally meet, in the absence of their followers, they are both very embarrassed, but as neither dares to admit it, either to himself or to the other, they approach each other in a particularly proud, provocative attitude, staring fixedly at each other and sitting down with the utmost dignity. And then for a long time nothing happens. Anyone who has ever bought a piece of land from an Austrian or a Bavarian farmer knows that whichever one first mentions the matter in hand has already half lost the bargain; and probably the same thing applies to Red Indians. Who knows how long the two chiefs sat face to face?

If you have to sit without moving so much as a face muscle, so as not to betray inner tension, if you are longing to do something but prevented by strong opposing motives from doing it, if in other words you are in a conflict situation, it is often a relief to do a third, neutral thing which has nothing to do with the two conflicting motives and which, moreover, shows apparent indifference to them. The ethologist calls this a displacement activity; colloquially it is called a gesture of embarrassment. All the smokers I know exhibit the same behavior in cases of inward conflict: they put their hand in their pocket, take out their cigarettes or pipe, and light it. Why should the people who invented tobacco smoking, and from whom we first learned it, do otherwise?

And so Spotted Wolf, or perhaps Piebald Eagle, lighted his pipe, at that time not yet the pipe of peace, and the other chief did the same. Who does not know it, the heavenly, tension-relieving catharsis of smoking? Both chiefs became calmer, more self-assured, and their relaxation led to complete success of the negotiations. Perhaps at the next meeting one of the chiefs lighted his pipe at once, perhaps at the third encounter one had forgotten his pipe and the other—now more tolerant—shared his with him. But perhaps a whole series of countless repetitions of the ceremony was necessary before it gradually became common knowledge that a pipe-smoking Indian is more ready to negotiate than a nonsmoking one. Perhaps it may have taken centuries before the symbol of pipe-smoking unequivocally meant peace. But it is quite certain that in the course of generations the original gesture of embarrassment developed into a fixed ritual which became law for every Indian and prohibited aggression after pipe smoking.

However, we would be neglecting an essential side of the matter if we only stressed the inhibiting function of the culturally evolved ritual. Though governed and sanctified by the superindividual, tradition-bound, and cultural superego, the ritual has retained, unaltered, the nature of a habit which is precious to us and to which we cling more fondly than to any habit formed only in the course of an individual life. And herein lies the deep significance of the movement patterns and pageantry of cultural ceremonies. The austere iconoclast regards the pop of the ritual as an unessential superficiality which even diverts the mind from a deeper absorption in the spirit of the thing symbolized. I believe that he is entirely wrong. If we take pleasure in all the pomp and ceremony of an old custom, such as decorating the Christmas tree and lighting its candles, this presupposes that we love the traditionally transmitted. Our fidelity to the symbol implies fidelity to everything it signifies, and this depends on the warmth of our affection for the old custom. It is this feeling of affection that reveals to us the value of our cultural heritage. The independent existence of any culture, the creation of a superindividual society which outlives the single being, in other words all that represents true humanity is based on this autonomy of the rite making it an independent motive of human action.

The formation of traditional rites must have begun with the first dawning of human culture, just as at a much lower level, phylogenetic rite formation was a prerequisite for the origin of social organization in higher animals. In the following brief description of these two processes I should stress their analogous nature, which is explained by their common functions.

In both cases, a behavior pattern by means of which a species in the one case, a cultured society in the other, deals with certain environmental conditions, acquires an entirely new function, that of communication. The primary function may still be performed, but it often recedes more and more into the background and may disappear completely so that a typical change of function is achieved. Out of communication two new equally important functions may arise, both of which still contain some measure of communicative effects. The first of these is the channeling of aggression into innocuous outlets, the second is the formation of a bond between two or more individuals.

In both cases, the selection pressure of the new function has wrought analogous changes on the form of the primal, non-ritualized behavior. It quite obviously lessens the chance of ambiguity in the communication that a long series of independently variable patterns should be welded into one obligatory sequence. The same aim is served by strict regulation of the speed and amplitude of the motor patterns. Desmond Morris has drawn attention to this phenomenon which he has termed the typical intensity of movements serving as signals. The display of animals during threat and courtship furnishes an abundance of examples, and so does the culturally developed ceremonial of man. The deans of the university walk into the hall with a "measured step"; pitch, rhythm, and loudness of the Catholic priest's chanting during mass are all strictly regulated by liturgic prescription. The unambiguity of the communication is also increased by its frequent repetition. Rhythmical repetition of the same movement is so characteristic of very many rituals, both instinctive and cultural, that it is hardly necessary to describe examples. The communicative effect of the ritualized movements is further increased, in both cases, by exaggerating all those elements which, in the unritualized prototype, produce visual or auditory stimulation while those of its parts that are originally effective in some other, mechanical way are greatly reduced or completely eliminated.

This "mimic exaggeration" results in a ceremony which is, indeed, closely akin to a symbol and which produces that theatrical effect that first struck Sir Julian Huxley as he watched his Great Crested Grebes. A riot of form and color, developed in the service of that particular effect, accompanies both phyletic and cultural rituals. The beautiful forms and colors of a Siamese Fighting Fish's fins, the plumage of a Bird of Paradise, the Peacock's tail, and the amazing colors on both ends of a Mandrill have one and all evolved to enhance some particular ritualized movements. There is hardly a doubt that all human art primarily developed in the service of rituals and that the autonomy of "art for art's sake" was achieved only by another, secondary step of cultural progress.

The direct cause of all these changes which make the instinctive and the cultural ceremonies so similar to each other, indubitably is to be sought in the selection pressure exerted by the limitations of the "receiving set" which must respond correctly and selectively to the signal emanating from the "sender," if the system of communication is to function properly. For obvious reasons, it is easier to construct a receiver selectively responding to a signal, the more simple and, at the same time, unmistakable the signal is. Of course, sender and receiver also exert a selection pressure on each other's development and may become very highly differentiated in adaptation to each other. Many instinctive rituals, many cultural ceremonies, indeed all the words of all human languages owe their present form to this process of convention between the sender and the receiver in which both are partners in a communicative system developing in time. In such cases, it is often quite impossible to trace back, to an "unritualized model," the origin of a ritual, because its form is changed to a degree that renders it unrecognizable. However, if, in some other living species, or in some still surviving other cultures, some intermediate steps on the same line of development are accessible to study, comparative investigation may still succeed in tracing back the path along which the present form of some bizarre and complicated ceremony has come into being. This, indeed, is one of the tasks that make comparative studies so fascinating.

Both in phylogenetic and in cultural ritualization the newly evolved behavior patterns achieve a very peculiar kind of autonomy. Both instinctive and cultural rituals become independent motivations of behavior by creating new ends or goals toward which the organism strives for their own sake. It is in their character of independent motivating factors that rituals transcend their original function of communication and become able to perform their equally important secondary tasks of controlling aggression and of forming a bond between certain individuals. . . .

In cultural ritualization, the two steps of development leading from communication to the control of aggression and, from this, to the formation of a bond, are strikingly analogous to those that take place in the evolution of instinctive rituals. The triple function of suppressing fighting within the group, of holding the group together, and of setting it off, as an independent entity, against other, similar units, is performed by culturally developed ritual in so strictly analogous a manner as to merit deep consideration.

Any human group which exceeds in size that which can be held together by personal love and friendship, depends for its existence on these three functions of culturally ritualized behavior patterns. Human social behavior is permeated by cultural ritualization to a degree which we do not realize for the very reason of its omnipresence. Indeed, in order to give examples of human behavior which, with certainty, can be described as nonritualized, we have to resort to patterns which are not supposed to be performed in public at all, like uninhibited yawning and stretching, picking one's nose or scratching in unmentionable places. Everything that is called manners is, of course, strictly determined by cultural ritualization. "Good" manners are by definition those characteristic of one's own group, and we conform to their requirements constantly; they have become "second nature" to us. We do not, as a rule, realize either their function of inhibiting aggression or that of forming a bond. Yet it is they that effect what sociologists call "group cohesion."

The function of manners in permanently producing an effect of mutual conciliation between the members of a group can easily be demonstrated by observing what happens in their absence. I do not mean the effect produced by an active, gross breach of manners, but by the mere absence of all the little polite looks and gestures by which one person, for example on entering a room, takes cognizance of another's presence. If a person considers him- or herself offended by members of his group and enters the room occupied by them without these little rituals, just as if they were not there, this behavior elicits anger and hostility just as overt aggressive behavior does; indeed, such intentional suppression of the normal appeasing rituals is equivalent to overt aggressive behavior.

Aggression elicited by any deviation from a group's characteristic manners and mannerisms forces all its members into a strictly uniform observance of these norms of social behavior. The nonconformist is discriminated against as an "outsider" and, in primitive groups, for which school classes or small military units serve as good examples, he is mobbed in the most cruel manner. Any university teacher who has children and has held positions in different parts of a country, has had occasion to observe the amazing speed with which a child acquires the local dialect spoken in the region where it has to go to school. It has to, in order not to be mobbed by its schoolfellows, while at home it retains the dialect of the family group. Characteristically, it is very difficult to prevail on such a child to speak, in the family circle, the "foreign language" learned at school, for instance in reciting a poem. I believe that the clandestine membership of another than the family group is felt to be treacherous by young children.

Culturally developed social norms and rites are characteristics of smaller and larger human groups much in the same manner as inherited properties evolved in phylogeny are characteristics of subspecies, species, genera, and greater taxonomic units. Their history can be reconstructed by much the same methods of comparative study. Their divergence in historical development erects barriers between cultural units in a similar way as divergent evolution does between species; Erik Erikson has therefore aptly called this process pseudo-speciation.

Though immeasurably faster than phylogenetic speciation, cultural pseudospeciation does need time. Its slight beginnings, the development of mannerisms in a group and discrimination against outsiders not initiated to them, may be seen in any group of children, but to give stability and the character of inviolability to the social norms and rites of a group, its continued existence over the period of at least a few generations seems to be necessary. . . .

The important function of polite manners can be studied to great advantage in the social interaction between different cultures and subcultures. A considerable proportion of the mannerisms enjoined by good manners are culturally ritualized exaggerations of submissive gestures most of which probably have their roots in phylogenetically ritualized motor patterns conveying the same meaning. Local traditions of good manners, in different subcultures, demand that a quantitatively different emphasis be put on these expression movements. A good example is furnished by the attitude of polite listening which consists in stretching the neck forward and simultaneously tilting the head sideways, thus emphatically "lending an ear" to the person who is speaking. The motor pattern conveys readiness to listen attentively and even to obey. In the polite manners of some Asiatic cultures it has obviously undergone strong mimic exaggeration; in Austrians, particularly in well-bred ladies, it is one of the commonest gestures of politeness; in other Central European countries it appears to be less emphasized. In some parts of northern Germany it is reduced to a minimum, if not absent. In these subcultures it is considered correct and polite for the listener to hold the head high and look the speaker straight in the face, exactly as a soldier is supposed to do when listening to orders. . . .

Of course the meaning of any conciliatory gesture of this kind is determined exclusively by the convention agreed upon by the sender and the receiver of one system of communication. Between cultures in which this convention is different, misunderstandings are unavoidable. By East Prussian standards a polite Japanese performing the "ear-tending" movement would be considered to be cringing in abject slavish fear, while by Japanese standards an East Prussian listening politely would evoke the impression of uncompromising hostility.

Even very slight differences in conventions of this kind may create misinterpretation of culturally ritualized expression movements. Latin peoples are very often considered as "unreliable" by Anglo-Saxons and Germans, simply because, on a basis of their own convention, they expect more social good will than actually lies behind the more pronounced "effusive" motor patterns of conciliation and friendliness of the French or the Italians. The general unpopularity of North Germans and particularly Prussians in Latin countries is, at least partly, due to this type of misunderstanding. In polite American society I have often suspected that I must give the impression of being rather rude, because I find it difficult to smile quite as much as is demanded by American good manners.

Indubitably, little misunderstandings of this kind contribute considerably to inter-group hate. The man who, in the manner described, has misinterpreted the social signals of a member of another pseudosubspecies, feels that he has been intentionally cheated or wronged. Even the mere inability to understand the expression movements and rituals of a strange culture creates distrust and fear in a manner very easily leading to overt aggression.

From the little peculiarities of speech and manner which cause the smallest possible subcultural groups to stick together, an uninterrupted gradation leads up to the most elaborated, consciously performed, and consciously symbolical social norms and rites which unite the largest social units of humanity in one nation, one culture, one religion, or one political ideology. Studying this system by the comparative method, in other words, investigating the laws of pseudospeciation, would be perfectly possible, though more complicated than the study of speciation, because of the frequent overlapping of group concepts, as for instance of the national and the religious units. . . .

It is perfectly right and legitimate that we should consider as "good" the manners which our parents have taught us, that we should hold sacred the social norms and rites handed down to us by the tradition of our culture. What we must guard against, with all the power of rational responsibility, is our natural inclination to regard the social rites and norms of other cultures as inferior. The dark side of pseudospeciation is that it makes us consider the members of pseudospecies other than our own as not human, as many primitive tribes are demonstrably doing, in whose language the word for their own particular tribe is synonymous with "Man." From their viewpoint it is not, strictly speaking, cannibalism if they eat the fallen warriors of an enemy tribe. The moral of the natural history of pseudospeciation is that we must learn to tolerate other cultures, to shed entirely our own cultural and national arrogance, and to realize that the social norms and rites of other cultures, to which their members keep faith as we do to our own, have the same right to be respected and to be regarded as sacred. Without the tolerance born of this realization, it is all too easy for one man to see the personification of all evil in the god of his neighbor, and the very inviolability of rites and social norms which constitutes their most important property can lead to the most terrible of all wars, to religious war—which is exactly what is threatening us today.

Here, as so often when discussing human behavior from the viewpoint of natural science, I am in danger of being misunderstood. I did indeed say that man's fidelity to all his traditional customs is caused by creature habit and by animal fear at their infraction. I did indeed emphasize the fact that all human rituals have originated in a natural way, largely analogous to the evolution of social instincts in animals and man. I have even stressed the other fact that everything which man by tradition venerates and reveres, does not represent an absolute ethical value, but is sacred only within the frame of reference of one particular culture. However, all this does not in any sense derogate from the unfaltering tenacity with which a good man clings to the handed-down customs of his culture. His fidelity might seem to be worthy of a better cause, but there *are* few better causes! If social norms and customs did not develop their peculiar autonomous life and power, if they were not raised to sacred ends in themselves, there would be no trustworthy communication, no faith, and no law. Oaths cannot bind, nor agreements count, if the partners to them do not have in common a basis of ritualized behavior standards at whose infraction they are overcome by the same magic fear as seized my little greylag on the staircase in Altenberg.

Translated by Majorie Kerr Wilson

Manfred Eigen
with Ruthild Winkler-Oswatisch

What Is Life?

Life Is Historical Reality

In any inquiry about the origin of life, we must make a clear distinction between the historical events that actually occurred and the conceivable events that natural laws make possible in principle. The study-matter of biology is the world of living organisms, in which the historical process is made manifest. The reconstruction of the course of evolution is restricted to using historical evidence. Such evidence as we possess indicates that all forms of life have a common origin. At every level of life, we find not only individual variability but also similarity of detail and the universal validity of the underlying physical and chemical laws. We can recognize these laws only if we abstract from reality; for physics is concerned not with individual processes as such, but solely with the repeating regularities in the process. . . .

Life is *not* an inherent property of matter. Life is indeed associated with matter, but it appears only under very specific conditions and, when it does, it expresses itself in very diverse and individual ways. It is therefore perfectly logical to set the question of life's origin alongside that of its nature. We shall come closest to understanding the principle of life if we can discover the principles according to which life *could* begin. This is a challenge addressed to the physicist, even if he calls himself a biophysicist, a biochemist, or a molecular biologist. How life *did* begin, however, can probably only be understood by appeal to historical evidence. . . .

Many misunderstandings have resulted from ignoring the difference between these two questions. There is no general physical theory that explains the *historical* origin of life. How life commenced must be regarded as a succession of events whose details can be neither reconstructed nor predicted. But they took place, none the less, under the directing influence of natural law.

Complexity as a Physical Problem

If we regard the phenomenon "life" as a regularity in the behavior of matter, we must at some point ask the question: "What kind of physical principle lies behind this behavior, and what are its effects?"

The question "What is life?" has many answers, none of which is ultimately satisfying. (Thomas Mann points up this enigma again and again, continually repeating the question and reshaping the answer.) The manifestations of life, and the characteristics and capabilities of living beings, are too numerous and too various to allow a meaningful general definition; such a definition would not be able so much as to hint at the individuality and the variety that make up the essence of life. The reason for this lies in the complexity common to all the forms of life with which we are acquainted. At the molecular level, the same problem is encountered in the structures associated with the processes of life: the nucleic acids and the proteins.

How complex are the most primitive organisms? Even this simple question seemed for many years to be unanswerable. Yet today we know that every organism is represented by a "blueprint." This is handed down from one generation to the next, and it ensures that each generation of progeny resembles its parents. While this applies especially to vegetative reproduction, it also applies with certain restrictions—those that are imposed by the nature of the genetic crossing process—to sexual reproduction. The problem of the complexity of organisms can thus be reduced to that of the complexity of their blueprints, since it is these that, in an appropriate environment, provide the instructions for the origin and the development of an organism.

Because the genetic information lies in the blueprint as a linear sequence of symbols, our question takes us ultimately to the quantity of information that can be put into a sentence—first of all, the absolute amount of information rather than its semantic content. There is a mathematical theory, information theory, that has a quantitative answer ready for us. The information content is the average number of binary yes/no decisions that are necessary in order to identify unambiguously a particular sequence of symbols. If all possible arrangements of the symbols in a given sequence were equally probable, one would have to go through all the alternative symbol sequences in order to hit the right one by chance. In a case like this, the number of possible sequences that can be produced from a defined set of symbols gives a measure of the information content. The reciprocal of this number gives the probability of the appearance of a *particular* sequence. Since the numbers of sequences are additive, while probabilities are multiplicative, it is usual to state the quantity of information not by the number of alternative arrangements but by its logarithm, as the logarithm of a product is equal to the sum of the logarithms of the factors. Further, logarithms to base 2 are used, and the unit in which the result comes out is the binary digit (*bit*). The bit number corresponds to the length of a sequence of binary characters. The nucleic acids employ four symbols, so that a gene of length N has 4^N (or 2^{2N}) different sequences. On the assumption that these are all equally probable, this means that the information content of the gene amounts to $2N$ bits.

How complex are organisms? The smallest autonomous units, unicellular microorganisms such as the bacterium *Escherichia coli*, have incorporated into their genomes a few millions of symbols—roughly the equivalent of a thousand-page book. The number of symbols in the genome of the human being is nearly a thousand times larger. It represents a respectable library. It would be pointless to try to imagine the number of alternative arrangements of the letters; our imagination simply does not run to such numbers. Consider instead just a single gene, with only a thousand symbols: this is like a sentence in the genetic language, and corresponds to one functional instruction. With four classes of symbols—so that each of the thousand positions can be occupied in any of four different ways—the number of variants that result is $4^{1000} \approx 10^{602}$ (a one followed by 602 zeros). The volume of the entire universe, calculated as a sphere with a diameter of ten thousand million light-years, amounts to a "mere" 10^{X4} cubic centimeters, or 10^{108} cubic angstrom units. The entire material content of the cosmos corresponds, weight for weight, to fewer than 10^{75} genes of the length assumed in this example.

These numbers, related to the size of the universe, are in any case quite irrelevant for our discussion. They serve simply to demonstrate our complete inability to conceive in any realistic way of numbers like 10^{600}. It would be more interesting to find out how many molecules, of length one thousand symbols, could have been tried out in the course of the process of evolution within the spatial and temporal confines of our planet. Naturally, the process of evolution cannot be reconstructed in such detail as to allow a precise answer to this question, but the number we are looking for probably lies between 10^{40} and 10^{50}. If we covered the Earth with a layer of solution one centimeter thick, containing nucleic acid at a concentration of one gram per liter, and allowed the nucleic acid molecules in it to form and decay with a lifetime of not more than one second each, then after one thousand million years there would have arisen some 10^{50} fresh molecules.

It is possible to make a similar estimation on the scale of the laboratory. A research student synthesizing nucleic acid molecules enzymically in a one-liter flask could, by working for twelve hours each day for a whole year, produce 10^{25} sequences. Compared with the planetary scale, that does not sound entirely hopeless, especially as the conditions for natural synthesis may have been assessed rather too optimistically in many respects. Realistic concentrations of nucleic acids are probably orders of magnitude lower than originally assumed. Genes arise by reproduction; that is, if a gene sequence occurs at all, then it occurs with high redundancy. Furthermore, it is not true that the entire surface of the Earth was available for the reaction, or that the yield was as high as supposed. But there still remains a conflict between the orders of magnitude, the discrepancy between what was possible and what would be necessary if genes were the product of a purely random synthesis.

What conclusions can we draw from this?

The genes found today cannot have arisen randomly, as it were by the throw of a dice. There must exist a process of optimization that works towards functional efficiency. Even if there are several routes to optimal efficiency, mere trial and error cannot be one of them.

The discrepancy between the numbers of sequences testable in practice and imaginable in theory is so great that attempts at explanation by shifting the location of the origin of life from Earth to outer space do not offer an acceptable solution to the dilemma. The mass of the universe is "only" 10^{29} times, and its volume "only" 10^{57} times, that of Earth.

The physical principle that we are looking for should be in a position to explain the complexity typical of a phenomenon of life at the level of molecular structures and syntheses. It should show how such complex molecular arrangements are able to form reproducibly in Nature.

How Does Information Arise?

We have already encountered the key-word that represents the phenomenon of complexity: information. Our task is to find an algorithm, a natural law that leads to the origin of information. The definition of information given earlier is based solely on the number of possible arrangements, is incomplete. It applies only to the limiting case in which all arrangements are equally probable. If we try to guess a binary sequence by asking questions that can be answered only with a "yes" or "no," then the average number of questions needed will correspond to the information content, or bit number, of the sequence, assuming that the two symbols have the same expectation values at each position. If the sequence is a sentence in a human language, then knowing the code that relates the letters to the binary digits (as in a teleprinter), we could arrive at our goal much more quickly by taking account of the familiar properties of the language in making our guesses. Analysis of the frequency of symbols in English shows that, apart from the space between words, the letter *e* is the most common. The average length of words is governed by the use of the space symbol. In the construction of words, we know that, for example, *q* is always followed by *u*. We know as well that vowels and consonants are not distributed arbitrarily. The structure of sentences is largely determined by the usage and the order of articles, nouns, adjectives and verbs. There are also grammatical and syntactical rules. The spectrum of rules and conditions covers even the meaning of the sentence, that is, the semantic information, which is dependent upon specific premisses that cannot be described by general statistical frequency laws. . . .

We conclude that every constraint that makes the distribution of prior probabilities of the symbols less even will reduce the quantity of information that is needed for their identification. This quantity corresponds to an average number of bits per symbol, multiplied by the total number of symbols in the message. It is not just a question of the absolute number of symbols and the total number of alternative arrangements, but also one of the average realizability of the alternatives. The origin of information is thus tantamount to a change in the probability distribution of the symbols on the basis of additional constraints that first emerge during the evolutionary process.

There exists a direct relationship between the quantity of information as considered above and the quantity known in thermodynamics as *entropy:* the information defined by Shannon corresponds to negative entropy. For our present discussion, it is of greater importance to recall that at thermodynamic equilibrium the entropy has reached a maximum. Any perturbation of the equilibrium produces a reaction that proceeds in a direction such as to cancel out the perturbation. Equilibrium is a stable state. There are no perturbations that can change the probability distribution in the system, as long as the external conditions are unaltered. Thus, information can *not* arise in systems that are in thermodynamic equilibrium.

So how has the information in genetic blueprints, the fixation of particular arrangements of symbols, come into being? A biologist would answer: by natural selection! He would add that the gene sequences contained in organisms, coding as they do for functions that are optimally adapted for life, are in fact the products of a whole series of changes in the sequence, stabilized one after another by selection. Such a process need by no means take place at a uniform rate. From time to time, stable intermediate states will be reached, during which evolution apparently comes to a standstill, because for a while no advantageous mutations occur. These are followed by phases of change, either due to rare mutations or caused by environmental factors that set off a cascade of successful mutations. In this way, intermediate states come about which are not yet optimally adapted and whose mutant spectra soon give rise to better-adapted sequences. This makes it appear as though Nature had been making jumps, because the relatively short-lived intermediate states leave no trace behind them.

Darwin's principle brings about what theoreticians would call the generation of information. Dominance by a wild type established by selection means the local stabilization of a particular probability distribution. The appearance of an advantageous mutant destabilizes the hitherto stable state, and establishes a new probability distribution, which in turn can be destabilized by another new mutant, and so on. The fact that a destabilizing mutant can appear at all shows that selection has nothing to do with genuine equilibrium states. It is true that statistical fluctuations (the general cause of mutations) do occur within systems in equilibrium. However, in equilibrium they cannot amplify themselves so as to become macroscopically observable. Every mutant—even an advantageous one—starts life as a single copy. Its ability to multiply in number depends upon special criteria that are not realized in equilibrium, and which are based solely on the properties of the constituents of living systems.

In order to illustrate the lawlike character of the selection process, we consider the law of mass action, which governs *chemical* equilibrium. In a closed chemical system, which does not exchange matter with its surroundings, the proportions of all components inevitably and reproducibly reach those values dictated by the law of mass action. Such an equilibrium distribution can be regarded as "selective." The basis of the selection is the free energy (that is, energy available for doing external work) contained by the individual components. Components with a lower free energy are preferred. However, this does not mean that other components, with higher free energy, die out. They simply appear less frequently, in accordance with the balance that follows from the law of mass action. As long as an equilibrium between two components can be defined, both will appear with finite frequency.

In the case of the Darwinian selection principle, the problem raised is very similar, but the answer is quite different. We look for the selection of a particular genotype, the one that encodes the phenotype with the quality of being "best adapted," meaning "producing progeny at a maximum rate." The genotype appears first as a copy of a sequence already in existence. But there always occur errors in copying. An error can be a symbol incorrectly copied, or the omission or addition of single symbols or even of entire blocks of symbols. Such mutations are the source of evolutionary progress. Selection now has two aspects. First, there is a single sequence that among all the mutants corresponds to the best-adapted phenotype (the "wild type"), and its growth outstrips that of the rest of the population. The less well adapted mutants—according to the classical interpretation—die out. They cannot coexist with the wild type and can at best appear sporadically as statistical fluctuations. The selected sequence becomes the basis of further progress. Secondly, the information in the wild type is conserved as long as there is no better-adapted variant among the mutants that have been randomly "tried out." In this way errors are prevented from accumulating. This requires that the error rate remain below a certain, critical threshold level. Only when a variant appears which is (even) better adapted does this take over the role of the wild type.

Returning to the question with which this chapter is headed, we could perhaps regard natural selection as the key to the problem of information and complexity. But what mechanism guarantees selection and, with it, the inevitable appearance of information?

Life Is a Dynamic State of Matter Organized by Information

Information is stored in DNA, the blueprint of organisms. This sequence of symbols must be organized, as in a language. Indeed, there is a form of punctuation, or subdivision of contents, that divides up the enormous document into words (codons), sentences (genes), paragraphs (operons), and entire volumes (chromosomes). This organization is genetically fixed; it is laid down in the structure, that is, in the sequence of the chemical units (nucleotides) of the DNA molecule.

But how has the information-rich, ordered state of this molecule come about? In terms of structural stability, a molecule carrying useful information has not the slightest advantage over a molecule carrying nonsense. The strength of the chemical interactions that stabilize the molecule and preserve the information contained in the symbol sequence, so that it can be handed down from one generation to the next, does indeed depend in part upon the composition of the sequence, but it has nothing to do with the information stored within it. The structural stability of the molecule has no bearing upon the semantic information which it carries, and which is not expressed until the product of translation appears. The selection of "informed" molecules is not based upon structural stability, but upon a kind of order that lies in the selection dynamics of its reproduction. . . .

Before we look into the question of the origin and the generation of the dynamic order of "life," we must ascertain whether this order really is of relevance for our problem.

What do all living things have in common?

They all use DNA as a store for their hereditary material, processing the stored information according to the scheme:

Legislative	→	Message	→	Executive	→	Function
DNA	→	RNA	→	Protein	→	Metabolism

Not only is this general scheme common to all organisms of Earth, but so is its detailed structure too. All organisms make use of a common genetic code, a common biochemical machinery, and synthetic macromolecular products that are organized according to common structural principles.

The lowest unit of autonomous life is the cell, the prototype of which is also built up according to a common design, even though the cells of multicellular organisms differ greatly in their observable function. Whatever task a cell is adapted to, it carries out with optimal efficiency. The blue-green alga, a very early product of evolution, transforms light into chemical energy with an efficiency approaching perfection. The enzymic reactions in a bacterium hardly differ in their efficiency from those that proceed inside the human cell. Archaebacteria show their ability to survive under extreme environmental conditions such as high salt concentration or high temperature. The amoeba is also a single-celled organism, but this time at a much higher level of development; it displays a form of social behavior, by communicating chemically with its fellows, and by cooperating in sporulation for the production of the next generation. The higher organisms demonstrate the most marvelous and astounding achievements. From loosely associated agglomerates of cells there have emerged centrally directed, multicellular forms of organization with highly differentiated functional demarcation.

All the varieties of life have a common origin. This origin is the information that, in all living beings, is organized according to the same principle.

An understanding of this principle will bring us closer to an answer to the question asked at the beginning of this book: "How *can* life begin?" Just as life has passed through many stages of development, there must also be many principles of organization: for the reproduction of individual genes, for their cooperative integration into a functional unit, for regulated growth, for the construction of cellular structures, for recombinative inheritance, for the differentiation of cells, and for the construction of organs up to and including the construction of *the* organ that functions as a memory, the organ that itself stores, processes, and creates information, bringing about a new kind of evolution at a level above that of matter.

Is There a Principle of Order in Biological Systems?

The principle of order upon which we shall now focus our attention is intended to explain how information comes into being. It will have to be a dynamic principle. Information *arises* from non-information. We are not merely dealing with a transformation that makes existing information visible. The state of the system has a completely new quality after information has arisen. The new information has made the previous, information-deficient state unstable, and thus has consigned it irretrievably to the past.

This is how a physical interpretation of the Darwinian principle might sound. According to Darwin's principle, whatever is better adapted spreads out and displaces its less well adapted predecessor. Thus, complexity, built upon simplicity, has accumulated throughout biological evolution from the first single-celled organisms to human beings. Evolution as a whole is the steady generation of information—information that is written down in the genes of living organisms. . . .

Today we can apply our knowledge to molecular systems such as genes and the products of their translation. We can also investigate in a much more objective way the physical nature of the Darwinian principle: theoretically, by defining accurately the prerequisites and constraints, and experimentally, by exact control of experimental conditions. We find that the selection principle is neither a mystical axiom immanent in living matter nor a general tendency observable primarily in living processes. On the contrary, it is—like many of the known physical laws—a clear "if-then" principle, that is, a principle according to which defined initial situations lead to deductible behavior patterns. It is thus analogous to the law of mass action, which regulates the attainment of the quantities of the components in a chemical equilibrium.

The initial situation must fulfill the following prerequisites.

- The individuals (DNA molecules, viruses, bacteria) among which selection is to take place must be self-reproducing. Once they have come into existence, they can multiply by the copying of individuals already present, but not by synthesis *de novo* of

new individuals. We shall call these self-copying individuals *replicators*.
- The first condition just stated is modified by allowing the self-reproduction to be subject to error. This is ultimately because the physical process of copying takes place at a finite temperature, and the energy associated with the interactions involved in copying is of the same order of magnitude as thermal energy. The molecules involved in replication are thus subject to the buffeting of thermal motion, which results in mutations. This means that some replicators come into existence not as the result of the true copying of an identical parent, but in consequence of inaccurate copying of one that is closely related.
- The self-replication must take place far away from chemical equilibrium. This means that the system of replicators requires a perpetual supply of chemical energy. In other words, the system must possess a metabolism. In chemical equilibrium, by contrast, formation and decay at the chemical level are strictly reversible: the autocatalytic formation caused by self-replication would compensate the autocatalytic decay and would therefore be unable to effect selection. Information cannot originate in a system that is at equilibrium.

Self-reproduction, mutagenicity, and metabolism are necessary conditions for natural selection. In a system that possesses these three properties, selection automatically goes into action. The consequences are seen most clearly in terms of the relative population numbers: one of the many replicators increases in number until it comes to dominate the entire population. Even for the smallest differences in selection value, the result is an all-or-nothing decision, as long as the competing replicators are unrelated. However mutants closely related to the dominating replicator will be tolerated, according to their own selection value and the closeness of their kinship. This implies that replicators of (nearly) equal selection value, that are closely related, will share the dominance. This is true irrespective of whether the system is stationary, is growing, or varies in any other way with time.

The selection value is a parameter defined by the dynamic properties of the system, and it takes account of the rate and quality of reproduction and the lifetime of a replicator. If selection values depend upon environmental conditions, such as the presence of accelerating or interfering substances, then their mathematical expression can be quite complicated. However, for simple molecular systems under defined conditions, selection values can be measured by the methods of chemical kinetics.

For large population numbers, behavior in selection is as regular as the attainment of chemical equilibrium. It is also as inevitable, as long as the conditions noted above are fulfilled. Selection contains an element of exact "if-then" behavior. It has nothing to do with the tautological interpretation "best adapted = selected." "Selection" could in principle just refer to *any* kind of preference. But here it means a *particular* kind of preference, which adheres unerringly to a single scale of values. Selection is based upon self-replication. It distinguishes sharply between competitors, it constructs a broad mutant spectrum on the basis of value, and in this way it organizes and steers the entire, complex system. It is true that the mass action of chemical equilibrium results in a kind of selection of the structurally stablest configuration. But this selection does not share the exclusive nature of the selection between replicators, which is inherently associated with nonequilibrium situations. High structural stability in chemical equilibrium is purchased at the price of extreme lethargy of the reaction. In contrast, the replicator that is stabilized dynamically in a nonequilibrium system dies out within a short time if a superior competitor appears.

Since all organisms are self-reproducing, selection plays a decisive role for all organisms. Naturally, there are variations associated with various internal and external secondary conditions. Under particular external conditions, selection can turn right round into coexistence or even cooperation. For example, if two or more different replicators are coupled in a cyclical way by repression or promotion effects, then the result is a regulated coexistence of all the partners, and the cycle as a whole competes with other such cycles. The higher organisms in particular have special mechanisms of inheritance: they exchange genes by recombination, for which the selective evaluation takes place at the level of the organism as a whole. It was certainly these organisms that Darwin had in mind when he formulated his selection principle. The abstract, mathematically deducible principle is associated with clearly defined conditions such as self-replication with mutation and nonequilibrium. These are fulfilled ideally by single DNA or RNA molecules, by genes, and likewise by viruses and vegetatively reproducing organisms. . . .

It also proved possible to confirm quantitatively the theoretically predicted relationship between error rate and quantity of information. The dominant sequence is selected stably only if it possess a selection value that is greater than the average efficiency of replication of the ensemble of mutants. If the incorrect copies are not to displace the dominant sequence altogether from the population, then the error rate must lie below a certain threshold value. This threshold value of error rate is given approximately by the reciprocal of the number of information-bearing symbols in the sequence. In other words, the longer a sequence is, the more accurate its reproduction must be; otherwise errors accumulate in successive generations and the original information is lost. . . .

Crossing the error threshold causes instability. This is what happens when a selectively advantageous mutant appears. The sequence previously established no longer fulfills the threshold condition. It continues to make errors, and is no longer able to compensate for this loss by having an advantage over other competitors. It dies out, while the new variant grows up. Afterwards, the dice continue to be thrown and the game of evolution continues on the new, higher level.

Individual, exact results depend upon the error rate, the lengths of the sequences, the efficiency of reproduction in comparison with the average efficiency of the mutant distribution, and the size of the population. Evolution experiments by Sol Spiegelman and by Christof Biebricher have shown that natural processes indeed proceed in the manner we have described.

In making these measurements, the researchers subjected their system to constraints that were easily realized, and which thus allowed a quantitative test of the theory. If we choose to examine the evolution of species in Nature, we need to remember that the constraints and subsidiary conditions are often extremely complex. Nevertheless, at higher levels of evolution, selection (especially selection against incorrect copies of the same species) remains an inviolable law. Admittedly, the many additional conditions complicate the process to such an extent that quantitative predictions are generally impossible. "Fittest" on the level of human beings is no longer a property that can be correlated with measurable characteristics. We must therefore be wary of extrapolation. Experience gathered at lower levels must not be projected carelessly on to higher ones. This kind of extrapolation has frequently obstructed the way to a correct understanding of the Darwinian principle, in spite of the fact that it is probably the most important principle of organization for the origin and development of life. . . .

Evolution Means the Optimization of Functional Efficiency

How good are our genes at their job? Their translation products are functional molecules, and these certainly fulfill with high efficiency their tasks as enzymes, as catalysts, and as regulatory units. But are they really optimal? And what do we mean by optimal? We can dissect the reaction mechanisms of enzyme-controlled processes down to the most elementary steps, which take place on the time-scale of one thousand millionth of a second. We can determine the highest rates that the laws of physics allow a given elementary step to attain. From this we can deduce how the individual steps must be adjusted in order to work in concert for the highest overall efficiency. In many cases, enzymic catalysis accelerates a reaction by a factor between one million and one thousand million. Wherever such a mechanism has been analyzed quantitatively, the result has been the same: enzymes are optimal catalysts.

The genes of the smallest proteins are made up of some three hundred basic units (nucleotides). Perhaps primitive genes were smaller still. Within the last few years, structural domains have been found in proteins, suggesting that the proteins may have originated by the coming together of smaller units. So primitive genes will probably have been some 100 to 300 nucleotides long. The number of permutations of a sequence of this length makes the number of alternative sequences so great that the chances of obtaining the optimal sequence by random arrangement are quite negligible.

Does the selection principle offer a solution to the problem of complexity? Can it be used to explain the origin of primitive genes and the optimization of their functional efficiency?

If we start from the popular interpretation of the Darwinian principle, we soon run into trouble. Today it is generally accepted that selection is an inevitable property of self-reproducing systems. Once an advantageous mutant has appeared in statistically significant numbers, these numbers will inevitably rise, and the new mutant will ultimately come to dominate in the population. Only at the beginning is there any uncertainty. As long as there is only one such sequence, or only a few, then it or they may be extinguished by some chance event before ever having the opportunity to reproduce. Deterministic selection always has a stochastic initial phase, and hence our allusion above to statistical significance. But the vital feature is our assumption that the mutant appears as the result of a *chance* event, a statistical fluctuation. In other words, each mutant appears with a probability that is independent of whether it is a superior, a neutral or an inferior variant. This in turn would mean that superior mutants appear only with extreme rarity. However, this interpretation reintroduces the problem of complexity, which was supposed to have been solved with the help of selection. This may not seem clear at first reading, so let us take a concrete example. If a gene consists of 300 nucleotides, then it has some $4^{300} \approx 10^{180}$ possible sequences. Most of these are completely useless, a reasonable number will be partly functional, and only a very few will encode a given optimal function. In a random distribution of starting sequences, there will therefore at best be just a few, rather poorly adapted variants. Only through further mutation and selective stabilization of the superior variants, by prolonged iteration, can the best possible structure ultimately be reached. The greater the demands placed on it, the greater is the distance to the next, improved variant. This would be the result of a simple alternation between random mutation and inevitable selection. Yet it could only lead to the goal if the selection value rose uninterruptedly toward the optimum.

However, we know that selection values do not rise uninterruptedly. The distribution of selection values for the mutants in a given system should rather be seen as a landscape with plains, hills, and mountain ranges. The selection mechanism sees to it that the highest value peak represented in the initial distribution, even if just one or a few examples are present, becomes occupied by many copies, and that the mutants group themselves around this wild type, which is the best at the start and therefore the first to be selected. But now the system comes up against a dilemma. The value peak is not yet optimal. So it turns into a trap, from which the population distribution can only escape by a jump across to the next, higher peak. If the value peaks are distributed randomly, and the jumps are also random, then the localization of the mutant distribution by an initial selection among the sequences present would be more a hindrance than a help, since it would prevent the system from trying out all alternatives. Moreover, in the absence of any guidance, the system would have to try out all possible mutations in order to find an advantage.

This dilemma was perceived in Darwin's time, but its real extent becomes clear when the chances of mutation are estimated quantitatively. For our small gene with 300 nucleotides, the frequency with which a particular ten-error mutuant occurs is no more than 10^{30}. This jump of ten errors means a change in about three per cent of the gene. If we were to begin with a random sequence, we would probably need to replace about three-quarters of the symbols before reaching the optimal sequence. (The numbers in this example are based upon a presumed error rate of 3×10^3 per symbol and the fact that each symbol in the initial sequence has three ways of mutating.)

The assumption made in classical genetics that the production of mutants is completely random rests partly upon the fact that the mutation process takes place unseen. A mutant in a population cannot be observed until is has presented its credentials by expressing its superiority in phenotypic characteristics that are clearly distinct from those of the wild type. Population biologists, using abstract models, long ago reached the conclusion that many neutral mutants must exist, differing only slightly or not at all from the wild type. Motoo Kimura has shown that these neutral mutants spread with a probability independent of the size of the population and displace the earlier wild type. This drifting through mutant space is presumed to make an important contribution to the overall evolution process. Most important, it could free the system from selection traps such as a value plateau lower than, but much broader than, the optimal value peak.

Later we shall see the importance not only of the neutral mutants, but also of those mutants present in the quasi-species distribution that, although somewhat less efficient than the wild type, are present in larger numbers than mutants only barely capable of survival. Such details seemed to be dispensable in the traditional theory. The classic phase "survival of the fittest" gives away the fact that only the wild type, the best-adapted individual type, was considered. Mutants were regarded as additional statistical fluctuations, necessary as a source of evolutionary progress, but for the most part neither observable nor identifiable. They could in no way be predicted or influenced. The exceedingly rare appearance of a superior mutant could thus be regarded as an independent and purely random event, and its rate of appearance accounted for by an *ad hoc* frequency. For the molecular biologist of today, however, mutants can be demonstrated by cloning and identified by sequence analysis. It is therefore now worth looking at the mutant distribution in detail. The theoretical approach must therefore include the exact registration of the fate of each individual sequence. When this book-keeping exercise was first performed, it led to a surprising result: one that demanded a complete reinterpretation of the Darwinian selection principle at the molecular level and presented the neutral mutants in a completely new light.

Theory and experiment show unanimously that, for viruses, the proportion of the population occupied by the true wild type is relatively small; the wild type appears macroscopically only because it is observed as an averaged sequence, termed "consensus sequence," of the whole mutant ensemble. In the ensemble, the total number of mutants is usually much greater than that of wild-type individuals. Even if the wild type is the most common individual sequence, the number of all mutants taken together is far greater. The frequencies with which individual mutants occur depends primarily upon their degree of kinship with the wild type. The more distant this kinship, the smaller will be the chance of generating the mutant directly from the wild type. If all the mutants were to reproduce substantially more slowly than the wild type, then their individual frequencies would be given quantitatively by a Poisson error distribution.

However, the distribution is modified, sometimes drastically, if a mutant can replicate at a rate comparable to that of the wild type. This can sometimes mean that its population number rises to approach that of the wild type. The next consequence is that the mutant produces new mutants of itself. Finally, even mutants relatively distant from the wild type may appear in reasonable amounts, as long as the chain of their precursors replicates almost as efficiently as the wild type. An amplification of this kind can make a difference of several orders of magnitude.

The generation of a superior mutant, which was left to pure chance in the neo-Darwinian model, is now seen to be determined by the following causal chain.

- Mutants closely related to the wild type arise primarily by erroneous copying of the wild type itself. A distribution develops, in which close relatives of the wild type appear the most frequently.
- Selective advantage can generally be expected only for relatively large mutation jumps. These cannot occur frequently by statistical fluctuation.

- The initial, value-free distribution is modified by selection of preferred states within the quasi-species distribution. Functionally competent mutants, whose selection values come close to that of the wild type (though remaining below it), reach far higher population numbers than those that are functionally ineffective.
- An asymmetric spectrum of mutants builds up, in which mutants far removed from the wild type arise successively from intermediates. The population in such a chain of mutants is influenced decisively by the structure of the value landscape.
- The value landscape consists of connected plains, hills, and mountain ranges. In the mountain ranges, the mutant spectrum is widely scattered, and along ridges even distant relatives of the wild type appear with finite frequency.
- It is precisely in the mountainous regions that further selectively superior mutants can be expected. As soon as one of these turns up on the periphery of the mutant spectrum, the established ensemble collapses. A new ensemble builds up around the superior mutant, which thus takes over the role of the wild type.
- The occupation of the ridges of the value mountains by efficient mutants steers the process of evolution systematically in the direction in which a higher peak is expected. This circumvents the need to try out blindly a vast number of valueless sequences.

This causal chain results in a kind of "mass action," by which the superior mutants are tested with much higher probability than inferior mutants, even if the latter are an equal distance away from the wild type. This is true in spite of the fact that the fundamental mutation step is purely random, or statistical, in nature. So there is no magical or prophetic force at work that steers the development of the mutant spectrum, but just the purely physical "weight of numbers." This directs the process straight into the mountain regions of the value landscape. The process is subject to the following rules:

Similarity in the sequence of the repeating units of the genes results in similarity in the sequence of the repeating units of the proteins that they encode. It is these proteins whose functional efficiency is judged by the selection to come. Similarity in the sequence of the repeating units of the protein chains results in similarity in their folded structures. Similarity in the folded structures of the proteins results in similarity in their functional properties and their efficiency. However, these relationships of similarity are by no means governed by a simple law of proportionality. Similarity of protein sequence need not in every case mean similar efficiency in function. There is merely a general, continuous trend, as in a mountain landscape in which peaks generally pass smoothly into valleys, but with occasional interruption by a steep face or a gorge.

Models that take account of this kind of behavior have been investigated by theoretical calculation, by numerical simulation, and by experiment. They lead to an abstract description that makes high demands upon our ability to visualize ideas. In a sequence with v symbols, any of the v positions can be mutated with much the same probability *a priori.* This is rather like starting from a given point in space and jumping in one of v possible directions. The space that this picture describes we call *sequence space.* Sequence space is thus an abstract world with v dimensions. Each of the v coordinates in sequence space is a line of four discrete points that correspond to the four ways of occupying the position of a real nucleic acid. Mutation at a given position means jumping from one point to another along the associated coordinate. The number of points in this space is equal to the total number of all possible sequences.

The concept of a v-dimensional space of points for binary sequences was introduced into information theory by Richard W. Hamming, and its application to the treatment of problems of evolution was first suggested by Ingo Rechenberg. If we wished to find our way around such a v-dimensional point-space, we would probably end up feeling like Alice in Wonderland. A binary sequence with 360 positions (corresponding to a relatively small gene) has $v = 360$ dimensions, and produces a sequence space that is simply immeasurable, and which would suffice to map the entire universe by the Ångström unit. In spite of this, only 360 steps are needed to cross the entire space. In this space, there are no great distances, but there are many twists and turns, and it is just as easy to get lost here as in the vast expanses of outer space. A characteristic property of sequence space is the extreme complexity with which routes passing through it are intertwined. Just wandering around aimlessly is of little help, since in the search for a particular position practically all positions would have to be looked at. However, guidance is provided by selection, which follows the value topography and thus reduces substantially the freedom of movement. For a connected range of value mountains, whose contours are not random but surround one or a few well-defined peaks, the peculiarities of the v-dimensional space are of enormous advantage: this is due to the fact that, although the volume is large, the distances between points are small and their connecting routes are intertwined. Thanks to the way in which the system orients itself according to the value criterion, the target sequence appears almost to have been aimed at. Even so, the optimization is subject to certain constraints. First of all, the length of the sequences is restricted; secondly, an optimal error rate adapted to the length is required; thirdly, the population numbers must be high enough to guarantee a sufficiently widely distributed occupation of the value terrain.

Sequence space and quasi-species are two novel concepts, with the help of which the theory of molecular self-organization has been formulated in a quantitative way. It is a dynamical theory, in which population numbers of nucleic acids are time-dependent variables and their rates of change are adjusted by reaction velocity parameters.

The theory describes the origin of the information that is laid down in the sequences of the nucleic acids, and whose quantity is expressed by the lengths of these sequences. The information is needed for the optimization of self-replication under given environmental conditions. This information is coupled to its own origin in a feedback loop that is based upon the inherently autocatalytic nature of reproduction kinetics. This feedback loop is the ultimate cause of the self-organization that led to genetic information.

The new formulation of the concept of selection and its application to molecular systems differ sharply from the original Darwinian approach and from its later reformulation in population genetics. The target of selection is no longer the individual wild type that produces chance mutants in a completely random way. The object of selective evaluation is rather the entire ensemble of mutants, which we have denoted as a quasi-species. Here the dominant mutant (the so-called wild type) is still the most frequently represented individual sequence, yet its numbers may amount only to a minute fraction of those of the entire population. The sequence of the wild type can still be determined unambiguously in the laboratory, because it is normally identical to the average sequence (the *consensus sequence*) of the complete mutant spectrum. This fact has now been confirmed experimentally by cloning and analysis of individual sequences from various quasi-species, both artificially produced distributions of RNA molecules and the mutant spectra of natural viruses.

There is an essential difference between the ideas expressed here and the neo-Darwinian idea of an alternation between mutation (= chance) and deterministic selection of the superior mutant (= necessity). In the neo-Darwinian view, the system is obliged to try out most of the possible sequences, and it can easily get stuck on a local optimization peak. The critical difference is connected with structure of the quasi-species. Since the quasi-species is evaluated as a whole, the individual population numbers for the mutants do not (as they do in the classical model) depend upon their distance from the selected wild type alone, but depend also upon their individual degrees of fitness and upon their distribution in the surrounding value landscape. Neutral or nearly neutral mutants are far better represented than others, because of their relatively efficient self-reproduction. If an efficient mutant lies in a region of efficient mutants, that is, in a mountainous region of the value landscape, then it will not only reproduce itself, but will also arise by the erroneous copying of its neighbors. This reinforcement leads to a dramatic shift in the population numbers. The usual decrease in number accompanying increasing distance from the dominant sequence becomes modulated; the *population topography* becomes a distorted picture of the *value topography.* The closer the fitness of a mutant comes to equalling the fitness of the dominant sequence, and the more sequences of equal value it is surrounded by, the better it is represented in the population.

The fact that the mutant distribution is asymmetric, in high-fitness regions, reaching far out into sequence space, has two consequences that we do not find in classical Darwinian theory, and which greatly bias the randomness of the generation of new mutants.

First, most mutants arise in the mountain regions of the value landscape, close to the high peaks of optimization. The system searches with high efficiency for mutants in the region where superior mutants are most to be expected. Narrow peaks are not aimed at.

Secondly, aimless drifting is strongly restricted, because genuinely neutral mutants hardly appear. This does not mean that there is not a large number of mutants with fitness values almost equal to that of the wild type. But, since the selection decision depends just as much on an evaluation of the neighborhood, two really equivalent mutants must not only have identical fitness values but also identical neighborhood contours. This is highly improbable, so that macroscopic ensembles, which in general consist of 10^{10} sequences or more, will only very rarely possess cases of exact degeneracy. In the quasi-species picture, the concept of neutrality can be dispensed with. In classical theory, it has remained an open question how far two selection values can be allowed to differ and still be regarded as equivalent. In the quasi-species model, each sequence, regardless of how closely it resembles the wild type in its selection value, is evaluated exactly, together with all the sequences in its neighborhood. Neutral theory in its present form refers to the limiting case of small populations and large genomes, where the appearance of any mutant is a unique, random event. The quasi-species picture, in contrast, requires finite and reproducible expectation values for population numbers. A general stochastic theory would unify both models.

Mathematically, selection can be formulated by an *extremum principle*. While this applies strictly only under certain conditions related to the mechanism of reproduction, it brings selection into line with other physical phenomena that also are characterized by extremum principles. The best-known example of these is thermodynamic equilibrium, characterized by a maximum of entropy or a minimum of free energy. On an abstract plane, selection means the localization of the mutant spectrum—the quasi-species—in a restricted region of sequence space. As sequences represent information, one sometimes speaks of a *condensation in information space.*

The error-threshold condition is disobeyed every time a superior mutant appears. The existing quasi-species is destablized; it "evaporates," only to "condense" again in a different part of sequence space. Evolution can thus be likened to a succession of phase transitions. Its movements are in no way aimless, or undirected, since superior mutants occur with greatest probability in the mountain regions of the value landscape. This kind of "preprogramming" depends naturally upon the population size. It takes place at the microscopic level, but is still to a certain extent deterministic. This directedness of the evolution process is perhaps the clearest expression of the present-day paradigmatic change in the established Darwinian world-picture.

Anyone who is accustomed to base his world-view dogmatically upon Darwin, calling himself a Darwinist, will be reluctant to accept this new interpretation. He will counter with his own accustomed view, which, seen ideologically, certainly offers a possible alternative. However, our argument is a physical one, so that two things are important: assertions must be logically (in the end, mathematically) deducible, and the consequences of a theory must differ from those of other models, with differences that are experimentally testable. The mathematical buttresses are restricted to the "if-then" behavior of the system. They set out from fixed boundary conditions and show what must necessarily follow from these. To this extent, a mathematical model is not a direct representation of reality, but only an abstraction of reality. It is therefore important to ensure, by observation of the actual processes, that the real and the abstract boundary conditions do actually correspond to one another. Seen in this way, our interpretation says simply: *If* selection results from differing efficiencies of reproduction, *then* this occurs in the sense of the quasi-species model and not in the way envisaged by the classical wild-type model. *If* evolution occurs on the basis of natural selection, *then* it is value-oriented. The mathematical formulation now points up the limits of our generalizations. A presupposition for the "if-then" behavior is a sufficiently large population. Mathematical exploration tells us that this condition is satisfied by the population numbers ($> 10^{10}$) typical of molecules, viruses, and microorganisms. Another presupposition is a limit placed upon the length of the genome. It is this that allows a sufficient number of quasi-species states to be populated reproducibly. The realism of this presupposition has been tested by examining RNA viruses. With these and with several laboratory systems, experiments can be conducted under defined conditions, and so far these have confirmed quantitatively the predictions of the mathematically developed theory.

The chief criticism of Darwin's idea was directed against its supposed claim to explain all of evolution. However, the development of life, from molecular systems to human beings, has passed through many stages of organization, and, while some of these were Darwinian in nature, many were fundamentally different. Since the preservation of all living systems is based upon reproduction, selection plays a role at all levels. But selection is expressed in many different ways, sometimes as coexistence or even cooperation, and sometimes as competition and the often irreversible weeding-out of some forms of life.

Quantitative estimates and experiments on model systems suggest strongly that the kind of molecular optimization described here must have reached its natural limit at a sequence length of a hundred to a thousand repeating units. This implies that the optimization of individual genes must have taken place before their integration into a giant molecule, the genome. The reason for this lies in the genome's length. In a bacterial cell, a single gene represents less than a thousandth of all the information present, so that the error rate must have become adapted to the more than thousandfold longer genome. This much lower error rate, had it applied to isolated genes, would greatly have slowed down their evolutionary optimization.

Leibniz wrote in his *Theodice*: "If, among all the possible worlds, none had been better than the rest [in our usage, optimal], then God would never have created one." This statement certainly comes close to the mark at the molecular level of life.

Translated by Paul Wooley

SOCIAL SCIENCES, LAW, AND CULTURE

Max Weber

Science as a Vocation

A really definitive and good accomplishment is today always a specialized accomplishment. And whoever lacks the capacity to put on blinders, so to speak, and to come up to the idea that the fate of his soul depends upon whether or not he makes the correct conjecture at this passage of this manuscript may as well stay away from science. He will never have what one may call the "personal experience" of science. Without this strange intoxication, ridiculed by every outsider; without this passion, this "thousands of years must pass before you enter into life and thousands more wait in silence"—according to whether or not you succeed in making this conjecture; without this, you have *no* calling for science and you should do something else. For nothing is worthy of man as man unless he can pursue it with passionate devotion.

Yet it is a fact that no amount of such enthusiasm, however sincere and profound it may be, can compel a problem to yield scientific results. Certainly enthusiasm is a prerequisite of the "inspiration" which is decisive. Nowadays in circles of youth there is a widespread notion that science has become a problem in calculation, fabricated in laboratories or statistical filing systems just as "in a factory," a calculation involving only the cool intellect and not one's "heart and soul." First of all one must say that such comments lack all clarity about what goes on in a factory or in a laboratory. In both some idea has to occur to someone's mind, and it has to be a correct idea, if one is to accomplish anything worthwhile. And such intuition cannot be forced. It has nothing to do with any cold calculation. Certainly calculation is also an indispensable prerequisite. No sociologist, for instance, should think himself too good, even in his old age, to make tens of thousands of quite trivial computations in his head and perhaps for months at a time. One cannot with impunity try to transfer this task entirely to mechanical assistants if one wishes to figure something, even though the final result is often small indeed. But if no "idea" occurs to his mind about the direction of his computations and, during his computations, about the bearing of the emergent single results, then even this small result will not be yielded.

Normally such an "idea" is prepared only on the soil of very hard work, but certainly this is not always the case. Scientifically, a dilettante's idea may have the very same or even a greater bearing for science than that of a specialist. Many of our very best hypotheses and insights are due precisely to dilettantes. The dilettante differs from the expert, as Helmholtz has said of Robert Mayer, only in that he lacks a firm and reliable work procedure. Consequently he is usually not in the position of control, to estimate, or to exploit the idea in its bearings. The idea is not a substitute for work; and work, in turn, cannot substitute for or compel an idea, just as little as enthusiasm can. Both, enthusiasm and work, and above all both of them *jointly*, can entice the idea.

Ideas occur to us when they please, not when it pleases us. The best ideas do indeed occur to one's mind in the way in which Ihering describes it: when smoking a cigar on the sofa; or as Helmholtz states of himself with scientific exactitude: when taking a walk on a slowly ascending street; or in a similar way. In any case, ideas come when we do not expect them, and not when we are brooding and searching at our desks. Yet ideas would certainly not come to mind had we not brooded at our desks and searched for answers with passionate devotion.

However this may be, the scientific worker has to take into his bargain the risk that enters into all scientific work: Does an "idea" occur or does it not? He may be an excellent worker and yet never have had any valuable idea of his own. It is a grave error to believe that this is so only in science, and that things for instance in a business office are different from a laboratory. A merchant or a big industrialist without "business imagination," that is, without ideas or ideal intuitions, will for all his life remain a man who would better have remained a clerk or a technical official. He will never be truly creative in organization. Inspiration in the field of science by no means plays any greater role, as academic conceit fancies, than it does in the field of mastering problems of practical life by a modern entrepreneur. On the other hand, and this also is often misconstrued, inspiration plays no less a role in science than it does in the realm of art. It is a childish notion to think that a mathematician attains any scientifically valuable results by sitting at his desk with a ruler, calculating machines or other mechanical means. The mathematical imagination of a Weierstrass is naturally quite differently oriented in meaning and result than is the imagination of an artist, and differs basically in quality. But the psychological processes do not differ. Both are frenzy (in the sense of Plato's "mania") and "inspiration."

Now, whether we have scientific inspiration depends upon destinies that are hidden from us, and besides upon "gifts." Last but not least, because of this indubitable truth, a very understandable attitude has become popular, especially among youth, and has put them in the service of idols whose cult today occupies a broad place on all street corners and in all periodicals. These idols are "personality" and "personal experience." Both are intimately connected, the notion prevails that the latter constitutes the former and belongs to it. People belabor themselves in trying to "experience" life—for that befits a personality, conscious of its rank and station. And if we do not succeed in "experiencing" life, we must at least pretend to have this gift of grace. Formerly we called this "experience," in plain German, "sensation"; and I believe that we then had a more adequate idea of what personality is and what it signifies.

Ladies and gentlemen. In the field of science only he who is devoted *solely* to the work at hand has "personality." And this holds not only for the field of science; we know of no great artist who has ever done anything but serve his work and only his work. As far as his art is concerned, even with a personality of Goethe's rank, it has been detrimental to take the liberty of trying to make his "life" into a work of art. And even if one doubts this, one has to be a Goethe in order to dare permit oneself such liberty. Everybody will admit at least this much: that even with a man like Goethe, who appears once in a thousand years, this liberty did not go unpaid for. In politics matters are not different, but we shall not discuss that today. In the field of science, however, the man who makes himself the impresario of the subject to which he should be devoted, and steps upon the stage and seeks to legitimate himself through "experience," asking: How can I prove that I am something other than a mere "specialist" and how can I manage to say something in form or in content that nobody else has ever said?—such a man is no "personality." Today such conduct is a crowd phenomenon, and it always makes a petty impression and debases the one who is thus concerned. Instead of this, an inner devotion to the task, and that alone, should lift the scientist to the height and dignity of the subject he pretends to serve. And in this it is not different with the artist.

In contrast with these preconditions which scientific work shares with art, science has a fate that profoundly distinguishes it from artistic work. Scientific work is chained to the course of progress; whereas in the realm of art there is no progress in the same sense. It is not true that the work of art of a period that has worked out new technical means, or, for instance, the laws of perspective, stands therefore artistically higher than a work of art devoid of all knowledge of those means and laws—if its form does justice to the material, that is, if its object has been chosen and formed so that it could be artistically mastered without applying those conditions and means. A work of art which is genuine "fulfillment" is never surpassed; it will never be antiquated. Individuals may differ in appreciating the personal significance of works of art, but no one will ever be able to say of such a work that it is "outstripped by another work which is also 'fulfillment.'"

In science, each of us knows that what he has accomplished will be antiquated in ten, twenty, fifty years. That is the fate to which science is subjected; it is the very *meaning* of scientific work, to which it is devoted in a quite specific sense, as compared with other spheres of culture for which in general the same holds. Every scientific "fulfillment" raises new "questions"; it *asks* to be "surpassed" and outdated. Whoever wishes to serve science has to resign himself to this fact. Scientific works certainly can last as "gratifications" because of their artistic quality, or they may remain important as a means of training. Yet they will be surpassed scientifically—let that be repeated—for it is our common fate and, more, our common goal. We cannot work without hoping that others will advance further than we have. In principle, this progress goes on *ad infinitum*. And with this we come to inquire into the *meaning* of science. . . .

It means . . . the knowledge or belief that if one but wished one *could* learn it at any time. Hence, it means that principally there are no mysterious incalculable forces that come into play, but rather that one can, in principle, master all things by calculation. This means that the world is disenchanted. One need no longer have recourse to magical means in order to master or implore the spirits, as did the savage, for whom such mysterious powers existed. Technical means and calculations perform the service. This above all is what intellectualization means.

Now, this process of disenchantment, which has continued to exist in Occidental culture for millennia, and, in general, this "progress," to which science belongs as a link and motive force, do they have any meanings that go beyond the purely practical and technical? You will find this question raised in the most principled form in the works of Lev Tolstoy. He came to raise the question in a peculiar way. All his broodings increasingly revolved around the problem of whether or not death is a meaningful phenomenon. And his answer was: for civilized man death has no meaning. It has none because the individual life of civilized man, placed into an infinite "progress," according to its own imminent meaning should never come to an end; for there is always a further step ahead of one who stands in the march of progress. And no man who comes to die stands upon the peak which lies in infinity. Abraham, or some peasant of the past, died "old and satiated with life" because he stood in the organic cycle of life; because his life, in terms of its meaning and on the eve of his days, had given to him what life had to offer; because for him there remained no puzzles he might wish to solve; and therefore he could have had "enough" of life. Whereas civilized man, placed in the midst of the continuous enrichment of culture by ideas, knowledge, and problems, may become "tired of life" but not "satiated with life." He catches only the most minute part of what the life of the spirit brings forth ever anew, and what he seizes is always something provisional and not definitive, and therefore death for him is a meaningless occurrence. And because death is meaningless, civilized life as such is meaningless; by its very "progressiveness" it gives death the imprint of meaninglessness. Throughout his late novels one meets with this thought as the keynote of the Tolstoyan art.

What stands should one take? Has "progress" as such a recognizable meaning that goes beyond the technical, so that to serve it is a meaningful vocation? The question must be raised. But this is no longer merely the question of man's calling *for* science, hence, the problem of what science as a vocation means to its devoted disciples. To raise this question is to ask for the vocation of science within the total life of humanity. What is the value of science?

Here the contrast between the past and the present is tremendous. You will recall the wonderful image at the beginning of the seventh book of Plato's *Republic:* those enchained cavemen whose faces are turned toward the stone wall before them. Behind them lies the source of the light which they cannot see. They are concerned only with the shadowy images that this light throws upon the wall, and they seek to fathom their interrelations. Finally one of them succeeds in shattering his fetters, turns around, and sees the sun. Blinded, he gropes about and stammers of what he saw. The others say he is raving. But gradually he learns to behold the light, and then his task is to descend to the cavemen and to lead them to the light. He is the philosopher; the sun, however, is the truth of science, which alone seizes not upon illusions and shadows but upon the true being.

Well, who today views science in such a manner? Today youth feels rather the reverse: the intellectual constructions of science constitute an unreal realm of artificial abstractions, which with their bony hands seek to grasp the blood-and-the-sap of true life without ever catching up with it. But here in life, in what for Plato was the play of shadows on the walls of the cave, genuine reality is pulsating; and the rest are derivatives of life, lifeless ghosts, and nothing else. How did this change come about?

Plato's passionate enthusiasm in *The Republic* must, in the last analysis, be explained by the fact that for the first time the *concept,* one of the great tools of all scientific knowledge, had been consciously discovered. Socrates had discovered it in its bearing. He was not the only man in the world to discover it. In India one finds the beginnings of a logic that is quite similar to that of Aristotle. But nowhere else do we find this realization of the significance of the concept. In Greece, for the first time, appeared a handy means by which one could put the logical screws upon somebody so that he could not come out without admitting either that he know nothing or that this and nothing else was truth, the *eternal* truth that never would vanish as the doings of the blind men vanish. That was the tremendous experience which dawned upon the disciples of Socrates. And from this it seemed to follow that if one only found the right concept of the beautiful, the good, or, for instance, of bravery, of the soul—or whatever—that then one could also grasp its true being. And this, in turn, seemed to open the way for knowing and for teaching how to act rightly in life and, above all, how to act as a citizen of the state; for this question was everything to the Hellenic man, whose thinking was political throughout. And for these reasons one engaged in science.

The second great tool of scientific work, the rational experiment, made its appearance at the side of this discovery of the Hellenic spirit during the Renaissance period. The experiment is a means of reliably controlling experience. Without it, present-day empirical science would be impossible. There were experiments earlier; for instance, in India physiological experiments were made in the service of ascetic yoga technique; in Hellenic antiquity, mathematical experiments were made for purposes of war technology; and in the Middle Ages, for purposes of mining. But to raise the experiment to a principle of research was the achievement of the Renaissance. They were the great innovators in *art,* who were the pioneers of experiment. Leonardo and his like and, above all, the sixteenth-century experimenters in music with their experimental pianos were characteristic. From these circles the experiment entered science, especially through Galileo, and it entered theory through Bacon; and then it was taken over by the various exact disciplines of the continental universities, first of all those of Italy and then those of the Netherlands.

What did science mean to these men who stood at the threshold of modern times? To artistic experimenters of the type of Leonardo and the musical innovators, science meant the path to *true* art, and that meant for them the path to true *nature.* Art was to be raised to the rank of a science, and this meant at the same time and above all to raise the artist to the rank of the doctor, socially and with reference to the meaning of his life. This is the ambition on which, for instance, Leonardo's sketch book was based. And today? "Science as the way to nature" would sound like blasphemy to youth. Today, youth proclaims the opposite: redemption from the intellectualism of science in order to return to one's own nature and therewith to nature in general. Science as a way of art? Here no criticism is even needed.

But during the period of the rise of the exact sciences one expected a great deal more. If you recall Swammerdam's statement, "Here I bring you the proof of God's providence in the anatomy of a louse," you will see what the scientific worker, influenced (indirectly) by Protestantism and Puritanism, conceived to be his task: to show the path to God. People no longer found this path among the philosophers, with their concepts and deductions. All pietist theology of the time, above all Spener, knew that God was not to be found along the road by which the Middle Ages had sought him. God is hidden, His ways are not our ways, His thoughts are not our thoughts. In the exact sciences, however, where one could physically grasp His works, one hoped to come upon the traces of what He planned for the world. And today? Who—aside from certain big children who are indeed found in the natural sciences—still believes that the findings of astronomy, biology, physics, or chemistry could teach us anything about the *meaning* of the world? If there is any such "meaning," along what road could one come upon its tracks? If these natural sciences lead to anything in this way, they are apt to make the belief that there is such a thing as the "meaning" of the universe die out at its very roots.

And finally, science as a way "to God"? Science, this specifically irreligious power? That science today is irreligious no one will doubt in his innermost being, even if he will not admit it to himself. Redemption from the rationalism and intellectualism of science is the fundamental presupposition of living in union with the divine. This, or something similar in meaning, is one of the fundamental watchwords one hears among German youth, whose feelings are attuned to religion or who crave religious experiences. They crave not only religious experience but experience as such. The only thing that is strange is the method that is now followed: the spheres of the irrational, the only spheres that intellectualism has not yet touched, are now raised into consciousness and put under its lens. For in practice this is where the modern intellectualist form of romantic irrationalism leads. This method of emancipation from intellectualism may well bring about the very opposite of what those who take to it conceive as its goal.

After Nietzsche's devastating criticism of those "last men" who "invented happiness," I may leave aside altogether the naive optimism in which science—that is, the technique of mastering life which rests upon science—has been celebrated as the way to happiness. Who believes in this?—aside from a few big children in university chairs or editorial offices. Let us resume our argument.

Under these internal presuppositions, what is the meaning of science as a vocation, now after all these former illusions, the "way to true being," the "way to true art," the "way to true nature," the "way to true God," the "way to true happiness," have been dispelled? Tolstoy has given the simplest answer, with the words: "Science is meaningless because it gives no answer to our question, the only question important for us: 'What shall we do and how shall we live?'" That science does not give an answer to this is indisputable. The only question that remains is the sense in which science gives "no" answer, and whether or not science might yet be of some use to the one who puts the question correctly.

Today one usually speaks of science as "free from presuppositions." Is there such a thing? It depends upon what one understands thereby. All scientific work presupposes that the rules of logic and method are valid; these are the general foundations of our orientation in the world; and, at least for our special question, these presuppositions are the least problematic aspect of science. Science further presupposes that what is yielded by scientific work is important in the sense that it is "worth being known." In this, obviously, are contained all our problems. For this presupposition cannot be proved by scientific means. It can only be *interpreted* with reference to its ultimate meaning, which we must reject or accept according to our ultimate position toward life.

Furthermore, the nature of the relationship of scientific work and its presuppositions varies widely according to their structure. The natural sciences, for instance, physics, chemistry, and astronomy, presuppose as self-evident that it is worth while to know the ultimate laws of cosmic events as far as science can construe them. This is the case not only because with such knowledge one can attain technical results but for its own sake, if the quest for such knowledge is to be a "vocation." Yet this presupposition can by no means be proved. And still less can it be proved that the existence of the world which these sciences describe is worth while, that it has any "meaning," or that it makes sense to live in such a world. Science does not ask for the answers to such questions.

Consider modern medicine, a practical technology which is highly developed scientifically. The general "presupposition" of the medical enterprise is stated trivially in the assertion that medical science has the task of maintaining life as such and of diminishing suffering as such to the greatest possible degree. Yet this is problematical. By his means the medical man preserves the life of the mortally ill man, even if the patient implores us to relieve him of life, even if his relatives, to whom his life is worthless and to whom the costs of maintaining his worthless life grow unbearable, grant his redemption from suffering. Perhaps a poor lunatic is involved, whose relatives, whether they admit it or not, wish and must wish for his death. Yet the presuppositions of medicine, and the penal code, prevent the physician from relinquishing his therapeutic efforts. Whether life is worth while living and when—this question is not asked by medicine. Natural science gives us an answer to the question of what we must do if we wish to master life technically. It leaves quite aside, or assumes for its purposes, whether we should and do wish to master life technically and whether it ultimately makes sense to do so.

Consider a discipline such as aesthetics. The fact that there are works of art is given for aesthetics. It seeks to find out under what conditions this fact exists, but it does not raise the question whether or not the realm of art is perhaps a realm of diabolical grandeur, a realm of this world, and therefore, in its core, hostile to God and, in its innermost and aristocratic spirit, hostile to the brotherhood of man. Hence, aesthetics does not ask whether there *should* be works of art.

Consider jurisprudence. It establishes what is valid according to the rules of juristic thought, which is partly bound by logically compelling and partly by conventionally given schemata. Juridical thought holds when certain legal rules and certain methods of interpretations are recognized as binding. Whether there should be law and whether one should establish just these rules—such questions jurisprudence does not answer. It can only state: If one wishes this result, according to the norms of our legal thought, this legal rule is the appropriate means of attaining it.

Consider the historical and cultural sciences. They teach us how to understand and interpret political, artistic, literary, and social phenomena in terms of their origins. But they give us no answer to the question, whether the existence of these cultural phenomena have been and are *worth while*. And they do not answer the further question, whether it is worth the effort required to know them. They presuppose that there is an interest in partaking, through this procedure, of the community of "civilized men." But they cannot prove "scientifically" that this is the case; and that they presuppose this interest by no means proves that it goes without saying. In fact it is not at all self-evident.

Finally, let us consider the disciplines close to me: sociology, history, economics, political science, and those types of cultural philosophy that make it their task to interpret these sciences. It is said, and I agree, that politics is out of place in the lecture-room. It does not belong there on the part of the students. If, for instance, in the lecture-room of my former colleague Dietrich Schäfer in Berlin, pacifist students were to surround his desk and make an uproar, I should deplore it just as much as I should deplore the uproar which anti-pacifist students are said to have made against Professor Förster, whose views in many ways are as remote as could be from mine. Neither does politics, however, belong in the lecture-room on the part of the docents, and when the docent is scientifically concerned with politics, it belongs there least of all.

To take a practical political stand is one thing, and to analyze political structures and party positions is another. When speaking in a political meeting about democracy, one does not hide one's personal standpoint; indeed, to come out clearly and take a stand is one's damned duty. The words one uses in such a meeting are not means of scientific analysis but means of canvassing votes and winning over others. They are not plowshares to loosen the soil of contemplative thought; they are swords against the enemies: such words are weapons. It would be an outrage, however, to use words in this fashion in a lecture or in the lecture-room. If, for instance, "democracy" is under discussion, one considers its various forms, analyzes them in the way they function, determines what results for the conditions of life the one form has as compared with the other. Then one confronts the forms of democracy with non-democratic forms of political order and endeavors to come to a position where the student may find the point from which, in terms of his ultimate ideals, he can take a stand. But the true teacher will beware of imposing from the platform any political position upon the student, whether it is expressed or suggested. "To let the facts speak for themselves" is the most unfair way of putting over a political position to the student.

Why should we abstain from doing this? I state in advance that some highly esteemed colleagues are of the opinion that it is not possible to carry through this self-restraint and that, even if it were possible, it would be a whim to avoid declaring oneself. Now one cannot demonstrate scientifically what the duty of an academic teacher is. One can only demand of the teacher that he have the intellectual integrity to see that it is one thing to state facts, to determine mathematical or logical relations or the internal structure of cultural values, while it is another thing to answer questions of the *value* of culture and its individual contents and the question of how one should act in the cultural community and in political associations. These are quite heterogeneous problems. If he asks further why he should not deal with both types of problems in the lecture-room, the answer is: because the prophet and the demagogue do not belong on the academic platform.

To the prophet and the demagogue, it is said: "Go your ways out into the streets and speak openly to the world," that is, speak where criticism is possible. In the lecture-room we stand opposite our audience, and it has to remain silent. I deem it irresponsible to exploit the circumstance that for the sake of their career the students have to attend a teacher's course while there is nobody present to oppose him with criticism. The task of the teacher is to serve the students with his knowledge and scientific experience and not to imprint upon them his personal political views. It is certainly possible that the individual teacher will not entirely succeed in eliminating his personal sympathies. He is then exposed to the sharpest criticism in the forum of his own conscience. And this deficiency does not prove anything; other errors are also possible, for instance, erroneous statements of fact, and yet they prove nothing against the duty of searching for the truth. I also reject this in the very interest of science. I am ready to prove from the works of our historians that whenever the man of science introduces his personal value judgment, a full understanding of the facts *ceases*. But this goes beyond tonight's topic and would require lengthy elucidation.

I ask only: How should a devout Catholic, on the one hand, and a Freemason, on the other, in a course on the forms of church and state or on religious history ever be brought to evaluate these subjects alike? This is out of the question. And yet the academic teacher must desire and must demand of himself to serve the one as well as the other by his knowledge and methods. Now you will rightly say that the devout Catholic will never accept the view of the factors operative in bringing about Christianity which a teacher who is free of his dogmatic presuppositions presents to him. Certainly! The difference, however, lies in the following: Science "free from presuppositions," in the sense of a rejection of religious bonds, does not know of the "miracle" and the "revelation." If it did, science would be unfaithful to its own "presuppositions." The believer knows both, miracle and revelation. And science "free from presuppositions" expects from him no less—and no more—

than acknowledgment that *if* the process can be explained without those supernatural interventions, which an empirical explanation has to eliminate as causal factors, the process has to be explained the way science attempts to do. And the believer can do this without being disloyal to his faith.

But has the contribution of science no meaning at all for a man who does not care to know the facts as such and to whom only the practical standpoint matters? Perhaps science nevertheless contributes something.

The primary task of a useful teacher is to teach his students to recognize "inconvenient" facts—I mean facts that are inconvenient for their party opinions. And for every party opinion there are facts that are extremely inconvenient, for my own opinion no less than for others. I believe the teacher accomplishes more than a mere intellectual task if he compels his audience to accustom itself to the existence of such facts. I would be so immodest as even to apply the expression "moral achievement," though perhaps this may sound too grandiose for something that should go without saying.

Thus far I have spoken only of practical reasons for avoiding the imposition of a personal point of view. But these are not the only reasons. The impossibility of "scientifically" pleading for practical and interested stands—except in discussing the means for a firmly given and presupposed end—rests upon reasons that lie far deeper.

"Scientific" pleading is meaningless in principle because the various value spheres of the world stand in irreconcilable conflict with each other. The elder Mill, whose philosophy I will not praise otherwise, was on this point right when he said: If one proceeds from pure experience, one arrives at polytheism. This is shallow in formulation and sounds paradoxical, and yet there is truth in it. If anything, we realize again today that something can be sacred not only in spite of its not being beautiful, but rather because and in so far as it is not beautiful. You will find this documented in the fifty-third chapter of the book of Isaiah and in the twenty-first Psalm. And, since Nietzsche, we realize that something can be beautiful, not only in spite of the aspect in which it is not good, but rather in that very aspect. You will find this expressed earlier in the *Fleurs du mal*, as Baudelaire named his volume of poems. It is commonplace to observe that something may be true although it is not beautiful and not holy and not good. Indeed it may be true in precisely those aspects. But all these are only the most elementary cases of the struggle that the gods of the various orders and values are engaged in. I do not know how one might wish to decide "scientifically" the value of French and German culture; for here, too, different gods struggle with one another, now and for all times to come.

We live as did the ancients when their world was not yet disenchanted of its gods and demons, only we live in a different sense. As Hellenic man at times sacrificed to Aphrodite and at other times to Apollo, and, above all, as everybody sacrificed to the gods of his city, so do we still nowadays, only the bearing of man has been disenchanted and denuded of its mystical but inwardly genuine plasticity. Fate, and certainly not "science," holds sway over these gods and their struggles. One can only understand what the godhead is for the one order or for the other, or better, what godhead is in the one or in the other order. With this understanding, however, the matter has reached its limit so far as it can be discussed in a lecture-room and by a professor. Yet the great and vital problem that is contained therein is, of course, very far from being concluded. But forces other than university chairs have their say in this matter.

What man will take upon himself the attempt to "refute scientifically" the ethic of the Sermon on the Mount? For instance, the sentence, "resist no evil," or the image of turning the other cheek? And yet it is clear, in mundane perspective, that this is an ethic of undignified conduct; one has to choose between the religious dignity which this ethic confers and the dignity of manly conduct which preaches something quite different; "resist evil—lest you be co-responsible for an overpowering evil." According to our ultimate standpoint, the one is the devil and the other the God, and the individual has to decide which is God for him and which is the devil. And so it goes throughout all the orders of life.

The grandiose rationalism of an ethical and methodical conduct of life which flows from every religious prophecy has dethroned this polytheism in favor of the "one thing that is needful." Faced with the realities of outer and inner life, Christianity has deemed it necessary to make those compromises and relative judgments, which we all know from its history. Today the routines of everyday life challenge religion. Many old gods ascend from their graves; they are disenchanted and hence take the form of impersonal forces. They strive to gain power over our lives and again they resume their eternal struggle with one another. What is hard for modern man, and especially for the younger generation, is to measure up to *workaday* existence. The ubiquitous chase for "experience" stems from this weakness; for it is weakness not to be able to countenance the stern seriousness of our fateful times.

Our civilization destines us to realize more clearly these struggles again, after our eyes have been blinded for a thousand years—blinded by the allegedly or presumably exclusive orientation toward the grandiose moral fervor of Christian ethics.

Translated by Hans H. Gerth
and C. Wright Mills

Karl Voßler

Language and Science

Linguistic thinking is different from logical or scientific thinking and yet not different, in so far as there is only one thinking process. As an active, theoretical attitude of the mind, linguistic and logical thought are the same in essence. As often as we try to separate the one from the other, we find that somehow they always come together again. It is therefore not thought as such that we have to analyze; we can only distinguish the paths it takes, its directions and aims. Linguistic thinking tries to image the world; logical thinking tries to understand it. Through the power of imagery the world becomes an appearance and, since the mind apprehends and represents it as a pure phenomenon, we remain uncertain whether the world is real or illusory. As long as the mind continues to image or to think linguistically, this will not trouble us. On the contrary, the fact that the world has a face, seems to us eminently satisfactory and pleasing. The mind finds enjoyment in the artistic vision and creation, which we call beauty. Only intuitively, as religious mind, will it have the certainty of belief that there is something substantial about its own images, visions, and dreams. Because of that, uncertainty need not arise; and as long as the mind sees and creates, uncertainty will not become a dialectical thorn, will not arouse doubt.

At the beginning of scientific thinking stands doubt, and not wonder, as the simple-minded Greeks thought; for wonder is much more an accompaniment of linguistic or intuitive thinking. Between linguistic and logical thinking there are no comfortable, gentle, unnoticeable transitions, indeed, no progress, no ascending or descending steps; it is a complete parting of the ways.

What, then, does thought have to do to free itself of the tendencies of language? It does not cease to image and represent, as though this tendency were a false one; it keeps it and yet relinquishes it. Thought is not a person or a body and is therefore not bound to space and time. Like a gas, it can act in different conductors at the same time. By turning back on itself, by doubt, reflexion, speculation, it turns away from the appearances of the world, and understands substantial reality within itself. This understanding of reality is called truth.

It is obvious, that in moments of doubting, in reflexive and speculative aversion from imagery, when thought turns back on itself, it can understand itself, but cannot for that very reason represent, express, and communicate itself. A concept in its logical purity can be represented in no language; nor is language called upon to represent it, since what is immediately clear—indeed, this clearness itself—does not need the mediation of language.

Only when thought ceases to reflect on itself and the mind looks at the world with new eyes, will it desire in some way to express in language what is substantial about appearances, and the apprehended difference between appearance and reality. This is done in the forms and expressions we call prose as distinct from the forms of poetry, which are poorer in reflexions. Poetry and prose are not two kinds of language, but two species of style. For since truth, concepts, reflection, and speculation, in short, thought that has turned away from appearances, do not express themselves directly, thought can only communicate itself indirectly, that is, again as appearance and by the circuitous paths of linguistic thinking. This process, by which thinking stops its linguistic activities, turns back on itself, and then continues to speak with a critical consciousness and in a more circumspect style, is known to everyone from his childhood. If he occasionally forgets it, he is reminded by the common warning: first think, then speak.

That it should be at all necessary to give such warnings, which the man of science can hardly repeat often enough to himself, is a sign that there are—not in logic, not in truth and reality, but within language and in the phenomenal world—innumerable seductive, pleasant, easy, hardly noticeable transitions between imagistic and conceptual thinking. With the criteria of inner language the one cannot be distinguished from the other at all, or the transitions determined. Science can mask itself in poetic, poetry in prosaic raiment; and those who have no logical training and philosophic education must not flatter themselves that they can unmask these masquerades of the spirit.

Since we are concerned with the philosophy of language, it is these transitions and masquerades of the logos in language, the conscious as well as the unconscious, the helpful and the misleading, that are particularly instructive. If we are to judge them correctly, we must not forget that the turning away of thought from speech, the unveiling of the concept, is a logical fact; the turning of conceptual to linguistic thinking, its appearances, disguises, and representations, is a linguistic fact. If we forget this fundamental law, and confuse the aspect of aversion with that of reversion, we become involved in errors and fall either into sophism or allegory. Sophism is the name of the logical or scientific vice that takes the aspect of the veiling of the logos to be the same as its aversion or unveiling, while allegory sins in the opposite sense, on the side of linguistic thought, by smuggling the logical aspect of unveiled thought, thought that has turned away from contemplation, into the series of modes of expressions and regarding it as identical with the aspect of concrete imagery.

Sophisms would not be possible or even thinkable were it not for the fact that language thinking momentarily experiences a kind of arrest or petrification when the logos, the concept, arises out of it. Anything that wants to live in logical thought must die and petrify in linguistic thought. A thought cannot become a concept other than by emerging from the chrysalis of its prelinguistic life, and discarding the dead shell. These dead shells no longer are immediately meaningful language forms; they are merely a kind of track, footmarks left by the logos as it launched itself. In their resemblance to colorless and rigid formulae, and in their grammatical schematism we can still trace and recognize the labors that logical thought had to undertake in order to free itself from linguistic thought. The demand that this freedom makes, in other words, its spiritual necessity, is contained in the "law of identity," according to which everything that has been thought must be equal to itself, $a = a$.

This law, however, is not true. In the intuitively apprehended world of appearances, as well as in logically understood metaphysical reality, there are movement, life, activity. Hence our linguistic as well as our logical thinking, to follow the flow of things, must be mobile and changeable, associative and dialectical. There is logically only *one* point at which thought has the possibility, the desire, the will and the compulsion to insist, if it is not to lose itself, on the identity of its objects with itself. We might say that it is along the line of death, where the world of appearances touches the metaphysical beyond, that is, where conceptual, pure, logical thinking has to maintain itself against the phantasies, dreams and imagery of linguistic thinking. Without the law of identity we should be continually confusing appearance and reality. It therefore has its application chiefly where logical and linguistic thought come into conflict, and appearances are mastered by concepts, above all in mathematics and the natural sciences. Here logical thinking shows its rigidity and exactitude far more than in the historical and philosophical sciences, in which the world of appearances certainly also has to be distinguished from metaphysical reality, but in which the separation is not so absolute that every incursion of the supernatural into the natural is felt as a disturbing factor. The historical and philosophical sciences are more concerned in apprehending the connections and activities by which the metaphysical becomes appearance. This phenomenological tendency of conceptual thinking demands a dependence on, and return to linguistic thinking, which would only be an obstacle to the mathematician and the physicist.

The spiritual educative value of mathematical and scientific studies—apart from their value as knowledge—lies in the liberation from words, in the overcoming of linguistic thinking, dreaming, vague intuition and the shackles of the mythical, magical, and fantastic; in short, in what is usually called "enlightenment."

Scientific thinking breaks that emphatic attitude of man which we have described above; that religious belief in language, in prayer, in magic, in meaning and speaking; that close interrelation between sentiments and the words in which they are expressed. The naiveté of the inner language form—by which a "horse" became the myth, "horse-horse"—and all the proper names of things are broken, their baptismal certificates are destroyed, so that there remain only the outer signs, the generic names, the formal order, in short, the translatability and the exchange value of words and languages. In terms of the concepts of mathematics and the natural sciences all languages are external and equal. These concepts can be put in any language, since they merely clothe themselves in the outer linguistic form, but live upon and exhaust the inner. The mathematical concepts of the circle, the triangle, the sphere, of number and so on, or the scientific concepts of force, matter, the atom, attain their full and exact scientific meaning precisely because all imagistic, fantastic, mythical and linguistic thinking that may still linger in them is rigidly excised.

It is due to this negative and abstractive behavior of the logos, that mathematics and natural science nevertheless grow on the soil of linguistic thought, like light on the wick that it destroys. And since in mental life every destruction is a spur and an incentive to renewed and multiplied creation, the abstractions of scientific concept formation cause an intense hunger after imagination and observant intuition, such as the poet would not have by himself. From the ends of the earth and the depths of the sea, from the whole cosmos of appearances, science gathers material for the senses, arms them with telescopes and microscopes, forces our imagination to look in the same direction as its logical questionings, and, not content with receiving intuitive experiences by the grace of accident or fate, like pious and simple-minded poets, it creates experiences according to the standards of its desire for knowledge, prepares them, investigates, and experiments. So science castigates and enriches, conserves and accelerates, prunes and sharpens, obstructs and drives forward linguistic thought in the service of the logos, which it rapes, deprives of its naiveté, and enriches instead with innumerable children. Through the work of the natural sciences the European languages have had their vocabularies immensely enriched since the end of the Middle Ages. At the same time, although grammatical training and discipline has not been given them directly by the sciences, they have achieved far more than that: they have emphatically demanded and asserted their right to this discipline. The demands made by our civilized languages on the concept forming powers of the natural sciences, will increase in the future rather than diminish. How they will respond to this pressure we can only foresee vaguely and in general terms. There will probably be a further increase in terminology. But the progressive elimination of the differences in national languages, which is frequently feared or hoped for, does not seem to be likely. On the contrary, just because naturalistic thought with its fundamental tendency to abstraction makes more or less the same demands on every language, it forces each one to achieve the highest precision and logical sequence of which, in its own characteristic way, it is capable. The characteristics of individual minds are not destroyed by common tasks and common competition, but are all the more emphasized, and instead of remaining potential are forced into the light of achievement. That is why the differences between Italian and French, or between French and German, have become greater rather than smaller since the rise of the natural sciences. The essential differences in the structure of the sentence in the Romance and the Germanic languages, and between the order and the formation of words in French and German, as well as differences of accent, were less pronounced in the Middle Ages than they are now.

It is possible, however, owing to the continually higher demands made on the civilized languages by abstractive naturalistic thought, and the increasing tension of competitive effort at solving common logical tasks, that one or other language may succumb, that is, be altogether disregarded in scientific literature, to live on only in poetry and everyday intercourse. Here and there we see signs of some languages dropping out of scientific world competition, ever since it began in earnest. The scientific research worker can already grasp almost all that is of importance in his work by reading French, German, and English. Important work in other languages is made accessible through translations, because it is felt to be isolated and would otherwise be in danger of being ignored.

The higher naturalistic thinking ascends into abstract technicalities, the more exclusive it becomes. It has no immediate need for the cooperation or the understanding of the masses, and cannot use the untrained help of amateurs and laymen at all.

At this height, however, where the estrangement and separation of logical from linguistic thinking is greatest, is the speculative or reflexive turning point at which the abstract concept becomes dialectical, and logical thinking discovers its true nature and at the same time its unity with linguistic thinking. This return and approach of the logos to language can be represented in many different ways: as the transition from mathematical to historical or from naturalistic to metaphysical thinking; or from the concepts of reason to those of intelligence; or from the abstraction to the idea; or from the rigid, postulated identity of thinking and being, to the moving reality of identity, and so on. From our point of view we can best regard the transition in question as one from the negative to the positive aspect of the inner language form.

Since we cannot think without speaking, or speak without thinking, each activity presupposes the other. They are so closely dependent on one another, that we can just as well regard and value thought as speech, or speech as thought. The more naive and natural view is that which supposes and recognizes thought only where there is also speech, so that the latter is seen as the premise of the former. From this standpoint, then, nothing is recognized that is not language, that cannot be apprehended and seen as expression, communication, and representation. It is the aesthetic point of view, which is incapable of seeing the naked logos or any silent and formless thought, and which is willing to honor only the representational faculty even in the greatest thinkers and scientists. If one is serious about this no doubt possible and justifiable attitude, and carries it through in the strictly scientific sense, one will come across language forms that are present in an external sense and yet have no linguistic meaning; empty words, hollow gossip, thoughtless phrases, unimaginative, unrealizable forms, which have no linguistic content or meaning, in short, which have no inner language form. We shall then understand that it is the inner language form which is the essential part of language, and that the outer form is purely fortuitous and illusory. Nevertheless, we cannot disregard the outer as long as we take up the aesthetic attitude; for how can we recognize the inner form if we have not got the body? If we refuse to recognize the outer form, it inevitably follows that we must also give up the inner; and then aesthetic contemplation would destroy its object and itself. If the inner language form were no more than language seen from the inside, that is, from the side of the speaker, that would be the end of the wisdom of philosophers. If the inner language form is denied, speech and all thought are denied as well. But thought does not destroy itself; it stops and retreats at this abyss, turns back upon itself, and becomes reflexive.

Thought carries out this retreat by contemplating its own imagery and speech. Everyone knows that he cannot and may not express everything he thinks; and he knows this because he observes his own imagery and speech, because he thinks about his thought. In this way we attain to the second and truly logical standpoint, that of self-consciousness. The negation of the inner language form has therefore in reality not taken place at all; it has only been considered and consciously avoided. We can therefore not speak of stepping back from negating to positing the inner language form, nor of a logical transition from the mathematical and scientific to the metaphysical and historical method of concept formation. There has been no transition at all, but a return of thought into itself. The linguistic direction of thought, which at first was external and free from doubt and which did not distinguish between outer and inner, regarding expression and imagery, appearance and reality, sound and meaning as identical and of no account, is startled out of its dream and critically illuminated by the logical concept. The latter does not, therefore, destroy and negate the former, but stops it in its sleepwalking, in order to point out the correct way. This desire to orientate is earlier than the "halt!," which thought calls out to itself. At the instant of calling a halt, thought already knows whither it wants to go. In order to enlighten the world, we must already have understood it; to abstract from its appearances, we must know its nature; to cut out linguistic thinking without destroying it, we must already have transposed it into its nonexternal form and know what it can and what it cannot do. What it can do is to apprehend the whole world of appearances as being and becoming, as motionless and moving appearance. In this sense we may say that the first stage of language is the onomatopoetic, or, to suggest a more comprehensive term, the *phenomeno-poetic*. For every kind of sense impression, not only that of hearing, can immediately express itself through language. This immediacy is no more binding for hearing than it is for sight or smell; it is not binding at all, but because of its fundamental originality is the immediacy of freedom, an *origo poetica* of the spirit. We can find no final reason why Hölderlin should express the eternal yearning in the heart of man by singing of sunlight and the ether, whilst Leopardi chooses the night and moonlight. In the same way we cannot give a proof why the German child should say *mä* to a sheep and the Italian *bä*. This irrationality of language, this dreamlike fluctuation of the poetic spirit, which demands to be bound and strengthened even at the stage of primordial creation, cannot be removed from the world by literary or etymological criticism. It is simply there, and its very indestructibility becomes a problem for conceptual thought. Why does language fluctuate, why does it not conform to the law of identity? Why does it not use the same word for the same thing at all times, or a different word every time? Why is language not even consistent in its fluctuation, in its changes? The only possible answer is, that it does not regard the concept as something rigid, external, and opposed to itself, but as something plastic within itself.

This plasticity of the concept is in fact the same as that which presents itself to our aesthetic judgment as the inner language form. It is the deeply felt and truly active spiritual principle of language, even though it does not always attain its fullest expression. To our logical judgment this same spirituality of language no longer presents itself as a mere language form, but as a form of thought, a concept.

All scientific concepts, the mathematical and naturalistic as well as the speculative and historical, are forms of language and of thought at the same time. They are a form of language if we take their aesthetic, a form of thought if we take their logical validity into consideration. That one and the same thing can be concept and language at once seems to be a contradiction; but it has a logical basis. We must remind ourselves again that in philosophy "the one" and "the other" *together* form that living unity which bears difference within itself, and that the things of the mind can be distinguished only if we do not separate them, but think them as a unity. I have shown elsewhere that the conceptual systems of the great philosophers are at the same time the inner language form of their thought, that, for instance, the *cogito ergo sum* of Descartes is his thought and the language form of his thought, and that a syntactical change in the one would also be a violation or falsification of the other.

Let us examine some further examples of the peculiar way in which the language forms are separated from concepts and at the same time united with them.

An intuitive fool once said he could quite well understand that the astronomers were capable of discovering the distances, sizes, movements, and velocities of the stars; what baffled him, however, was how they knew what the stars were *called*. Well, the astronomers do not know the names of the stars, and do not want to know them. In fact it matters so little to them, that any and every name suits them, provided it refers to the particular star they are discussing, and to no other. They give to celestial objects the names of ancient gods, or letters, or numbers; only the convention must be rigid, so that there may be no confusion. Astronomical names are external and have no immediate inner language form; they are not really *nomina,* but *pro-nomina*. The whole language of the scientists and mathematicians is in this sense pronominal; it points and refers to things, is demonstrative and relative. Their minds are not busy with words, they do not say anything, they operate. As regards their linguistic nature, numbers are pronouns; as regards their mathematical nature they are operations or functions. In so far as these operations are carried out by arithmetical thinking, they do not need names. Hence, instead of numeral adjectives, the mathematicians can substitute letters or even the things themselves, wooden balls or stones, or mechanical, physical, and chemical quantities of matter or force whose relations they are investigating. It makes no conceptual difference whether the operations in question are carried out arithmetically and the numbers recited or written down, or whether they consist in working a calculating machine, or whether they are carried out as experiments in a laboratory; for as far as the concept, the scientific substance, is concerned, experimental operations are the same as the method of calculating by reciting numbers. And that is why the origin and essence of the inner language form of numbers is an operation. This fact has frequently enough been noticed in the languages of primitive peoples. "The Ewe, for example, count on their outstretched fingers, beginning with the smallest finger of the left hand and bending up the finger they have counted with the index finger of the right. After the left they proceed in the same way with the right. . . . In Nuba the gestures that accompany counting are as follows: Beginning with *one*, the fingers of the left hand are pressed into the palm by the right hand in order, starting with the little finger. The same is then done to the right hand. For twenty, both fists are pressed horizontally together. Von der Steinen reports that the Bakairi failed to accomplish the simplest operation of counting, if the objects to be counted, *e.g.*, a handful of maize, were not immediately accessible to touch. . . . In Sotho the word for five really means 'complete the hand,' that for six 'jump,' that is, jump to the other hand. This active character of the so-called numeral adjectives is particularly clear in those languages that form their expressions for numbers by having a special description for the way in which the objects to be counted are grouped, set down, or stood up. Thus the Klamath language has a great number of such terms, which are formed from the verbs for placing, laying down, and setting up. A particular group of objects that are to be counted has to be spread out on the ground, another has to be arranged in superimposed layers, some have to be divided into heaps, others arranged in rows; and to each such 'placing' of the objects there corresponds a different verbal numeral adjective, a different *numeral classifier,* according to their characteristics. The movements needed in setting up these objects are accompanied by definite bodily movements, which are thought of as being done in a particular order. The latter do not need to be confined to hands and feet, the fingers or toes, but may be extended to any part of the body. In British New Guinea counting starts with the fingers of the left hand, and then continues to the wrist, the elbow, the shoulder, the neck, the left breast, the chest, the right breast, the right side of the neck and so on; in other parts the shoulder blade, the clavicle, the navel, the throat, or nose and eye and ear are used."

We see that the clumsiest counting efforts of the least civilized show the same fundamental relation of concept and linguistic form as the most difficult and abstract calculations of a master of applied mathematics. For the least civilized as well as for Einstein, the theorem holds true that the inner language form of number is an activity of thought, a grasping and manipulation and transportation of objects from standpoint to standpoint, and that external language, the expression, communication, and representation of this active adjustment of points of view, is a phenomenon accompanying it and coordinated with it. Because of this relation of coordination, external language forms, mathematical signs, numeral adjectives, gestures, etc., can accompany the inner activity of calculation like the shadow the dog. They can just as well remain absent or vanish, or they can be employed as assistants or vicarious substitutes, or they can even become the inner activity themselves. That depends on the task we have set ourselves and the practiced abilities we apply to it. If the mathematical task lies in regions we have often traversed, the arithmetical operation becomes an almost automatic function, which we hardly need to carry out. We merely need to set it going and to represent it by external mathematical language forms, like logarithms. On such occasions mathematical thought appears condensed and externalized, as its own shadow and substitute and identical with its language forms. But if new regions are to be discovered, it must actively seek and build the road, free itself from the shadow of language, relinquish familiar formulae and signs, in order to create new language forms, new orientations and functions through its own initiative, and clothe them in new formulae, signs and external characteristics. On such occasions mathematical thought appears independent of its language form, and becomes the light that dissipates the shadow, to throw it in other directions.

The coordination of thinking and speaking in the mathematical sciences is at once free and bound; on the one hand, therefore, mathematics may have validity as a language, that is, as a system expressing conceptual operations, on the other as a logical activity, that is, as a systematic attempt to attain freedom from language. We might call it a language, which allows only pronouns in place of nouns, imperatives in place of verbs, copulative equations instead of adjectives and adverbs, and whose fundamental attitude toward the whole colorful movement life is summed up in the one sentence: "Put this and that equal to that and this!" This is not in the true sense of the word a language; it is the bare expression of the purely logical will that operates on the world of appearances, the world of linguistic thinking. The purpose of the mathematical coordination of language and concept is the liberation of the concept from the senses. It is a kind of pledge, in which both sides purify each other, become more spiritual, and free themselves from the senses by serving each other as substitutes.

In the speculative and historical sciences the purpose is the same: the liberation of thought from the senses. The relation of logos and language, or inner and outer language form, also remains the same in so far as it is a free and bound relation determined by the purpose for which knowledge is sought. But in practice the relation becomes different. It becomes more intensified, becoming more free on the one side and more closely bound on the other. Seen from the outside, the language of historians and usually of philosophers also remains that of common humanity; it is not laced into the Spanish boots of a technical convention. Only occasionally do philosophers demand such asceticism of it; but that is an exception and a misuse. Since it can move about freely, and revel to its heart's content in its nominal and verbal wealth, it cannot pledge itself to the logos as it does in mathematics, and cannot become a substitute for it as often as it likes. Nevertheless it is in the service of the logos, and shall and will and must serve it—but only as Faust served his "master," *"auf besondere Weise,"* in his own way; it strives hard and often errs but remains conscious of the right way—in its *"dunkeln Drange sich des rechten Weges wohl bewusst."* It is a relation of love, not that of a contract, though this sounds somewhat fantastic; for how can language love the logos, or images a concept? And yet the expression is justified in so far as the logical and scientific thinker can only contemplate, express, communicate and represent his knowledge if he loves it. Understanding unites with contemplative and creative thought in the Platonic *eros,* provided we regard it philosophically, and not historically or, worse still, mythically; and in this embrace the logos, which otherwise would be something general, something that stands alone in the world, becomes *ours.*

> Allen gehört was du denkst; dein eigen ist nur, was du fühlst.
> Soll er dein Eigentum sein, fühle den Gott, den du denkst.

Without eros not only the cosmos but our thought first of all would fall to pieces. There would be so much reason and abstraction, that thought would be unable to find the way back to itself. This danger does in fact continually threaten mathematical and naturalistic thinking, for it has no eros, or rather, it has not got it as unharnessed passion but as a desire for knowledge that trains our purposes and is trained by them—and this is both more and less.

In all sciences, that is along the whole front of linguistically expressed science or scientific literature, the relation of linguistic to logical thought is fundamentally determined and regulated by the tone of the spiritual logos. Where it is active, as in the natural sciences, its mood becomes more sober, while in the more contemplative sciences it can become intensified to the point of intoxication. Its fluctuations can, as it were, be read on the thermometer of psychology; but we must not believe that this glass instrument makes the weather. The natural temperatures of thought are no more than the tensions between its subjects and its objects, or its vehicles and objects. Therefore the study of these tensions, what we may call the psychology of scientific *Weltanschauungen*, is no longer a matter for philosophy but one for philology and the literary sciences. An examination of the systems of philosophy, the methods of mathematics and the natural sciences, the *Weltanschauungen* of history, in order to discover by what they are naturally determined, or, what comes to the same, to discover their spiritual eros, cannot lead us to hope for more than an understanding of their *langage*. That is a great deal; for the whole meaning of a thinker appears in his *langage*, his specific way of expressing things and his inner and outer language forms. On the other hand it is very little; for the meaning of his expressions contains, in an undistinguishable mixture, all that he believes because of his religious convictions; the intuitive knowledge and the errors of his uncertainty; his fantasies; what he knows and apprehends through his reason and intelligence; what he desires on the strength of his convictions; or what he pretends to himself and others because of his vanity. All these can be beautifully represented in his language form and may mislead us. True, the eroticism of the scientific spirit should not allow prostitution and adultery; but the linguistic part of that spirit is at once spirit and flesh, and where the one is willing, the other is weak.

The chastisement to which the historical and speculative sciences are subjected by the scientific formation of concepts only takes place partially and in the modified form of a positive and, as it were, inner asceticism. The logos calls language back to its inner life, and makes it once more conscious of its better self. Language is persuaded to stop following merely its own euphonies, turn away from the seductions of its rhymes and rhythms, and seek its beauty in truth, in the love of logic, whose vehicle it has to become. The effect of this definite, positive, and liberal education is easily seen if we examine a language with a feebly developed logos, one, for example, which has no philosophic and historical literature or schooling. Such a language is a *patois,* or at most a dialect. Poetry alone, however deep its springs and however great, is not sufficient to lift a language from the level of dialect to that of literature; and daily intercourse, the language that goes from mouth to ear, is also not sufficient as long as it is restricted to serving immediately practical ends and needs. Only when speaker and listener take thought of their language and give a backbone of logic to the intuitive spontaneity of their expression, can they free themselves from the spatially and temporally conditioned externality of their speech, which we call dialect, and create a written language, a literature. A literature that is merely poetic, that has no scientific writings, is no more than written dialect. It is as yet unfledged. In this sense we have to look upon the whole of the literature of the Middle Ages that was written in the vulgar tongue as bound to dialect and as spiritually unfree. For in those times speculative and historical, indeed all scientific thinking, belonged to Latin and existed in the mother tongues only vicariously and because they borrowed from Latin. The Middle Ages certainly possessed original poetry, but no prose of its own; its scientific thought was dependent and not free. In these times of a coarser romanticism, when the medieval spirit is again being extolled, it is well to be reminded of the views of Hegel, which still hold good. "This is the great principle, that in the absolute relationship to God all externality vanishes; with the disappearance of externality, which is the estrangement of the self from itself, the state of subjection, too, is dissolved. And with it praying in an alien tongue, and the prosecution of science in it, are at an end. In language, man is productive; it is his first external expression, the simplest form of existence that he reaches in consciousness. What a man thinks, he also thinks inwardly in terms of language. If he has to express or feel through a strange tongue the things that touch his highest interests, this first form is broken and strange. But now this break with the first emergence into consciousness is healed; it is essential to freedom to be able to be in one's own sphere, to speak and think in one's own language. This is infinitely important, and without this form of coming into one's own, subjective freedom would not have existed. Luther would not have been able to complete his Reformation without translating the Bible into German."

The education of a deeper inwardness through philosophic thought can, of course, be overdone. Through such exaggerations the spoken expression of the individual will become dim, unexternal, uncommunicable through too much concrete matter-of-factness—as we can observe in certain prosaic German philosophers—or the whole language as it is in general use becomes stiff and unsuited to the individuation of personal thinking through a too highly developed system of concepts. The scientific conventions of French prose are an example and a warning of this.

But we can leave these pathological cases of linguistic eroticism for the logos; poetry will see to it that they do not cause any harm in the long run.

Translated by Oscar Oeser

Georg Simmel

Money and the Pace of Life

Finally, there is a third influence by which money contributes to determining the form and order of the contents of life. It deals with the *pace* of their development, which is different for various historical epochs, for different areas of the world at any one time and for individuals of the same group. Our inner world extends, as it were, over two dimensions, the size of which determines the pace of life. The greater the differences between the contents of our imagination at any one time—even with an equal number of conceptions—the more intensive are the experiences of life, and the greater is the span of life through which we have passed. What we experience as the pace of life is the product of the sum total and the depth of its changes. The significance of money in determining the pace of life in a given period is first of all illustrated by the fact that a *change* in monetary circumstances brings about a *change* in the pace of life.

It has been asserted that an increase in the quantity of money—whether through the import of metals or the debasement of currency, through a positive balance of trade or through the issue of paper money—would leave the internal situation of a country completely unchanged. For aside from the few people whose income is fixed and not multipliable, every commodity or piece of work would increase in money value if the supply of money increased; but since everyone is a producer as well as a consumer, then the individual would earn only that much more as he had to spend, and the situation would remain unchanged. Even if such a proportionate increase in prices were the objective effect of an increase in money supply, quite basic psychological changes would occur. No one readily decides to pay a higher price for a commodity than he did hitherto even if his income has increased in the meantime; on the other hand, everyone is easily tempted by an increased income to spend more, without considering that the increased income is balanced by price increases in daily needs. The mere increase in the supply of money that one has in one's hand intensifies—quite regardless of any awareness of its mere relativity—the temptation to spend money, and in so doing promotes a greater turnover in commodities, an increase, acceleration and multiplication in economic conceptions. The basic human trait of interpreting what is relative as an absolute conceals the transitory character of the relationship between an object and a specific amount of money and makes it appear as an objective and permanent relationship. This brings about disturbance and disorientation as soon as one link of the relationship changes. The alteration in what is active and passive is in no way immediately balanced by its psychological effects. When such changes occur the awareness of the economic processes in their previous stability is interrupted from every side and the difference between present and previous circumstances makes itself felt on every side. As long as the new adjustment does not occur, the increase in the quantity of money will cause a constant sense of disorder and psychic shocks, and will thus deepen the differences and the comparative disparity between current conceptions and thereby accelerate the pace of life. It would therefore be to invite misinterpretation were one to infer a "consolidation of society" from the continuous increase in income. It is precisely because of the increase in money income that the lower strata become agitated, a condition that—depending upon one's political viewpoint—is interpreted either as rapacity and mania for innovation, or as healthy development and energy, but which in any case is avoided where a greater stability of income and prices exists. The latter implies at the same time the stability of social distances.

The accelerating effects of an increase in the supply of money on the development of the economic-psychic process are most conspicuously displayed by the after-effects of debased paper money, in the same way as some aspects of normal physiology are most clearly illustrated by pathological and abnormal cases. The unnatural and unfounded influx of money brings about, first of all, a shaky and illogical increase in all prices. The first plethora of money only suffices to satisfy the demand for certain categories of goods.

Therefore one issue of unreliable paper money is followed by another, and the second issue by yet another. "Any pretext"—it was stated of Rhode Island at the beginning of the eighteenth century—"served for the additional multiplication of notes. And if paper money had driven all coins out of the country, *the scarcity of silver* would have been an additional reason for further paper money issues." The tragic consequence of such operations is that a second paper money issue is unavoidable in order to satisfy the demands that are the result of the first issue. This will make itself felt all the more where money itself is the immediate center of the movements: price revolutions that are the result of the inundation of paper money lead to speculation, which in turn requires constantly growing supplies of money. One might say that the acceleration in the pace of social life that is brought about through an increase in the supply of money is most clearly discernible when the purely functional importance of money, without reference to its substantial value, is in question. The acceleration in the whole economic tempo is here raised to a still higher pitch, because, as it were, its origin is purely immanent; that is, it first manifests itself in the acceleration in the printing of money. This interrelationship is demonstrated by the fact that, in countries with a rapid pace of economic development, paper money is particularly apt to increase in quantity. A monetary expert states with reference to North America: "One cannot expect people who are so impatient with small gains, so convinced that wealth can be produced out of nothing or at least out of very little, to be willing to impose upon themselves the self-restrictions which in England or Germany reduce the dangers of paper money issues to a minimum." In particular, however, the acceleration in the pace of life that is brought about through an increase in the supply of paper money results from the upheaval in ownership. This is clearly discernible in the North American paper money economy prior to the War of Independence. The abundantly printed money which had originally circulated at a high value suffered tremendous losses in value. Whoever was wealthy yesterday could be poor today; and conversely, whoever had secured fixed values for borrowed money paid his debts back in devalued money and thus became rich. Not only did it become everyone's urgent interest to transact his economic operations as quickly as possible, to avoid long-term transactions and to learn to take up opportunities immediately; but also, these fluctuations in ownership brought about a sense of continuous change, sudden rifts and convulsions within the economic scene that spread to many other areas of life and were thus experienced as the growing intensity in the trend of economic life or as a quickening of its pace. Compared with stable money, debased money has even been considered to be of specific utility: it has been claimed that it is desirable to have debts repaid in debased money, because debtors are generally active economic producers, whereas creditors are mostly passive consumers who contribute much less positively to economic transactions. The fiduciary note issue was not yet legal currency at the beginning of the eighteenth century in Connecticut and at the beginning of the nineteenth century in England, yet every creditor was obliged to accept it in payment of debts. The specific significance of money for the pace of economic life is further substantiated by the fact that the crisis that occurs after the excessive issue of paper money retards and paralyzes economic life to a corresponding degree. Here too the role of money in the objective development of the economy corresponds to its functions as a mediator in the subjective aspect of that development: for it has been rightly pointed out that exchange is slowed down by the multiplication of the means of exchange beyond what is actually required, just as the increase in the number of brokers eases transactions up to a certain point beyond which, however, it operates as a barrier to transactions. Generally speaking, the more mobile money is, the less secure is its value because everyone tries to get rid of it as quickly as possible. The obvious objection, that trade requires two people and that the ease with which base money is given away is paralyzed by the hesitancy to accept it, is not quite valid, because base money is still better than no money at all (and the same cannot always be claimed for poor merchandise). The interest in money as such has to be discounted against the distaste for base money on the part of the seller of merchandise. Hence the interest of the buyer and the reluctance of the seller to exchange commodities for base money do not exactly balance since the latter is weaker and cannot adequately limit the acceleration of circulation through the former. On the other hand, the owner of base money, or money that is valuable only under specific circumstances, has a lively interest in the preservation of the circumstances that give value to his possessions. When in the middle of the sixteenth century the princes' debts had grown to such an extent that there were widespread national bankruptcies, and when in France the sale of annuities was practiced to an excessive extent, then it was stated in their defense—since they were very insecure—that in so doing the loyalty of the citizen as an owner of annuities to the king and his interest in saving him would thereby be greatly strengthened. It is significant that the term "partisan" originally referred to a money lender who was party to a loan to the Crown, while later, owing to the solidarity of interests between such bankers and the minister of finance under Mazarin and Fouquet, the term acquired the meaning of an "unconditional supporter" and it has preserved this meaning ever since. This occurred during the period of greatest unreliability in the French finances, whereas during their improvement under Sully the partisans (money-lenders) moved into the background. And later Mirabeau, when introducing the assignat, emphasized that wherever the currency existed the desire for its reliability ought to exist: "You consider a defender necessary for the measures taken and a creditor interested in your success." Thus, such money creates a specific grouping of interests and, on the basis of a new tendency towards inertia, a new animation of contrasts.

However, this assumption that these consequences of an increasing amount of money in circulation make themselves felt to a greater extent in so far as cheaper money affects producers and consumers to the same extent is far too simple. In reality such phenomena are much more complicated and volatile. This may be seen, first of all, in objective terms. The increase in the supply of money at first brings about an increase in the prices of only some commodities and leaves others as they were. It has been assumed that because of the influence of American precious metals the prices of European goods since the sixteenth century has risen in a definite and slow order of succession. The increase in the supply of money within a country always at first affects only a specific group that takes care of the flood of money. First and foremost, a rise in the prices of those goods will occur for which members of this group compete, whereas other commodities, the price of which is determined by mass consumption, will remain cheap. The gradual influx of larger supplies of money leads to attempts to balance them out, the previous price relationship of commodities is disrupted, and the budget of each household becomes accustomed to disturbances and shifts. In short, the fact that any increase in the supply of money affects the prices of goods *unevenly* necessarily has a disturbing effect upon the process of interpretation of the situation on the part of economically active persons. It leads to widespread experiences of differentiation, to the breakdown of existing parities and to demands for attempts to balance them out. It is certainly true that this influence—partly accelerating, partly retarding—is a result not only of the unevenness of prices but also of the unevenness within money values themselves. That is, it is the result not only of the devaluation of money but, perhaps even more so, of the continuous fluctuation in the value of money. It has been said of the period prior to the great English coinage reform of 1570 that "if all shillings had been reduced to the value of groats, transactions would have adjusted themselves relatively easily. But the fact that one shilling equaled six pence, another ten, and a third one eight, six, or even four pence made every exchange a controversy!"

The unevenness in the prices of commodities results in a situation in which certain persons and occupations profit by a change in money values in a quite specific manner while certain others suffer considerably. In former times this was especially true of the peasantry. Toward the end of the seventeenth century, the English peasant, ignorant and helpless as he was, actually became squeezed between those people who owed him money and paid him its face value, and those to whom he owed money and insisted on payment by weight. Later the same was true in India at every new devaluation of money: if the farmer sold his harvest, he never knew whether the money received would suffice to pay the rent for his mortgage. It has long been known that wages are the last to be adjusted to a general increase in prices. The weaker a social group is, the slower and more sparingly does the increase in the amount of money trickle through to it. Frequently, an increase in income is attained only after an increase in the prices of that strata's consumer goods has long been in force. Out of this process, shocks and agitations of all kinds emerge. The growing differences between the strata require constant alertness because, in view of the new circumstances, conservative and defensive attitudes are no longer sufficient. Instead, positive struggle and conquest are required in order to preserve the *status quo ante* with regard to the relationship between the strata as well as the standard of living of individual strata. This is one of the basic reasons why every increase in the quantity of money has such a disturbing effect upon the pace of social life, since it produces new differences on top of the existing ones and divisions, even in the budget of the individual family, that must constantly accelerate and deepen the level of awareness. It is quite obvious that a considerable decline in the amount of money will bring about similar effects except that they will be in reverse. The close relationship between money and the pace of life is illustrated by the fact that an increase as well as a decrease in the amount of money, as a consequence of its uneven diffusion, brings about those manifestations of differentiation that are mirrored psychologically in break-downs, irritations and the compression of mental processes. This implication of *changes* in the quantity of money is only a phenomenon or an accumulation of the significance of money for the relationship of objects, that is for their psychic equivalents. Money has brought about new equations between objects. We compare them, one with another, according to their utility value, their aesthetic, ethical, eudaemonistic and labor value, with reference to hundreds of relationships of quantity and quality, so that their identity in one of these relationships may coincide with total lack of identity in another. Thus, their money value creates an equation and comparison between them that is in no way a constant function of other values, yet is always the expression of some notions of value that are the origin and combination of others. Every value standpoint that orders and ranks things differently and cuts across the usual mode of ordering things provides, at the same time, a new vitality for their relationship, a suggestion of as-yet unknown combinations and syntheses, of the discovery of their affinities and differences. This is because our minds are constantly endeavouring to counterbalance what is irregular and to force differentiation upon the uniform. In so far as money confers upon things within a given sphere a sameness and differentiation to a greater extent than any other value standpoint, it thereby stimulates innumerable endeavors to combine these with the ranking derived from the other values in the sense of these two tendencies.

The Concentration of Monetary Activity

In addition to the results of changes in the supply of money, which suggest that the pace of life is, as it were, a function of those changes, the compression of the contents of life is evident in another consequence of monetary transactions. It is a peculiar feature of monetary transactions that they tend to concentrate in relatively few places. As far as local diffusion is concerned, it is possible to establish a scale of economic objects. Here I shall indicate only some of the characteristic levels. The scale commences with agriculture, which by its very nature resists every attempt to concentrate its different areas; agriculture is inevitably bound up with the original dispersal of space. Industrial production can be compressed to some extent: the factory is a spatial condensation compared with artisan production and domestic industry while the modern industrial center is a manufacturing microcosm, in which every kind of raw material in the world is transformed into objective forms, whose origins are dispersed throughout the world. The most remote link in this scale is money transactions. Owing to the abstractness of its form, money has no definite relationship to space: it can exercise its effects upon the most remote areas. It is even, as it were, at any moment the central point of a circle of potential effects. On the other hand, it also enables the largest amounts of value to be condensed into the most minute form—such as the $10 million check that was once signed by Jay Gould. To the possibility of condensing values by means of money and of condensing money by means of its increasingly abstract forms, there corresponds the possibility of condensing monetary transactions. In so far as the economy of a country is increasingly based upon money, financial activities become concentrated in large centers of money transactions. In contrast to the country, the city has always been the seat of money transactions and this relationship also holds for comparisons between small towns and cities. An English historian has stated that in its whole history London, though it never functioned as the heart of England but sometimes as its brain, always operated as its purse. Similarly, it was said that already at the end of the Roman Republic every penny that was spent in Gaul entered the books of financiers in Rome. This centrifugal force that finance possesses supports the interest of both parties: that of the borrowers because they can obtain cheaper money because of the competition of inflowing capital (the interest rate in Rome was fifty percent lower than the average in ancient times), and that of the creditors because, although money does not have such a high value as in outlying areas, they are sure of chances for investment at any time, which is more important than lending the money at a higher rate in isolated areas. As a result, it has also been pointed out that contractions in the central money market can be more easily overcome than at the various outlying points on the periphery. Through the process of centralization that is inherent in money, the preliminary stage of accumulation in the hands of scattered individuals has been surmounted. The centralization of monetary transactions on the stock exchanges counteracted the superior power that individuals could wield by monetary means. For instance, even though the stock exchanges of Lyons and Antwerp brought enormous gains to individual money magnates during the fifteenth century, they objectified the power of money in a central institution that was superior to the power and rules of even the most powerful individuals, and they prevented the situation from arising in which a single financial house could determine the trend of world history to the extent that the Fuggers had once done.

The more basic reason for the evolution of financial centers is obviously to be found in the relativity of money. This is because, on the one hand, money expresses only value relationships between commodities, while on the other the value of every definite quantity of money cannot be as directly ascertained as can that of any other commodity; it has significance only in comparison with the total amount that is offered. Therefore, the maximum concentration of money at one point, the continuous competition of huge amounts, the balancing of a major part of supply and demand as such, will lead to the more accurate determination of its value and to its greater utilization. A bushel of grain has a particular importance at any one place, no matter how isolated and regardless of its money value. A certain quantity of money, however, is important only in relation to other values. Hence, in order to attain a stable and just valuation, money has to be confronted with as many other values as possible. This is the reason why not only "everything presses for gold"—men as well as things—but also why money itself presses for "everything." It seeks to come together with other money, with all possible kinds of values and their owners. The same interrelationship operates in the opposite direction: the convergence of large numbers of people brings about a particularly strong need for money. In Germany, one of the main demands for money rose out of annual fairs organized by local lords in order to profit from the exchange of currency and the tax on goods. Through this enforced concentration of commercial transactions at a single point in a larger territory, the inclination to buy and sell was greatly increased and the need for money thereby first became a general necessity. Wherever increasingly large numbers of people come together, money becomes relatively that much more in demand. Because of its indifferent nature, money is the most suitable bridge and means of communication between many and diverse people. The more people there are, the fewer are the spheres within which they can base their transactions except through monetary interests.

The Mobilization of Values

All this illustrates to what great extent money symbolizes acceleration in the pace of life and how it measures itself against the number and diversity of inflowing and alternating impressions and stimuli. The tendency of money to converge and to accumulate, if not in the hands of individuals then in fixed local centers; to bring together the interests of and thereby individuals themselves; to establish contact between them on a common ground and thus, as determined by the form of value that money represents, to concentrate the most diverse elements in the smallest possible space—in short, this tendency and capacity of money has the psychological effect of enhancing the variety and richness of life, that is of increasing the pace of life. It has already been emphasized elsewhere that the modern concept of time—as a value determined by its usefulness and scarcity—first became accepted with the growth of capitalism in Germany when, during the fifteenth century, world trade and financial centers developed together with the quick turnover of cheap money. It was in this period that the church clocks began to strike at every quarter of an hour; and Sebastian Franck, who was the first to recognize the revolutionary significance of money even though in a most pessimistic manner, first called time an expensive commodity. The most characteristic symbol of all these correlations is the stock exchange. Economic values and interests are here completely reduced to their monetary expression. The stock exchange and its representatives have achieved the closest possible local assembly in order to carry out the clearance, distribution and balancing of money in the quickest manner possible. This twofold condensation of values into the money form and of monetary transactions into the form of the stock exchange makes it possible for values to be rushed through the greatest number of hands in the shortest possible time. The New York Stock Exchange, for instance, has a turnover every year that is five times the amount of the cotton harvest through speculation in cotton, and even in 1887 fifty times the total yearly production of oil was sold there. The frequency of the turnover increases with fluctuations in the quoted prices of a particular value. Indeed, the fluctuations in the rate of exchange was the reason why regular stock exchange dealings in royal promissory notes [*Königsbriefen*] developed at all in the sixteenth century. For these notes, which reflected the changing credit status of, for instance, the French Crown, provided a completely different inducement to buying and selling than had previously existed with stable values. Changes in valuation are greatly increased and even often brought about by the flexible quality of money to express them directly. And this is the cause as well as the effect of the fact that the stock exchange is the center of monetary transactions. It is, as it were, the geometrical focal point of all these changes in valuation, and at the same time the place of greatest excitement in economic life. Its sanguine-choleric oscillations between optimism and pessimism, its nervous reaction to ponderable and imponderable matters, the swiftness with which every factor affecting the situation is grasped and forgotten again—all this represents an extreme acceleration in the pace of life, a feverish commotion and compression of its fluctuations, in which the specific influence of money upon the course of psychological life becomes most clearly discernible.

Finally, the relative speed of circulation of money in relation to all other objects must immediately increase the general pace of life wherever money becomes the general center of interest. The roundness of coins which makes them "roll" symbolizes the rhythm of the movement that money imparts to transactions. Even where coins originally possessed corners, their constant use must have smoothed the corners and rounded them off; physical necessity has thus provided the most useful form of instrument for the intensity of transactions. For centuries in the countries bordering on the Nile there even existed globular money composed of glass, wood or agate—the differences in the material used suggests that its form was the reason for its popularity. It is no coincidence that the principle of "rounding off" is applied with reference to large sums of money, since this principle corresponds to the expanding money economy. "Rounding off" is a relatively modern term. The most primitive form of checks payable to the English Treasury were tallies for any irregular amount and they frequently circulated as money. Only in the eighteenth century were they replaced by endorsable paper bills which represented rounded-off amounts from £5 upward. It is surprising how little attention was formerly paid to rounding off, even for large amounts of money. That the Fuggers in 1530 agreed to pay 275,333 florins and 20 crowns to the Emperor Ferdinand, and that Emperor Maximilian II in 1577 owed them 220,674 florins, are not isolated cases. The development of the institution of shares followed a similar course. The joint stock of the East India Company in the Netherlands in the seventeenth century could be split up into any proportions that might be desired. Only the acceleration of transactions finally brought about the situation in which a fixed unit of 500 Flemish pounds became the only possible unit of ownership or "share" in its trade. Even today in the retail trade, monetary transactions are calculated in rounded off amounts in places with a considerable volume of money transactions, whereas prices in more remote regions would appear to be rarely rounded off.

The above-mentioned development from inconveniently large to smaller coins and money orders clearly has the same significance for the acceleration of the speed of transactions as the rounding off process, which itself suggests a physical analogy. The need to have money in small amounts increases with the speed of transactions. In this context, it is significant that in 1844 an English bank note circulated on average of fifty-seven days before being redeemed, whereas in 1871 it circulated for only thirty-seven days! If one compares the velocity of circulation of landed property with that of money, then this immediately illustrates the difference in the pace of life between periods when the one or the other was the focal point of economic activity. One thinks, for example, of the character of tax payments with reference to external and internal fluctuations depending on the object on which they were levied. In Anglo-Saxon and Norman England taxes were imposed exclusively upon land ownership: during the twelfth century levies were imposed on the possession of cattle; shortly afterwards, certain portions of mobile property (the fourth, seventh and thirteenth parts) became taxable. The objects of taxation became more and more diverse until finally money income was made the proper basis of taxation. In so doing, taxation attains a hitherto-unknown degree of flexibility and adjustability, and the result is a much greater variability and yearly fluctuation in the contribution of individuals, combined with a greater stability of the total revenue produced. The direct significance of and emphasis upon landed property or money for the pace of life may explain the great value that very conservative peoples place upon agriculture. The Chinese are convinced that only agriculture secures the peace and perpetuation of states, and perhaps for this reason they have imposed a huge tax upon the sale of land, so that most sales of land are carried out privately and without official registration. But where the acceleration of economic life that is instigated by money has asserted itself, it seeks to impose its rhythm upon the resistant form of landed property. During the eighteenth century the state of Pennsylvania provided mortgages for private land purchase and permitted the bills to be circulated as paper money. Benjamin Franklin stated that these bills were, in reality, *coined land*. Similarly, in Germany it has been asserted by conservatives that the legislation of recent decades concerning mortgages will bring about a liquidation of landed property and will transform it into some kind of paper money that could be given away in bills of any desired amount so that, as Waldeck also puts it, landed property would seem to exist only in order to be sold by auction. Not surprisingly, modern life too mobilizes its contents in the most superficial sense and in several less well known respects. In medieval times and also during the Renaissance, what we today term "movables" or furnishings in the strict sense were little in demand. Wardrobes, sideboards and benches were built into the paneling; tables and chairs were so heavy that they were often immovable, and small movable fixtures were almost nonexistent. Subsequently, furniture, like capital, has become mobile.

Finally, I wish to illustrate by means of a legal regulation the power of the trend in the money economy to subject other contents of life to its own pace. It is an old legal precept that an object that has been taken away from its legal owner has to be returned to him in all circumstances, even if the present owner has acquired it legitimately. Only with reference to money is this precept invalid: according to Roman as well as modern law, money that has been stolen cannot be taken away from a third person who has acquired it in good faith and returned to the original owner. This exception is obviously necessitated by the practice of business transactions which would otherwise be considerably handicapped, disturbed, and disrupted. But recently, however, this restitutory dispensation has been extended to cover all other objects that come under rule of the commercial code. This implies that the acceleration in commercial transactions makes every commodity similar to money. It allows them to function only as money value and subjects them to the same regulations that money itself requires for the purpose of facilitating its transactions!

Constancy and Flux as Categories for Comprehending the World

The following consideration may serve to characterize the contribution that money makes to the determination of the pace of life by its specific nature and in addition to its technical consequences that have already been mentioned above. The more precise analysis of the concepts of constancy and change reveals a dual opposition in the form in which they are realized. If we consider the substance of the world, then we easily end up in the idea of an unchangeable being, which suggests, through the exclusion of any increase or decrease in things, the character of absolute constancy. If, on the other hand, we concentrate upon the formation of this substance, then constancy is completely transcended; one form is incessantly transformed into another and the world takes on the aspect of a *perpetuum mobile*. This is the cosmologically, and often metaphysically interpreted, dual aspect of being. However, if a thorough-going empirical method is applied, this contrast between constancy and flux takes on a different aspect. If we observe the image of the world as it immediately presents itself to us, then there are certain forms that do persist through time, whereas the real elements of which they are composed are in continuous motion. Thus, for example, the rainbow persists despite the constantly changing position of the water particles; the organic form persists despite the constant exchange of material of which it is composed. Indeed, in every inorganic object only the relationship and the interaction of the smallest parts persist, whereas the parts themselves, hidden to our eyes, are in constant molecular flux. Thus, reality itself is in a restless flux, and though we are unable to observe this because, as it were, we lack the sharpness of sight, the forms and constellations of movements solidify in the appearance of the enduring object.

As well as these two contrasts in the application of the concepts of constancy and flux to the world as it is perceived, there exists a third. Constancy may have a meaning that goes beyond any extended period of time. The simplest, but in this context a sufficient, instance of this is the law of nature. The validity of the law of nature rests on the fact that a certain constellation of elements necessarily results in a definite effect. This necessity is totally independent of *when* the preconditions present themselves in reality. Whether it be once or a million times, at this moment or in a hundred thousand years hence, the validity of the law is eternal in the sense of timelessness. Its essence and very notion exclude any change or motion. It does not matter, at this point, that we cannot ascribe unconditional validity with unconditional certainty to any single law of nature. This is not only because our comprehension, which cannot distinguish between the recurrent but fortuitous combination of phenomena and actual causal relationships, is necessarily subject to correctibility, but rather, and above all, because each law of nature is valid only for a definite state of mind, whereas for another one the truth would lie in a different formulation of the same factual state of affairs. However, since the human mind is liable to develop no matter how slowly and indiscernibly, there can be no law that is valid at a given moment that is not subject to change in the course of time. Yet this change refers only to the perceptible content of the law of nature and to its meaning and concept. The notion of a law—which exists regardless of any instance of its imperfect realization but which none the less justifies the idea and gives it meaning—rests upon that absence of all motion, upon that validity that is independent of all given conditions because they are changeable. There must be a corresponding phenomenon in the form of motion to this distinctive absolute form of persistence. Just as constancy may extend over any extent of time, no matter how long, until any relationship to a specific moment of time is simply dissolved by the eternal validity of the law of nature or the mathematical formula, so too change and motion may be conceived of as absolutes, as if a specific measurement of time for them did not exist. If all motion proceeds between a "here" and a "there," then through this absolute motion—the *species aeternitatis* in reverse—the "here" completely disappears. Whereas timeless objects are valid in the form of permanency, their opposites are valid in the form of transition, of non-permanency. I am in no doubt that this pair of opposites is comprehensive enough to develop a view of the world out of them. If, on the one hand, one knew all the laws that control reality, then reality would actually be reduced to its absolute contents, to its eternal timeless significance. This would be true even though reality could not yet be constructed on this basis since the law as such, according to its ideal content, is completely indifferent toward any individual instance of its realization. But it is precisely because the content of reality is completely absorbed in these laws, which constantly produce effects out of causes and simultaneously allow these effects to operate as causes, that it is possible, on the other hand, to perceive reality, the concrete, historical, experiential appearance of the world in that absolute flux that is indicated by Heraclitus's symbolic formulation. If one reduces the view of the world to this opposition, then everything of duration, everything that points beyond the immediate moment, is extracted from reality and assembled in the ideal realm of mere laws. In reality itself things do not last for any length of time; through the restlessness with which they offer themselves at any moment to the application of a law, every form becomes immediately dissolved in the very moment when it emerges; it lives, as it were, only by being destroyed; every consolidation of form to lasting objects—no matter how short they last—is an incomplete interpretation that is unable to follow the motion of reality at its own pace. The unity of the whole of being is completely comprehended in the unity of what simply persists and what simply does not persist.

Money as the Historical Symbol of the Relative Character of Existence

There is no more striking symbol of the completely dynamic character of the world than that of money. The meaning of money lies in the fact that it will be given away. When money stands still, it is no longer money according to its specific value and significance. The effect that it occasionally exerts in a state of repose arises out of an anticipation of its further motion. Money is nothing but the vehicle for a movement in which everything else that is not in motion is completely extinguished. It is, as it were, an *actus purus;* it lives in continuous self-alienation from any given point and thus forms the counterpart and direct negation of all being in itself.

But perhaps it represents, no less as a symbol, the opposite form, that of defining reality. The individual amount of money is, in fact, by its very nature in constant motion. But this is only because its value relates to the individual objects of value, just as the general law relates to the concrete conditions in which it realizes itself. If the law, which itself stands above all motions, none the less represents the form and basis of all motion, then the abstract value of wealth that is not subdivided into individual values and that is represented by money is, as it were, the soul and purpose of economic activities. As a tangible item money is the most ephemeral thing in the external–practical world; yet in its content it is the most stable, since it stands as the point of indifference and balance between all other phenomena in the world. The ideal purpose of money, as well as of the law, is to be a measure of things without being measured itself, a purpose that can be realized fully only by an endless development. Money expresses the relationship that exists between economic goods. Money itself remains stable with reference to the changes in relationships, as does a numerical proportion which reflects the relationship between many and changing objects, and as does the formula of the law of gravity with reference to material masses and their infinitely varying motion. Just as the general concept in its logical validity is independent of the number and modification of its realizations, indicating, as it were, their lawfulness, so too money—that is, the inner rationale by which the single piece of metal or paper becomes money—is the general concept of objects in so far as they are economic. They do not need to be economic; but if they wish to be, they can do so only by adjusting to the law of valuation that is embodied in money.

The observation that this one institution participates equally in the two basic forms of reality may explain the reality of these two forms. Their significance is actually a relative one; that is, each finds its logical and psychological possibility for interpreting the world in the other. Only because reality is in constant motion is there any sense in asserting its opposite: the ideal system of eternally valid lawfulness. Conversely, it is only because such lawfulness exists that we are able to comprehend and grasp that stream of existence that would otherwise disintegrate into total chaos. The general relativity of the world, at first glance familiar to only one side of this opposition, in reality also engulfs the other side and proves to be its mistress where it only appeared to be a party. In the same way, money transcends its significance as a single economic value in order to represent abstract economic value in general and to entwine both functions in an indissoluble correlation in which neither is the first.

Money, as an institution of the historical world, symbolizes the behavior of objects and establishes a special relationship between itself and them. The more the life of society becomes dominated by monetary relationships, the more the relativistic character of existence finds its expression in conscious life, since money is nothing other than a special form of the embodied relativity of economic goods that signifies their value. Just as the absolutist view of the world represents a definite stage of intellectual development in correlation with the corresponding practical, economic and emotional conditions of human affairs, so the relativistic view of the world seems to express the monetary relationship of adjustment on the part of our intellect. More accurate, it is confirmed by the opposing images of social and subjective life, in which money has found its real effective embodiment and the reflected symbol of its forms and movements.

Translated by Tom Bottomore and David Frisby

Gustav Radbruch

The Concept of Law

He who shies away from the idea finally does not even have the concept.—J. W. von Goethe

The question of the concept of law seems at first glance to belong to legal science and not to legal philosophy. Indeed, legal science has again and again attempted to get the concept of law inductively out of the various legal phenomena; and there can be no doubt as a matter of principle that it is possible by comparing the various legal phenomena to get the general concept underlying all of them. However, in such a manner we may only get the concept of law, but we cannot reason it out. General concepts, as many as one pleases, may be derived from experience, such as, all men with a certain initial or with a certain date of birth. But the generality of such concepts, in relation to a larger or smaller circle of individual facts, does not guarantee their value. That they are not accidental but necessary general concepts, that is, efficient and fruitful ones, can never be shown by way of generalizing induction. That the concept of law is such a *necessary* general concept is to be demonstrated now, by the manner in which it is derived.

Law: The Reality Directed toward the Idea of Law. The concept of law is a cultural concept, that is, a concept of a reality related to values, a reality the meaning of which is to serve a value. Law is the reality the meaning of which is to serve a value. Law is the reality the meaning of which is to serve the legal value, the idea of law. The concept of law thus is oriented toward the idea of law.

Now the idea of law can be none other than justice. *Est autem jus a justitia, sicut a matre sua, ergo prius fuit justitia quam jus* (but law issues from justice as from its mother, as it were, so there has been justice prior to law), reads the gloss on I.I *pr. Dig.* I, I. But we are also justified in stopping at justice as an ultimate point of departure, for the just, like the good, the true, or the beautiful, is an absolute value, that is, a value that cannot be derived from any other value.

Justice as the Idea of Law. One might be tempted to regard justice merely as a form in which the moral good appears. Indeed, this is correct if justice is regarded as a quality of man, a virtue, as in Ulpian's words: *constans ac perpetua voluntas jus suum cuique tribuendi* (the constant and perpetual will to allot to everyone his right). Yet such justice in a subjective sense cannot be defined but as the sentiment directed toward objective justice, in the way in which veracity, for instance, is directed toward truth. Objective justice alone is in question here. But the object evaluated by objective justice is quite different from the object toward the moral value judgment is directed. Always, what is morally good is but a human being: a human will, a human sentiment, a human character. Even social ethics evaluates man, in his relations with other men to be sure, yet it does not evaluate those relations themselves. But just, in the sense of objective justice, can be only a relation between human beings. The ideal of the moral good is represented by an ideal human being; the ideal of justice is represented by an ideal social order.

From another point of view, too, justice is of two kinds. We may call "just" either the application or observance of a law, or that law itself. The former kind of justice, especially the justice of the judge true to the law, might better be called righteousness. Here, at any rate, we are concerned not with that justice which is measured by positive law, but rather with that by which positive law is measured.

Justice in this sense means equality. But equality itself admits of different significations. On the one hand, as regards its object, it may be related to goods or to men: the wage that corresponds to the value of the work is just, but so, too, is the punishment that is meted out to one man and the other alike. On the other hand, as regards its standard, equality may be absolute or relative: the wage equal to the work, as against the punishment of several men proportionate to their guilt.

Both distinctions are combined in Aristotle's famous doctrine of justice. Absolute equality between goods, e.g., between work and wage, or between damage and compensation, is called by him "commutative" justice. Relative equality in treating different persons, e.g., taxation according to ability to bear the tax, or relief according to need, or reward and punishment according to merit and guilt, is the essence of "distributive" justice. Commutative justice requires at least two persons, while distributive justice requires at least three. The two persons in the former case confront each other as co-equals; but of the three or more persons in the latter case one, who imposes burdens upon or grants advantages to the others, is superior to them. Commutative justice is justice in the relation of coordination; distributive justice is to prevail in the relation of super- and subordination. Commutative justice is the justice of private law; distributive justice is the justice of public law.

This is sufficient to clarify the mutual relation between the two kinds of justice. Commutative justice is justice between persons co-equal as to their rights. Therefore, it presupposes an act of distributive justice which has granted to those concerned equality of rights, equal capacity to act, equal status. Distributive justice, then, is the prototype of justice. In it we have found the idea of justice, toward which the concept of law must be oriented. This is not to say that law could be explained exhaustively by founding it upon justice. On the one hand, the principle of distributive justice does not say who is to be treated as equal and who as unequal; rather it presupposes that, from a viewpoint which it does not of itself provide, equality or inequality has already been established. Equality, indeed, is not something that is given; things and men are as unequal "as one egg is to another." Always equality is but an abstraction, from a certain point of view, of a given inequality. On the other hand, from the idea of distributive justice we may gather only the relation and not the kind of the treatment of different persons: we may gather whether theft in relation to murder is less severely punishable, but not whether the thief is to be hanged and the murderer to be broken upon the wheel or whether the thief is to be fined and the murderer to be committed to the penitentiary. In either direction, justice needs to be complemented by other principles if rules of right law are to be derived from it. Justice is not the exhaustive principle of law. It is rather the specific principle of law, that which governs the determination of the concept of law: law is the reality the meaning of which is to serve justice.

Equity. In the struggle to govern law, however, justice is rivaled by equity. The dilemma that equity is to be better than justice and yet not quite opposed to justice, but rather a kind of justice, has troubled men as early as Aristotle's famous chapter 5:14* of the *Nicomachean Ethics.* But again Aristotle already indicated the solution that justice and equity are not different values but different ways to arrive at the unitary value of law. Justice regards the individual case from the viewpoint of the general norm; equity in any individual case looks for the proper law of that case, which, however, must also be susceptible of being elevated finally to a general law; for equity as well as justice is ultimately generalizing. Thus, in the distinction between justice and equity, we again confront the previously suggested methodical distinction between a deductive derivation of the right law from general principles and an intuitive grasp of the right law out of "the nature of the thing." Equity is the justice of the individual case. So regard to equity does not compel us to vary our formula: that law is the reality the meaning of which is to serve justice.

Derivation of the Concept of Law. The foregoing would indicate what approach to take in determining the concept of law, but it would not yet give us the determination of the concept itself. We want to know of what kind that reality is that is intended to serve justice; and we are indeed able to draw conclusions from that meaning of legal reality back to the essence of legal reality. Justice means rightness as related especially to the law. By virtue of this material qualification of the idea, we are able to draw from the idea conclusions as to the matter for which it is valid.

The realities the meaning of which is to serve ideas are of the psychological nature of evaluations and demands. Thus, they represent a peculiar kind of reality, intermediate between the idea and the other realities. As psychological facts, they belong to reality themselves; but at the same time they rise above the other realities

---

*[In the Oxford translation of the *Nicomachean Ethics* (W. D. Ross, 1942), the passage on "equity" is in book 5, sec. 10.]

by applying standards and raising demands. Of this kind are conscience, the cultural phenomenon related to the moral idea; taste, that related to the aesthetic idea; and reason, that related to the logical idea. The factual phenomenon which in the same way corresponds to the legal idea is the precept. It, too, may be said to have the same peculiar character of reality, that is, both positivity and normativity. Furthermore, the precept as a reality related especially to the idea of law (i.e., justice) shares with justice its subject of reference: the mutual relations between men. It is social in character. As it is the essence of justice ultimately to shape those relations in the sense of equality, so it is essential to the legal precept in its meaning to be directed toward equality, to claim to be susceptible of generalization or to be general in character. A precept addressed to an individual human being or an individual relationship, say, a "measure" according to Article 48 of the Reich Commission [of 1919],* is nevertheless a legal rule if its individual character is due merely to the fact that its legal terms apply only to that individual person or relationship; that is, if only the substratum of the precept is individual in character, but not, if the precept itself is individual in character. We summarize the essence of the legal precept as both positive and normative, both social and general. In this sense we define law as *the complex of general precepts for the living-together of human beings.*

This determination of the concept of law has not been obtained inductively from the various legal phenomena but has been derived deductively from the idea of law. It is thus not juridical but prejuridical; that is, in relation to legal science, it is *a priori* in nature. The concept of law is not an ordinary and accidental concept, but is a necessary general concept. The law is law not because the various legal phenomena may be classified under it; rather, contrariwise, legal phenomena are "legal" only because they are embraced by the concept of law. The concept of law has not been set up above the legal phenomena by themselves, democratically as it

*[Art. 48, the "dictatorship article" of the Constitution of Weimar, provided in part as follows: "If in the German Reich public safety and order are to a considerable extent disturbed or endangered, the Reich President may take the measures requisite for the restoration of public safety and order; if necessary, he may intervene with the aid of the armed forces." "Of all measures taken according to . . . this article the Reich President shall immediately advise the Reichstag. Upon the demand of the Reichstag the measures shall be repealed."]

were, but it has assumed its rule over them "by the grace of God," that is, by the grace of the idea. Only when the chaos of what is given is considered from the viewpoint of the concept of law is the juridically essential separated from the juridically unessential, as water and land were separated by the creative word. If, in the words of Savigny, law is taken for "the very life of men, viewed from a particular aspect," or considered from a particular point of view, this point of view constitutive of the legal universe is the *a priori* concept of law.

A Priori Legal Concepts. However, the concept of law comprises a number of particular legal concepts which share its *a priori* nature, that is, the quality of being not products but instruments of legal science, not accidental generalizations of empirical legal phenomena but indispensable categories of juridical thought. Thus, from the nature of law as both positive and normative there results the concept of the legal rule, and with the legal rule result the concepts of its elements. It may be said *a priori* (that is, in advance) that there can be no legal rule that does not rule something, thus involving both the something and the ruling: the state of facts and the legal consequence. Inseparably bound up with the qualities of positivity and normativity, too, is the question of where law is created, the question of the source of law. There is no law that does not owe an answer, and is not able to give an answer, to the question of the origin of its normative character. From the normative character there results the twofold possibility of acting in accordance with it or against it, and therewith result the concepts of legality and illegality, before which again each legal fact has the *a priori* duty to identify itself. From the validity of the law for the living together of men, their mutual relations, there follows that its contents must be to establish legal relations, and as their elements, legal duties and legal rights, subjective rights. No legal order is conceivable that may not be into legal relations, rights and duties. Again, rights and duties are not conceivable without subjects to whom they belong, nor without objects to which they relate. Legal subject and legal object are again concepts which cannot be dispensed with by one legal order while being used by another but which are necessary to any conceivable law.

Later on in our discussions we shall meet still further legal concepts *a priori*. For the *a priori* is a relational concept, characterizing a relation of certain concepts to certain factual materials. Thus, the legal concept as an *a priori* concept fully unfolds only against the fullness of legal facts; and these unfoldings can no more be exhaustively enumerated in advance than can the facts with which the legal concept will be confronted. So the idea of a "table of categories," that is, a symmetrical schedule of innumerable *a priori* legal concepts, cannot be realized.

Translated by Kurt Wilk

Robert Bosch

How Can We Achieve Economic Harmony?

When faced with the question as to why such a serious conflict besets humanity almost all over the world, in any case not only in Germany, one comes to understand that this conflict is due in large part to the fact that the so-called ruling classes have not understood how to achieve a correct relationship to the common people.

There is no doubt that this conflict of opinions has as much to do with political concerns as it does with economic ones. It must be admitted, however, that economic measures are generally assessed as more important and that the necessity of improvements in the political situation is only maintained by the most progressive sector of the upper class. At the same time though, it can be said that political interest and understanding have generally increased in recent years, in spite of the broad world-weariness that is, unfortunately, so evident today. But it must also be admitted that the political objectives are more easily attainable than the economic ones. It is just this that makes the resolution of the conflict so difficult.

One would think that once political equality had been largely accomplished by general, direct, and secret voting rights for both men and women, at least in Germany, the political conditions would have been created that could provide a context for the achievement of situations as satisfactory as are generally possible.

Politically, much was accomplished by the events of 1918. Economically, however, little was achieved. As a result, the conflict remained. Between the ruling classes and the masses there exists a gaping disharmony that prevents our social body from healing.

The upper class is responsible for this situation, at least to the extent that it could have prevented the cleft from becoming as broad and deep as it actually is. Above all, the responsibility of the upper class lies in the fact that it short-sightedly, but consistently obstructed even legitimate efforts to improve the political and social situation of laborers. It can, however, be said that employers have begun to make decisive progress in reconsidering their positions. Understandably, those members of the upper class who are over fifty years of age continue to oppose reforms. The older one is, the more difficult it is to adjust. But in general it seems as if many employers have learned nothing!

If we see a lack of compromise on one side though, we must recognize that there are excessive, or rather, impossible demands on the other. The general implementation of socialized production is one demand that is impossible under current conditions. This demand for the complete socialization of the economy is based on the writings of Karl Marx. Clearly, this is not the place for a critique of the purely scientific inquiries of Karl Marx. I can, however, say that the teachings advanced by Marx, like, for example, the pauperization theory that was so central to his argument, have been shown to be incorrect by the successes achieved through labor struggles in the intervening years. Marx was also wrong to the extent that he assumed conditions in all enterprises would always mirror the situation in his time and in a particular textile factory that was managed by his friend Engels. In this factory, the owner, if he so wished, could sell an entire year's production to a single dealer and buy the raw materials needed for this production in a single day. The owner of such a factory was certainly not difficult to replace and, if it were so simple everywhere, socialization would certainly be fundamentally easier than it has been in actuality. The situation, however, is not so simple.

If a better understanding, or even a trusting relationship existed between owners and employees, it would still be possible today to refer to the fact that it was Marx himself who suggested that the extreme consolidation of capital in a few hands and also, above all, the abundant accumulation of goods were two prerequisites for the socialization of the economy. Of these two prerequisites, one has not yet been achieved and the other no longer applies. If class antagonism did not make people deaf and blind, such a point would doubtlessly receive attention.

If the consolidation of capital identified by Marx as necessary for socialization were indeed achieved, the experienced and knowledgeable management of the enterprises would have to be further retained so that this socialization could actually be implemented. Under current conditions, however, whether or not these managers would facilitate the process is questionable. And this will remain dubious at least as long as approaches, like the current ones of work committees, operate under the assumption that they are justified, capable, and even obliged to look in every corner and speak to every issue, even in cases where they lack specialized knowledge.

Karl Marx would not have considered the preconditions for the implementation of socialization to be existent today, and if the chasm between employers and employees were not so considerable, a large mass of the people would never have come to the conclusion, on which they now insist, that the economy must be socialized because they have the power to do so.

In the final analysis, Marxian theory makes the rather weighty claim that only the proletariat can free itself from the bonds of capitalism. But this conclusion has also, together with the pauperization theory from which it is derived, been shown to be untenable due to the successes of the labor movements. On the other hand, it must also be freely admitted that it would not have been possible to recruit so successfully with these teachings if the opponents in the capitalist camp had shown themselves ready to address the demands of the unions to a more reasonable extent. The claim that concessions would not have allayed the greed that undeniably characterizes the masses as well as individuals, and in fact would only have provided an impetus for the incessant renewal of demands, is as correct as it is incorrect. For while conflicts would certainly not have remained unexpressed as a result of concessions, they would have been led in a less confrontational way, and class antagonism would not have assumed such intensity.

If, for example, the eight-hour workday had been implemented as an agreement, I am convinced that a railway worker would never have carefully maintained the eight-hour day even on less traveled stretches—if, that is, he had ever arrived at the curious notion of demanding it. Indeed, the ruling classes have only themselves to blame for the fact that the proletariat took what was not given willingly, until it finally took more than is generally good and sustainable. There is no doubt that both sides were somehow to blame for shortcomings in the give-and-take of struggles over wages. It could not be otherwise. But more farsighted leaders would have led regardless of the conditions.

No side disputes the fact that leadership will be necessary everywhere and at all times. The fact that all men are not born equal makes the suggestion that a time will come when we can manage without leading personalities seem absurd. If one wishes to object to this by suggesting that no one is opposed to leading individuals, but rather to ruling classes, I would respond that leading individuals constantly gravitate to such classes, for in human society no single person can lead. A cultural world of almost unimaginable scope can only be led by an equally extensive organization, which means a multitude of people who recognize their roles and understand their goal. Such a group will and must endeavor to be workable. It must consist of people who want the same thing, for otherwise the organization is not effectual. The task of the leading individuals then, and indeed of the public as a whole, must be to see that after the implementation of universal voting rights the most capable leaders are also chosen to direct the economy.

Ruling classes will, of course, continue to exist in the future. They may even continue to emerge in large part from the same families. But in the future it will be easier to be admitted to these ruling classes, for the earlier privileges of birth and ownership will no longer entitle one to a position of leadership. Instead, it is hoped, the most qualified individuals will be selected more than before from the entire society.

As leaders are necessary for the life of a state, so are they also needed for the life of an economy. And here also the fact that we are not all equally talented is relevant. I would imagine that no one, even if he or she were a complete egalitarian, would suggest that less competent individuals should be placed over their more competent counterparts. Even to attempt to implement such nonsense would mean failure from the outset.

I say this in spite of the experiences of the revolutionary period and after we know what the catchy phrases of this time accomplished. For while the people "with the big bang" often could do nothing more than incite this bang, they at least had this ability, which they in turn used to ignite the workers' antagonism toward their managers. If this class antagonism could no longer be utilized, and if catchwords like "scabs" were no longer germane, the pressure of the rulers and the slogans of the masses would no longer lead them, against their better convictions, to foolishness. Then the positions of leadership will be assumed by those most competent to lead, and their management will be happily accepted.

Karl Kautsky, a member of the Socialization Commission and my colleague on the Economic Advisory Council, wrote recently that while we must remain committed to capitalist production in order to maintain our economy, we should establish a socialist government. When I asked him what he meant, he responded that much could be improved by a government of Socialists. When I objected that we do not have too many preferred Socialists in Germany who would be capable of assuming positions of leadership, and that his suggestion was therefore not workable, he answered, "Do you think not? It would work in Austria." I do not wish to discuss whether what is not feasible for Germany would be possible in Austria. Suffice it to say that Kautsky is also of the opinion that we cannot yet think of socialist production. For sufficient amounts could not be produced, at least under current conditions. In short, for the foreseeable future we need capitalist production, assuming there is sound leadership. Naturally, socialist production would require the same. However, I demand more of this capitalist leadership today than what Kautsky demands of the government. Namely, *they must have a social conscience.*

Here then I must introduce a welcome fact that I express with unwavering conviction: today there are, among the companies in southern Germany, a large number of men with social conscience. Further, I do not hesitate to suggest that there is more true social conscience to be found among the management of these young companies than there is a real and honest socialist conviction and a corresponding sense of responsibility among the workers. If all workers were to examine themselves and their surroundings, they would certainly not be able to contradict me so easily. Those who had promised that the fulfillment of political and economic wishes would follow the proletariat's seizure of power in 1918 will demand, "Should the result of the revolution be nothing more than the resumption of the old yoke?" To which I reply that while there certainly were conditions in industry that could not have been described as satisfactory, on the other hand, they were in no way as bad as they were made out to be. When speaking of one's workplace, talk of "prisons" was not reasonable in most cases. In the struggle for better working conditions, it was not only the stubbornness of short-sighted employers that was so disastrous, but also the most inflammatory and inciteful actions of the union leaders, to which they were bound by the *Communist Manifesto*.

When the Works Committee Law was under consideration last year, I suggested to the Association of German Industry that I understood the Works Committee as a reform that could assist in fundamentally improving the relationships between employers and employees. I am as convinced of this now as I was before. This success presumes, however, both that the correct individuals are selected for the Works Committee, and that the employers assume an appropriate standpoint. With such a reform both parties must assist one another in mutual understanding and compromise. There is something for everyone to learn. If I, for example, were the Works Committee advisor for the Robert Bosch Company, I would not involve myself in things of which I had no understanding. I would, for example, not demand that my company prove that they understand how to purchase materials properly. That they obviously understand this would have been demonstrated by the fact that they have been successful over the course of more than thirty years. I would simply say to myself that whoever has accomplished this professionally for the last thirty years is naturally more capable than I am. In fact, if I, as the advisor, could find nothing better to do than intrude in areas with which I wasn't familiar, then the situation would be one I was not capable of improving. That the advisors occasionally maintained another position is due to several facts. For one thing, the necessary understanding between management and workers does not exist. Actually, they don't even know each other. In addition, the previously described, and badly mistaken Marxist notion that employers were in every case dispensable and would have to be replaced by advisors also contributed to the misunderstanding. Employers are not dispensable, at least not as long as they are still involved with the company's management.

In short, the workers did not understand. They underestimated the work involved in the management of a company. They believed for the most part that exploitation was the culprit, and that revealing the tactics of the exploiters would be the first task for the advisors. Above all, once the surpluses had been regained, the glorious days of the employers would be over and those of the workforce initiated. In fact though, while the glorious days of the employers have ended, and for this they themselves are largely to blame, who would claim now that those of the workforce are coming? In my opinion, the workforce's chances of success without management are as slim as management's could be without a workforce. In the industrial machine there are no superfluous parts, and none that can be replaced hastily. A company's advisor cannot be its management.

I must make a few remarks about this "surplus" catchword. There certainly were companies like those described by Engels, even in Germany. We had, and unfortunately still have, companies that have pursued dividend politics in the most shortsighted manner. But what has become of them? They are crumbled and aged. They were full of machines that gradually required replacement, but the surplus had been disbursed among the capitalists in the form of dividends. There was no money there for innovating and acquiring new machines. These firms suffered, although they have recovered now, in part due to the despicable war. Is it better then, if the "surplus" is divided in some way among the workers rather than among the capitalists? Will the result not be similarly ruinous for the companies? They will be enterprises that lack the support required for self-preservation. In what are by far the majority of cases, and this is particularly true today, a company's yield is not large enough to improve fundamentally the economic situation of its workers if this yield, or so-called surplus, were regularly distributed among the employees. On the other hand, a firm is condemned to sickness and eventual death if its own means of renewal are taken away. We will soon see whether the high taxes of today are already taking so much of this surplus away that the companies will have no more money to maintain their vitality. That the feared results of this heavy taxation cannot be good, not even for the general interest, is truly not a matter of contention. Taking away the surplus from the employer(s) has its two sides, and I think that we should not try to improve the situation of workers in this way. I remember that about thirty years ago, when I had been in business only a few years, I paid, with real satisfaction, a worker thirty-five marks a week for ten-hour workdays. I was proud of the fact that I could manage such a high income for one of my people. This man is still employed by my company and will surely remember this arrangement. Later, but already before the war, he and his colleagues were earning one and half times this amount for forty-eight working hours. While it wasn't rash or incautious, we made progress surely and steadily.

Let me provide another example. Around the same time, the end of the eighties that is, I bought a bicycle. My landlord, a foreman, was astonished by this. It struck him as a luxury. I used the bicycle in my business, for I supervised the work of my electrical technicians personally. Finally then, he summarized his impressions with the following words: "Well, I guess it is also true that many people still keep a horse. This is similar." I, the employer, was perceived in this way simply for having bought a bicycle. Almost every worker had one even before the war. While a bicycle thirty years ago cost six times what it did before the war, they have since then become accessible for almost everyone. And today, the bicycle of the prewar years has not so rarely become a motorcycle.

In short, even in the capitalist state situations have generally improved, and will only truly improve after the political order has changed. But it is necessary that the two sides compromise. At the beginning of my analysis I said that the ruling classes have not understood how to lead. Today, however, it is imperative that not only the employers, but also the workers make an effort.

The employers have made mistakes. These mistakes were due in part to both hasty development and to the brevity of the development period. But leading must also be learned! Upstarts are mostly disagreeable, and almost unbearable. After the founding of the German Reich had created the possibilities for development, we grew by leaps and bounds. Led by the Prussians, the most politically regressive German state, we grew by way of military success. Success won with arms brought us economic success. We adored this violent success, and it became our "front line." But it is in large part this success that is also responsible for our current predicament.

Today we all have the political possibility to have an effect on our own fate. We must, however, stop operating according to the old political routine! We must get used to seeing more in our fellow human beings than simply our inferiors or our enemies. Let us leave all pettiness and narrow-mindedness aside! All of us, whether they be above or below, right or left, are individuals, with goals for their life that have grown out of their personality. Whoever finds their way uprightly and according to their good conscience and sense of responsibility deserves our respect, whether they are with or against us. It would not be sensible to demand that all people be satisfied in the future with what they are offered. There will still be struggles in the future, but they should be honest and decent struggles. The supreme principle must be: be human and honor human dignity!

It has become apparent to the various people from the industrial and other sections of the economy who have visited the United States that a different relationship exists between employers and employees there. Among the publications of these observations that I have read, however, not even one of the authors has correctly attributed the cause of the American workforce's different attitude toward the factories in which they work.

The first thing to say is that it is not as if the workers over there perform their tasks with the same devotion everywhere. In his book, the renowned Taylor uses the verb "to soldier" to describe the activity of the ideal worker. If a man like Taylor uses such a word in this way, it must be customary over there. But anyone who has had the opportunity to look around in a factory over there in which hourly or weekly wages are paid knows that there also is idling from time to time.

It is, however, absolutely correct that workers over there throw themselves into their tasks completely differently when good earnings are at stake. Why is this?

The answer is that the American worker knows that he will be allowed to earn more when he produces well. The employers there do not reproach each other if one of them provides good earnings for his employees. This was already the case forty-five years ago, and, as I know from my own experience, it still is today. In the United States the realization that "buying power" must be created has become common knowledge. In Germany on the other hand, and this also I know from my own experience, anyone clever enough to know that reductions in piece-rate wages will cause workers to hold back and work only enough to prevent further cuts in their salaries is frowned upon.

In addition, in the United States there is no caste mentality that extends so far that a worker, whatever his or her actual value may be, cannot earn more than an office worker or a technician. Over there one examines the productivity of all individuals, evaluates their work for the company, and pays them accordingly, regardless of the fact that they are workers. This results in a situation where one can be a salesman today and a lathe operator tomorrow.

Further, this is no mere democratic state of mind that in actuality contrasts with more concrete, flesh-and-blood cases. If, for example, Al Smith is elected president this year, there will be no decent American who dares to reproach him for having begun on the very bottom. If Ebert had become president of the United States, the

Americans would have boasted of the fact that they had such a strikingly independent and unselfish president who had worked his way up to the top position. And there are many examples like this!

This also means that American workers know all positions are accessible to them. If they possess the capability, there is no caste mentality that stands in the way of their becoming the director of the factory in which they had been a worker.

There are, of course, also people in the United States who have other viewpoints. There also, judgment based on pure ability sometimes gives way to preferential treatment based on friendship, relations, or similar reasons. For the most part, however, competent people are not barred from advancement, even if their backgrounds are dubious. (Certainly, in most cases those marked for advancement cannot be black).

What can we learn from this?

There are, I think, fundamentally four things.

First, provide yourself with an enterprise that enables you to manufacture goods rationally. And produce commodities that can be manufactured rationally, so that you can pay your workers the highest possible wages.

Second, show your workers that you see them as your equals. Be fair and not arrogant! There are talented and not so talented, and very valuable and less valuable people. We are not all born equal and thus there cannot be equality in this sense. But all people have a right to the respect of their peers, as long as they behave themselves decently. While all citizens today have the right to vote, they are not only your respectable fellow citizens when you want their vote for your party.

Third, don't ever be concerned with one of your useful people not earning, or even having degrees or diplomas.

For seventy years now the members of the workforce have been told over and over again: You are a class of your own! No worker will ever be able to cross a certain line! You are born in the dust, and will never come out of it! The union movement has already managed to disprove Marx's claim that it was an iron rule that workers would never earn more than the costs required to take care of their children. In spite of this, however, such catch phrases are still in use today, and employers can do no better than to prove their invalidity with their actions. Employers are acting astutely when they promote a competent worker to foreman, or to a department director, or even a factory-supervisor position.

Fourth, pay your workers as well as you can. In order to do this, you will have to pay attention to the first point. But this is not enough! See if you have people in your company who are no longer competent or who will soon be incompetent. If this is the case, ensure their living by allocating a certain amount in good years to a fund. From the interest on this amount grant your people a pension that, along with the disability pension, is sufficient to assure them of a comfortable retirement. It is not necessary to provide your people with a legal right to a pension, for you must retain the right to dismiss those who show themselves to be unworthy. However, never release a worker unfairly, be magnanimous, and above all, stand by your word!

On the question of salaries, I would like to say, as I began to do with the first point, that while there is no doubt that social costs have heavily burdened the manufacturers in Germany (as with health insurance costs, for example, two-thirds of which the employees are supposed to pay, but are covered in the final analysis by employers), common sense demands, where at all possible, that one not be stingy with salaries. For workers have a right not only to their daily bread, but also to be able to afford modest pleasures or amass a small savings.

A person who has something behind him or her is different from one who constantly lives with wants and worries. Support your fellow workers who stand by you in work by paying them sufficiently—the higher, the better. I do, of course, know fully well that employers often cannot do what they would very much like to.

The class struggle has been conducted in a negative way by both sides. I do not wish to claim that the employers have played a more decent role in this struggle than the unions. I would, however, like to suggest that the employers should have assumed a more decent role because of their obligation as the leaders, and as the stronger of the two parties.

The result of the class struggle has been a serious mutual distrust. The employers' first task must be to eliminate this distrust. I make this the first priority because the elimination of distrust will require considerable time and willpower on the part of employers. Hatred has been fueled for some seventy years! Hatred is a weed with deep roots, a weed that cannot simply be pulled. Rather, it must slowly wither because it receives no more nourishment. The ground in which it grows will slowly become impoverished then, and the weed will die itself.

If individual employers could succeed at least once in reaching a state of peaceful understanding with their workers, a state in which each side can most vigorously defend their legitimate interests, one would think that such a mutual understanding would have an exemplary effect and even be emulated. In contrast, however, until now those employers who are compromising, fair, and worker-friendly have been seen by their workers as worse enemies than even the so-called exploiters. This, of course, is in keeping with Marx, who in the *Communist Manifesto* calls on the workers to struggle against the bourgeois philanthropists and social benefactors. Until now, for example, it could quite rightly be said that all of my efforts to improve the lot of my workers have not succeeded in making them more noticeably satisfied than any others. In spite of the fact that they have received higher salaries than elsewhere for years and that I introduced the eight-hour workday and half days on Saturday long before the revolution, there was little sign from the workers that this progress was appreciated. In fact, I was often criticized by other employers, and so I stood between two fires and was the object of antagonism from both the left and the right. It could have been cause for satisfaction when a well-known labor leader, and one who had fought me bitterly before the war, said to me several years ago, "You wouldn't believe how ashamed I am." When I asked him what he meant, he replied, "What were you before? The manager of the people's capabilities, and you managed them well. But how are they handled today, and why did we treat you the way we did during the strike of 1913?" And another said to me, "Now we are in the process of explaining to our union leaders that we also must implement all of the things that were blamed on you and that were described simply with the catchwords 'Taylor system.'"

Clearly, there are approaches that are characterized by more adequate understanding. We in turn must concern ourselves with transforming these approaches into breakthroughs.

Much would be better in the future if we could negotiate decently from positions of mutually confident trust and replace open struggle with honest understanding. Employees certainly should and will constantly demand the highest salary they can receive for their work. They will struggle with all their power to improve their standard of living and to provide security for themselves and their family's future. On the other hand, competition on the world market will force the employers to keep their production costs as low as possible. (Decreases in production costs are beneficial to all and have only positive results.) This opposition of interests exists and will continue to exist. If we were not to see and admit this, we would only be deceiving ourselves. But employees and employers are dependent on the fate of their company in the same way, and recognition of this should prepare the way for the peaceful negotiations to which both parties must come. Only when employers and employees practice "solidarity" in this sense can we hope for general economic improvement. We must first become unified in our goals and then those of us who still feel young enough—even if they are over fifty—can search for new strategies aimed at resolving the social question and eliminating the barriers that still separate individual groups of people.

Translated by Daniel Slager

Aphorisms

Be human and honor human dignity.

We must not deny respect to anyone, whether with or against us, who pursues his or her way uprightly and is constantly responsible to his or her conscience.

The thought that someone could prove, upon examination of one of my products, that they were somehow of low quality has always been intolerable to me. I have therefore unvaryingly attempted to manufacture only products that stand up to any objective examination, products that is, that are the best of the best.

According to my experience, there is nothing worse for an enterprise's chances to last and remain progressive than having no competitors.

I never had the ambition to have made something myself.

"It is better to lose money than trust" is the principle I have always followed. The inviolability of my promises and the belief in the worth of my products and of my word have always been more important to me than momentary profits.

* * *

One prevails against performance only with performance.

Not only powers of observation, but also the abilities to utilize one's observation, recognize its context, and arrive at conclusions based on it are necessary ingredients for success. Moreover, imagination is also required for being able to place what is seen where it belongs.

Completing a contract without second thoughts and as punctually as possible is an act of quintessential business sense.

Having character is of absolutely primary importance. Persons of character do not lie or deceive and always keep their word. They have a sense of duty towards their clients, their family, and themselves. This makes a businessman liked and respected.

Only mutual understanding can create a tolerable relationship. One who represents his or her position sincerely must be reciprocated with trust.

Employers and employees are bound in the same way to the fate of their enterprise.

Translated by Daniel Slager

Carl Friedrich von Weizsäcker

Public Consciousness: Culture

The human being is the life-form that learns to speak.

This proposition, which seems obvious, adds a qualification to an old definition of the human being. Aristotle defines the human being as the *zoon logon echon,* literally, the life-form *(zoon),* which has the Logos (*echon = having*). The Latin tradition translates this as *animal rationale,* the rational life-form. *Logos* in Greek, however, has the primary meaning of speech; not just any babble or chatter, to be sure, but meaningful, "rational" speech. The human being is "the speaking animal." But it is also, and herein lies the qualification, the life-form that *learns* to speak. The human child is born with the ability to learn to speak. The language it learns, however, is determined by the culture into which it is born; what it learns first is the colloquial language of this culture. If its environment is bilingual, the child can grow up bilingual; so great is the determining force of the tradition into which it is born. The phase of speech acquisition is one of the earliest and most important phases in the process of human development.

What is the meaning of this step in our reflections on politics and consciousness?

We began with the necessity of a collectively applied faculty of political reason, with the "public consciousness." This led us to the personal prerequisites to such a faculty. The basis for the existence of the public consciousness is the personal consciousness of each individual, each member of society. The hope placed in education led us to the unconscious prerequisites to the ability to be educated, to the development and the healing of consciousness. But no development of consciousness is possible without the help of language. Language, however, is not the possession of any one individual. Without society, no individual would possess it. The basis for the development of the personal consciousness is the public consciousness, the culture to which it belongs.

Which concepts should we then use to describe culture? I shall take the liberty here to sketch once again a conceptual model which I have used on a number of occasions. I call it the "construction scaffold." As such, it does not claim to be able to say what culture really is; it does not claim to be the "house" that could represent a genuine theory of culture commensurate with our line of inquiry. When one builds a house, one erects a scaffold that is meant to be taken down again when the walls have been built and the roof has been put up. We have not yet reached this point.

The topic of the "construction scaffold" is human behavior in culture. The culture being referred to here is a particular culture, our own, Western culture, from which we are attempting to infer a number of our behavioral traits. We shall see that other cultures show other traits, that another scaffold would be necessary to reconstruct these cultures. This insight shall be an essential one for our political behavior in today's world, in which these cultures must actively live together.

The "construction scaffold" consists of four "levels." I shall number them from bottom to top. After all, one can enter a building under construction only on the ground floor. I shall arrange the outline in such a way that the uppermost level appears at the top as number four, and the bottom level at the bottom as number one, the number of entry.

"Scaffold"

4. The Image of Unity: Myth, Religion, Philosophy.
3. Cultural Elaborations: Ethics, Theory, Art.
2. Practical Rationality: Action and Judgment.
1. The Unity of Behavior: Perception, Judgment, Emotion, Action.

And now for the elucidation. We shall begin at the bottom.

1. The Unity of Behavior. The animal lives for the most part in the unity of perceiving and moving, of stimulus and response. We humans separate this unity into four members. The cat sees something running (perception), "a mouse!" (judgment), "a meal!" (emotion), it captures the prey (action). The mouse sees the lurking creature (perception), "a cat!" (judgment), "danger" (emotion), it runs away (action). The unity of the members: judgment occurs as early as the stage of perception ("running," "lurking"), emotion occurs as early as the stage of judgment ("mouse" is "prey," "cat" is "dangerous"), emotion turns immediately into action. We humans behave in the same manner whenever we act spontaneously, whenever we do not interrupt the unity with a hiatus, with an abstinence of action.

2. *Practical Rationality.* Even the animal can stop and think. The cat lurks, it stalks its prey. The mouse peers cautiously from its hole. With humans, language is the primary means by which this separation of perception and action is carried out. Initially, to be sure, language is a member of the unity of behavior; a call, a command. The imperative and the optative may well designate language applications historically prior to those designated by the statal indicative. But in the developed language of our culture, the statement that expresses a factual content is a fundamental figure; modern-day linguists maintain that every complete sentence comprises a propositional (declarative) and an illocutive (addressive of the partner) component. Only when the judgment is separated from the action does it become possible for the action to transcend the status of mere reaction and become deliberate, free action. The hiatus, the distance between judging and acting, enables the human to pursue practical ends consciously: such judgment-based action is "practical-rational." We shall see that while the higher levels may rest upon the lower levels in our scaffold, our manner of describing the lower levels can only proceed from and be understood in light of the content of the upper levels. One must be able to separate judgment and action in a practical-rational manner if one is to separate, in the behavior of the cat and the mouse, the probable judgments ("a mouse!," "a cat!") from the action of capturing or running away. Upon closer inspection, one can distinguish in human behavior the perception as the basis of judgment from the judgment itself and the emotion as the basis of action from the action itself.

But what are the practical ends? Towards what does the action strive? Gratification of the emotions? Or are not the emotions perhaps our subjective perception of what is beneficial to us? And what is beneficial to us; not only to the individual, but to society, without which the individual would not be able to live? What are the values? On the level of practical rationality, an unanswerable question. The moment such values are no longer self-evident, practical rationality demands a higher level of insight, one superordinate to it.

3. Cultural Elaborations. The inquiry into the values that determine our action, or that should do so, is a post factum inquiry. The child desires before it is able to judge. Elemental wishing is the basis of human action throughout the entire human life span, and the objects of the wishes change with the stages of maturity. Practical-rational judgment can discern the necessary routes between the wish and its object, the means to the end. This does not yet revoke the elemental character of the desire. But in the process of its socialization, a child must learn to renounce wishes; it must learn to wish for things it would not have desired at an elemental level. On the other hand, societal norms as well, in short, the demands of *ethics,* hold without having to be explained. They represent for the various societies an elemental, for the most part unquestioned, tradition. The very inquiry into the values, the question of what is actually valid, expresses that this self-evidence has been shaken, whether it be by way of conflicts experienced between one's own wishes, or by way of the conflict between wishes and upheld norms, or by way of a discovery of conflicts between the norms.

The title "Cultural Elaborations" expresses the notion that the answer to the question of what is valid depends on the respective culture. Every culture stylizes its norms, its values. To use a term from evolution theory, one could also call this stylization a luxuriation of certain behavioral patterns. Organs can luxuriate: the mammoth's tusk, the peacock's tail. For the most part, such organ formations are bound up with luxuriating behavioral patterns vis-à-vis members of the same species: the struggle for dominance, courtship. The development of a culture in which tradition passes on acquired behavior to the succeeding generations progresses much more quickly than organic evolution. In such a culture, new behavioral patterns can emerge and, within a few centuries or even decades, luxuriate. I call such cultural stylizations "elaborations" as well, or, figuratively, "Eiffel Towers." They are broadly rooted in the ground of reality, but they taper off in the thin air of high stylization in narrow points, between which contact threatens to break off.

In the older representations of the scaffold, I designated theory, praxis, and art as the three perhaps most important elaborations of modern Western culture. These names allude to three values handed down by the Greeks: the true, the good, the beautiful. This arrangement follows Aristotle, who distinguishes between theory, praxis, and poiesis, which, translated into English, would amount to viewing, acting, and making. Since politics was the topic of our previous discussion, I have placed praxis at the beginning and have replaced its classical name, which designates action meaningful in and of itself, with one of its normative stylizations—"ethics."

A definition may be appropriate here. Aristotle distinguishes praxis, as an action that bears its meaning within itself, from poiesis, an act of making, that finds its meaning in some work that lies outside itself. Poiesis comprises artisanship and art. For the Greeks, the artist was numbered among the artisans. The modern age sees as the chief value of artisanship and technology their utility for preordained purposes, and thus relegates artisanship and technology to the realm of practical rationality. Art—a concept that did not come into being until 1800, when it was coined to designate the entirety of the "fine arts"—assumes hereby the status of an autonomous field.

In what way then are these cultural forms broadly rooted in the ground of reality, and in what way do they taper off into stylized points? Each of the three governing values has a normative character, each seeks to exclude its opposite. In common parlance, the false stands opposite the true, the bad stands opposite the good, the ugly stands opposite the beautiful.

Let us begin with praxis. The Greek opposite–pair "good" *(agathon)* and "bad" *(kakon)*. Even in modern English colloquial usage, the word "good" designates by no means only the morally good. A shoe is good when it fits, a soccer player is good when he cooperates with his team and thereby enables them to score or block goals, a scientist is good when he brings interesting results to light. These are norms of specific fields that "bear their meaning within themselves," or at least serve such a meaning. There also exist, however, general norms of human behavior. Here, another opposite–pair has assumed importance for the Western world since the victory of Christianity: the "Jews' gift to humanity," the opposites of "good" and "evil." A bad shoe, soccer player, or scientist is not necessarily evil. Evil is a quality of the will: to be evil means not to want the good. Here, ethics becomes personalized. The good is required of a people by its god, so that the people might live. To be evil would then mean to oppose God. But evil, in the end, makes life impossible: "The wages of sin is death" (Romans 6, 23).

These human experiences indicate the breadth of the reality in which the Western understanding of praxis, ethics, and morality are rooted. Their normative stylization occurs in the tradition of Judaism as well as under the influence of Greek philosophy. Traditional ethics holds without having to be explained. Anyone who wants to have it explained falls under the suspicion of wanting to change it in such a way as to grant a measure of freedom to his personal wishes. Throughout Jewish history, the norms were protected against this threat by being laid down in accordance with the Holy Scriptures as positive commandments of God, developing eventually into a strictly ritualized system of separate rules. The Christian West abandoned the details of these norms on the grounds of such details' belonging to the "Old Covenant." But the Christian West needed as much as any other people a standardized system of ethics, and here the influence of Greek philosophy's heroic endeavor soon predominated, the endeavor to lay down ethical norms by freeing them from their unexplainedness, by rationally understanding their meaning.

What is decisive here is the influence of one of "the Greeks' great gifts to humanity," the *theory*, the differentiation between "true" and "false." With a view to the contemporaneously emerging deductive mathematics, classical Greek philosophy developed the logic that could be characterized as the structural mathematics of the true and false. We will return at a later point to the metaphysical-religious core of Greek philosophy. Its structural influence on ethical thought, increasing continually over the course of two thousand years, has consisted in the construing of even ethical statements as propositions that should be true and not false. This mode of thought achieved a decisive breakthrough, after preludes in early Christian dogmatics and medieval scholasticism, in the Enlightenment of the modern age.

The content of ethical norms here played a decisive role. There are above all two spheres that are always viewed with Argus eyes: political-social morality and sexual morality. Political-social morality is the topic of this book. It should not be forgotten, however, that sexual morality exerts by way of the substrata of consciousness, subject as they are to the process of repression, a no less profound influence upon culture.

In substance, political–social morality has been moving since the European Enlightenment towards the transition from the traditional ethos of domination and subservience to an ethos of freedom and equality. In the course of this development, however, the mythical image of God as our Lord loses its obvious illustration in the secular rulers whom we obey, and the unexplained traditional morality is perceived as a restriction of freedom. The indispensable political–social morality must now be explained through the recognition of its necessity to society. This has already been attempted in Plato's *Republic*. The most mature form of this thought in the modern age is most likely Kant's categorical imperative, a law that reason sets up for itself: "Act in such a way that the maxim of your will can at any time be looked upon as a principle of universal law." Kant's thought progresses consistently, culminating in the work of his later years, *Perpetual Peace*. . . . Peace, then, is a necessary demand of practical reason.

Nevertheless, this development leads us into the thin air that wafts about the tops of Eiffel Towers. What is the truth of normative propositions? They assert—in the post-Kantian mode of expression—not what *is,* but rather what *should* be. But what is the truth of *should?* How have we come to know this truth? The categorical imperative is a penetrating philosophical proposition and a criterion for the cultivation of our ethical perceptive faculty. No one has succeeded in deriving positive norms from it in a politically effective manner.

Here lies a weakness; one inherent not only in that ethics which bears the form of theory, but in theory itself as it is understood today. "Be" and "should" isolate the two elements of judgment and action; perception and emotion vanish into the indistinct milieu. Nowadays, theory is generally recognized only as conceptually operating science. Kant calls this faculty of conceptual thought "understanding," as distinguished from "reason," which is a faculty of totality, a comprehensive view. This, too, I wanted to express in the definition of reason as "perception of a whole." But now we are trying to point out the capabilities and limits of purely conceptual thought; what is at issue is the ability of scientific theory to aid understanding.

Even sensory perception orients us within the entirety of the context at hand. I do not see "red in green," but rather a rose in the garden, or a car under a tree. In this respect, perception itself is already predicative, it is to a partial extent conceptually expressible. The pure concept, however, leads us out of the limited whole of the prevailing perception into the nonprevailing generality of its specific area of application; the concept designates, if one may so express it, something "specifically general." The concept "rain" designates the general, i.e., continually recurring phenomenon of water falling in drops from the clouds. The concept "money" designates a measurable object of exchange universally accepted in a society. In order to explain concepts we need already other concepts. Thus do we need for "rain" the concepts "water," "drop," "to fall"; for "money," the concepts "society," "exchange," "accept." The concept is a creation of human society, created through the symbolic function of language available to humans from the ability, already present in animals, to perceive form. The philosophical abysses into which the inquiry into the nature of "form," "perception of form," "symbolic function," and "language" would lead us shall not concern us in the present text. Let us take a closer look at the way conceptual thought works in society and in politics.

The concept leads us out of the state of naive orientation in the situation at hand. Such concepts as "rain" or "money" remind us of the many instances of the wetness of rain or of payments that we have already experienced and with which we reckon in the future. Whoever thinks conceptually learns to create instruments that from the start are applicable to recurring situations: a roof, a raincoat, or an umbrella; money itself is already an instrument for the exchange of goods within a society. Conceptual thought and instrumental action are closely connected. And instrumental action transforms the world.

But the concept, which acquaints us with distant, general structures, removes us by virtue of this very acquaintance from the familiarity with the whole of our real situation. The concept, which links things distant, fragmentizes that which is present, fails to perceive it as a whole. "There is money to be made here"—and I forget, that I thereby do harm to my neighbor. "Traffic conditions demand a thoroughfare here"—what does the traffic department care about the forest that has to be cut down to make way for such a thoroughfare?

Perception and emotion are forced aside by conceptual thought and ethical norms, and form an unanalyzed residual category. In the modern world, they find refuge in *art*. One can define art as the beatifying or painfully seismographic perception of form through the creation of form. In the cave drawings of the stone age, we moderns can still sense what the people of that time perceived as the essence of their world. Early cultures represent the determinant forces of their life with images of gods. Music intensifies the stirrings of the soul by representing them. For centuries, the Greeks recognized their political identity in the epic of the Trojan War. A love song expresses in a repeatable fashion that which moves the soul of every lover. A temple or a palace inevitably constitute representations of the prevailing order. The tragedies of Oedipus, Antigone, Macbeth, and Hamlet reveal the abyss over which this order has been erected.

When I spoke of the stylization of a culture, I described culture with a concept from art history ("style"). I represented a culture itself the same way I would a great work of art: in the forms it has created it perceives itself. Conservative thinking clings to these forms, which guarantee to this way of thinking the identity of its own life. The optimism of progress is faced with the problem of having to create new forms in which it can recognize its identity. How important were political songs in days past: the "Marseillaise," the "Internationale"! The skyline of New York cannot be explained merely by the real-estate prices in Manhattan: it is the symbol of triumphant technology, the new tower construction of Babel.

The development of art as a societal institution mirrors the development of culture. In the political world of domination and subservience, art accentuates the separation as well as the connection of the social spheres. There is the prince's bard and there is the folk song; the icon painter serves the bishops and the poor who pray before the icons. The mason's guilds, the court painters, and the wandering minstrels were able, for better or worse, to live from their art. In the age of industry, even art develops into a branch of trade. The more technological civilization no longer represents anything but the dominance of its own practical rationality, the more does art become the refuge of perception and emotion. In one's professional life, one transforms the world technologically; privately, one performs music at home, gives record albums as gifts, reads novels, attends art exhibitions. Since the nineteenth century, art has also played an increasing role as a mouthpiece for the criticism of culture and society: Dickens, Baudelaire, Zola, Dostoevsky, Tolstoy, or in the Germany of my youth, such antipodal authors as George and Brecht. But socially critical art is also a part of society. It, too, becomes a branch of trade, for even the socially critical artist must eat. Beatification and painful seismography, perception of the imminent earthquake fulfill real needs, and as long as the legitimate demand for them exists, they will be shaped in part by the forms of this demand.

The decidedly general definition of art as the perception of form through the creation of form can be applied as well to the other cultural elaborations. I like to refer to theory as an "artwork of the Greeks." Truth that can be seen, felt, suffered, assumes here the highly stylized form of defensible propositions. The same holds for ethics. Spontaneous, self-evident action, caring devotion to one's fellow man, constructive criticism, deeply painful self-criticism become a system of rules. Its meaning lies in rendering visible the forms of spontaneity, thus teaching spontaneity.

In all of these created forms, however, lurks the danger that the stylization will lose its character as a guide to perception and to action, and will become an end in itself. That is what was meant by the metaphor of the Eiffel Tower. Let us note well, if we may stylize this process itself, the places where the vertices extend in such a way that each stylization contradicts itself!

Theory that regards itself as free of purpose is appropriated by virtue of this very position by forces that know very well what they want. Such theory enters into their service in the form of deployment of technical means as well as that of ideology. It becomes untrue when it refuses to perceive this state of affairs.

Ethics compels people to justify themselves to themselves. When they appear to succeed in doing so in a fashion consistent with existing norms, self-righteousness renders ethics profoundly evil.

Art represents the essential. This compels it to represent seismographically the lie as well, the antipode of existence. Art as an end in itself, however, can become a refuge from life, and thus detached, and devoid of essence.

4. The Image of Unity. What I have outlined above is, in a stylized form, an image of the fourth of the crises described in chapter 2: the crisis of our culture. I did not seek the essence of the crisis in the same place where conservative, in and of themselves justified value judgments seek it: in the increasing meaninglessness of the traditional norms of truth, morality, beauty. The norms are losing their force at the very point where their factual untruth cannot remain hidden to the alert perceptive faculty. We had proceeded from the subjective consciousness to culture, the achievement of which has been to offer to the subjectivity of the individual the objective, societal foundation of real behavior. For this very reason the crisis of consciousness reveals itself to us as a crisis of cultural norms.

I have described this crisis in a form that would perhaps have been incomprehensible before the nineteenth century. In and of itself, the untruthfulness of sociocultural norms is an ancient, perpetually recurring phenomenon. In the form of suffering, this experience is and always has been accessible to anyone with an alert mind. Time and time again throughout the course of history, however, images have emerged expressive of a conscious perception of the whole, of the unity of culture, a unity that is perpetually endangered and yet at the same time a perpetual object of aspiration. I have mentioned three forms of such images in my scaffold: myth, religion, and philosophy.

Translated by Daniel Theisen

Biographies

BOSCH, ROBERT (b. Albeck, near Ulm, 1861, d. Stuttgart 1942), engineer and industrialist. Educated in the United States where he worked with Thomas A. Edison. In 1866, founded the manufacturing company that bears his name and had its breakthrough with sparks plugs for automobiles in 1897. Advocated industrial arbitration and free trade. Author of *The Prevention of Future Crises in the World Economy* (1937).

BUTENANDT, ADOLF (b. Bremerhaven-Lehe 1903, d. Munich 1995), professor of biochemistry. Studied chemistry, physics, and biology at the universities of Marburg and Göttingen. Professor of chemistry in Danzig, Berlin, Tübingen, and Munich. Discovered the chemical nature of sexual hormones such as androsterone and progesterone. Nobel Prize in Chemistry, 1939. President of Max Planck Society 1960–72.

EIGEN, MANFRED (b. Bochum 1927), professor of physics and director, Max Planck Institute of Physical Chemistry in Göttingen. Studied physics and chemistry at the University of Göttingen. Nobel Prize in Chemistry, 1967. Paul Ehrlich Prize for his research on the molecular mechanism of evolution in 1992. Author of *The Game—Laws of Nature Control Change* (1975) and *Steps toward Life* (1987) (with Ruthild Winkler-Oswatisch).

EINSTEIN, ALBERT (b. Ulm 1879, d. Princeton 1955), physicist who developed the special and general theories of relativity. Studied physics and mathematics at the Polytechnic in Zürich. Professor of physics in Prague and Zürich. Appointed director of the Kaiser Wilhelm Institute for Physics in Berlin in 1913. Nobel Prize in Physics, 1921. Backed pacifism as well as Zionism and helped create the Hebrew University in Jerusalem. Joined Institute for Advanced Study at Princeton in 1933. Author of *Relativity, the Special and the General Theory* (1921), *The Meaning of Relativity* (1921), *Ideas and Opinions* (1954).

GÖDEL, KURT (b. Brünn 1906, d. Princeton 1978), mathematician and logician best known for Gödel's proof. Studied mathematics, physics, and philosophy at the University of Vienna. In contact with the logical positivists of the Vienna Circle around Moritz Schlick and Rudolf Carnap, though he "never believed that mathematics is the syntax of language." Lecturer at the University of Vienna until 1933. Appointed member of the Institute for Adanced Study at Princeton in 1933 and professor of mathematics in 1953. The United States awarded him a National Medal of Science in 1975.

HAHN, OTTO (b. Frankfurt 1879, d. Göttingen 1968), chemist who discovered the process of nulear fission. Studied chemistry, physics, and philosophy at the University of Marburg. Postdoctoral work in radioactivity with William Ramsay in London and Ernest Rutherford in Montreal. Appointed professor of chemistry at the University of Berlin in 1910 and director of the radiochemistry department of the Kaiser Wilhelm Institute for Chemistry in Berlin in 1912. Together with his colalborators Lise Meitner and Fritz Strassmann, a pioneer in radiochemistry, which led to the discovery of nuclear fission in 1938. Nobel Prize in Chemistry, 1944. President of Kaiser Wilhelm Society (soon renamed *Max Planck Society*) 1946–60. Author of *Applied Radiochemistry* (1936), *New Atoms* (1950), *Otto Hahn: A Scientific Autobiography* (1966), *My Life* (1968).

HEISENBERG, WERNER (b. Würzburg 1901, d. Munich 1976), physicist and philosopher who formulated the indeterminacy, or uncertainty, principle. Studied physics at the universities of Munich and Göttingen. Postdoctoral studies with Max Born in Göttingen and Niels Bohr in Copenhagen. Appointed professor of theoretical physics at the University of Leipzig in 1927. Contributed to the "Copenhagen Interpretation" of quantum mechanics. Nobel Prize in Physics, 1932. Director of the Kaiser Wilhelm Institute for Physics in Berlin 1942–45 where he worked on nuclear energy. Appointed director of the Max Planck Institute for Physics in Göttingen in 1946 and president of the German Research Council in 1949. Partner in dialogue with the philosopher Martin Heidegger and teacher of Carl-Friedrich von Weizsäcker. In 1958, Heisenberg moved his Institute to Munich and formulated the "world formula," a nonlinear spinor equation designed to explain existence and behavior of matter itself by fields. Author of *Physical Principles of the Quantum Theory* (1930), *Nuclear Physics* (1953), *Physics and Philosophy* (1958), *Introduction to the Unified Field Theory of Elementary Particles* (1966), *Physics and Beyond* (1971).

KOCH, ROBERT (b. Clausthal 1843, d. Baden-Baden 1910), physician and scientific investigator who founded bacteriology and tropical medicine. Studied botany, physics, mathematics and medicine at the University of Göttingen. Field surgeon during the Franco–Prussian War of 1870–71 and a country physician with a private laboratory where he perfected the pure-culture techniques. Discovered the tubercle bacillus as the cause of tuberculosis in 1882, organized the Hygiene Exhibition in Berlin in 1883, and was appointed professor of hygiene at the University of Berlin in 1885. Scientific mission to fight cholera epidemics in Egypt and in India 1883–84. As head of the German government plague commission, Koch investigated the plague in India and the rinderpest, malaria, blackwater fever, and sleeping sickness in Africa and was able to identify the transmitter of these illnesses. Nobel Prize in Physiology or Medicine, 1905. Author of *Investigations Into the Etiology of Traumatic Infective Diseases* (1878), *The Aetiology of Tuberculosis* (1882), *Interim Report on Rhodesian Redwater or African Coast Fever* (1903), *The Relationship Between Human and Cattle Tuberculosis* (1906).

LORENZ, KONRAD (b. Vienna 1903, d. Altenberg, 1989), zoologist who founded comparative ethology. Studied medicine and zoology at Columbia University in New York and at the University of Vienna. In 1937, appointed editor of the *Journal of Animal Psychology* and in 1940 professor of psychology at the University of Königsberg. Head of the Institute for Comparative Ethology in Altenberg, Austria, and 1961–73 of the Max Planck Institute for Behavioral Physiology in Seewiesen, Bavaria. Nobel Prize in Physiology or Medicine, 1973. In 1974, he returned to Altenberg for research in animal sociology. Author of *King Solomon's Ring: New Light on Animal Ways* (1949), *Man Meets Dog* (1953), *On Aggression* (1963), *Behind the Mirror: A Search for a Natural History of Human Knowledge* (1973), *The Foundations of Ethology* (1978).

MACH, ERNST (b. Chirlitz-Tura 1838, d. Haar 1916), physicist and philosopher who established principles of optics, mechanics, and wave dynamics. Studied mathematics, physics, and philosophy at the University of Vienna. Appointed professor of mathematics at the University of Graz in 1864 where Mach became professor of physics two years later. Professor of experimental physics at the University of Prague 1867–94. In 1895, appointed professor of inductive philosophy at the University of Vienna. "Mach's Principle" on inertia inspired Einstein's theories of relativity. In 1887, Mach discovered the principles of supersonics and the Mach numbers. From 1901, elected member of the Austrian parliament. Author of *Science of Mechanics* (1883), *Contributions to the Analysis of the Sensations* (1887), *Popular Scientific Lectures* (1895), *Knowledge and Error* (1905).

MEITNER, LISE (b. Vienna 1878, d. Cambridge 1968), physicist who was one of the discoverers of nuclear fission. Studied as one of the first women physicists at the University of Vienna with Ludwig Boltzmann. Close associate (1912–38) of Otto Hahn, whom she joined at the Kaiser Wilhelm Institute for Chemistry in Berlin. In 1918, appointed head of the physics department at the Institute and, in addition, professor at the University of Berlin in 1929. In 1938 dismissed as a Jew from the Institute, Meitner fled to Denmark, then Sweden. With her nephew, Otto Frisch, she correctly interpreted the splitting of the uranium nucleus and in a letter to *Nature* named it *fission*. She worked from 1939 to 1947 with the Nobel Institute in Stockholm and from 1948 with the Swedish Atomic Energy Commission in a laboratory at the Royal Institute of Technology. In 1947, visiting professor at the Catholic University of America and in 1957, at Bryn Mawr College. Enrico Fermi Award in 1966.

PLANCK, MAX (b. Kiel 1858, d. Göttingen 1947), theoretical physicist who originated quantum theory. Studied mathematics and physics at the universities of Munich and Berlin. In 1885, appointed professor of theoretical physics at the University of Kiel and in 1887 at the University of Berlin, where he became director of the Institute for Theoretical Physics. In 1900, established quantum theory and introduced Planck's constant. Visiting professor at Columbia University in 1909. Nobel Prize in Physics, 1918. President of Kaiser Wilhelm Society 1930 to 1935. Author of *Lectures on Thermodynamics* (1897), *Introduction to Theoretical Physics* (1916–30), *The Philosophy of Physics* (1936), *The New Science* (1959), *Scientific Autobiography* (1968).

RADBRUCH, GUSTAV (b. Lübreck 1878, d. Heidelberg 1949), jurist, politician, legal philosopher who advocated a contextual understanding of law relative to moral values, time, and place. Professor of law at the universities of Königsberg, Kiel, and Heidelberg. Minister of justice in the Weimar government 1921–23. Author of *Introduction to Jurisprudence* (1910), *Legal Philosophy* (1914), *Primer on the Philosophy of Law* (1948).

SCHRÖDINGER, ERWIN (b. Vienna 1887, d. Vienna 1961), theoretical physicist who founded quantum-wave mechanics, and philosopher of science. Studied physics and mathematics at the University of Vienna. Appointed professor of physics at the University of Zurich in 1921 and at the University of Berlin in 1927. Friendship with Max Planck. Nobel Prize in Physics, 1933. Fellow of the Magdalen College at Oxford in 1933, member of the Dublin Institute for Advanced Studies 1939–55. In 1956, return to the University of Vienna. Author of *Collected Papers on Wave Mechanics* (1928), *Science and the Human Temperament* (1935), *What Is Life? The Physical Aspect of the Living Cell* (1944), *Statistical Thermodynamics* (1946), *Space–Time Structure* (1950), *Science and Humanism: Physics in Our Time* (1951), *Nature and the Greeks* (1954), *Mind and Matter* (1958), *My View of the World* (1964).

SIMMEL, GEORG (b. Berlin 1858, d. Strassbourg (1918), sociologist and philosopher of social life. Professor of philosophy at the University of Berlin 1885–1914 and of the University of Strassbourg 1914–18. Influenced by Immanuel Kant and Henri Bergson, his philosophy of life analyzed ordinary phenomena such as money, poverty, loyalty, jewelry, and fashion. As a sociologist, he isolated general forms and recurrent regularities of social interaction and stressed the principle of interdependency. Author of *Philosophy of History* (1892), *Philosophy of Money* (1900), *Sociology* (1908), *Goethe* (1913), *The Conflict of Modern Culture* (1918).

Uexküll, Jakob von (b. Keblas 1864, d. Capri 1944), biologist and ecological philosopher who established the unity of the organism and the environment. Studied zoology at the University of Dorpat. Research associate at the physiological institute of the University of Heidelberg and at the zoological station in Naples. Director of the institute for environmental research at the University of Hamburg 1925–36 as well as professor and director of the Zoological Garden in Hamburg 1925–44. His concept of the functional circle anticipated biological cybernetics and his environmental doctrine influenced ethology. Author of *Environment and Inner World of Animals* (1909), *Theoretical Biology* (1926), *A Stroll through the World of Animals and Men* (1934).

Vossler, Karl (b. Hohenheim 1872, d. Munich 1949), philologist. Studied philology, history, and philosophy at the universities in Tübingen, Genf, Rom, Strassbourg, and Heidelberg. Professor of Romance philology at the universities of Heidelberg, Würzburg, and Munich 1902–37. Dismissed from his post by the National Socialists 1937–45. Reinstated in 1945 and in 1946 elected rector of the University of Munich. Influenced by Benedetto Croce, emphasized a comparative study of Italian, French, Spanish, and Portuguese literature and languages in terms of cultural history. Author of *Medieval Culture: An Introduction to Dante and His Times* (1907–10), *Contemporary Italian Literature* (1914), *The Culture of France in the Mirror of Its Language Development* (1913), *Philosophy of Language* (1923), *The Spirit of Language in Civilization* (1925), *Lope de Vega and His Century* (1932), *Spain and Europe* (1952).

Weber, Max (b. Erfurt 1864, d. Munich 1920), sociologist who developed the sociology of religion and contributed to political economy. Studied law, economy, history, and philosophy at the universities of Heidelberg, Strassbourg, Berlin, and Göttingen. In 1893, lecturer of German law at the University of Berlin; in 1894, professor of political economy at the University of Freiburg; 1897–89, the University of Heidelberg. Travels in the United States and private research in Heidelberg. His philosophy of history stressing "disenchantment." Weber's analysis of Protestant ethic as the basis of capitalism proved as stimulating as his concept of sociology being a descriptive science neutral to values. Appointed professor of sociology at the University of Munich. After his sudden death in 1920, his widow edited most of his writings. Author of *Science as Vocation* (1917), *The Rational and Social Foundation of Music* (1921), "The Theory of Social and Economic Organization" (1922), "General Economic History" (1923), "The Protestant Ethic and the Spirit of Capitalism" (1930), "The Religion of China: Confucianism and Taoism" (1951), "Essays in Sociology" (1947), "Ancient Judaism" (1952), "The Religion of India: The Sociology of Hinduism and Buddhism" (1958), "On Charisma and Institutions" (1968). He is represented in The German Library by volume 60, *Sociological Writings.*

WEIZSÄCKER, CARL-FREDERICH VON (b. Kiel 1912), physicist and philosopher of nature. Studied physics and mathematics at the universities of Leipzig, Berlin, and Göttingen. A student of Werner Heisenberg and Niels Bohr, was research associate at the Institute for Theoretical Physics at the University of Leipzig and from 1936 at the Kaiser Wilhelm Institutes for Chemistry and for Physics. Worked with Otto Hahn and Lise Meitner. In 1937, established the "Weizsäcker formula" for the atomic nucleus. Professor for theoretical physics at the University of Strassbourg, 1942–45, where he developed his cosmogonic theory. Professor of physics at the University of Göttingen, 1946–56, and 1957–70, professor of philosophy at the University of Hamburg. Director of the newly founded Max Planck Institute for Research on the Conditions of the Scientific-Technological World, 1970–80. Author of *The History of Nature* (1949), *The World View of Physics* (1952), *Ethical and Political Problems of the Atomic Age* (1958), *The Unity of Nature* (1971), *The Politics of Peril* (1976), *The Ambivalence of Progress* (1977), *The Perception of Modernity* (1983), *Man and History* (1991).

WEYL, HERMANN (b. Elmshorn 1885, d. Zürich 1955), mathematician who contributed to theoretical physics, especially quantum physics and the theory of relativity. Studied mathematics (with David Hilbert) at the University of Göttingen. In 1913, appointed professor of mathematics at the Zürich Polytechnic, where Albert

Einstein was his colleague. Professor of mathematics at the University of Göttingen 1930–33. Member of the Institute for Advanced Studies in Princeton 1934–51. Author of *The Concept of a Riemann Surface* (1913), *Space, Time, and Matter* (1918), *Group Theory and Quantum Mechanics* (1928).

Translated by Virginia Cutrufelli

Bibliography

Bendix, Reinhard. *Max Weber: An Intellectual Portrait.* London: Heinemann, 1960

Blackmore, John T. *Ernst Mach: His Work, Life, and Influence.* Berkeley: University of California Press, 1972

Cassidy, David C. *Uncertainty: The Life and Science of Werner Heisenberg.* New York: Freeman, 1992

Gibbin, John. *The Search for Schrödinger's Cat: Quantum Physics and Reality.* Toronto, New York: Bantam Books, 1994

Heisenberg, Elisabeth. *Inner Exile: Recollections of a Life with Werner Heisenberg.* Transl. S. Capellari and C. Morris. Boston: Birkhäuser, 1984

Hofstadter, Douglas. *Gödel, Escher, Bach.* New York: Basic Books, 1979

Jungnickel, Christa and Russell McCormack. *Intellectual Masters of Nature: Theoretical Physics from Ohm to Einstein.* vol. 2. Chicago: University of Chicago Press, 1986

Moore, Walter. *Schrödinger: Life and Thought.* Cambridge: Cambridge University Press, 1989

Heilbron, John L. *The Dilemma of an Upright Man: Max Planck as Spokesman for German Science.* Berkeley: University of California Press, 1986

Poggi, Gianfranco. *Money and the Modern Mind: Georg Simmel's Philosophy of Money.* Berkeley: University of California Press, 1993

Powers, Thomas. *Heisenberg's War: The Secret History of the German Bomb.* New York: Alfred Knopf, 1993

Ringer, Fritz K. *The Decline of the German Mandarins: The German Academic Community 1890–1933.* Cambridge: Cambridge University Press, 1969

Shea, William R., ed. *Otto Hahn and the Rise of Nuclear Physics.* Dordrecht: Reidel, 1983

Sime, Ruth Lewin. *Lise Meitner: A Life in Physics.* Berkeley: University of California Press, 1996

Wilson, Robert Anton. *The Schrödinger's Cat Trilogy.* New York, Pocket Books, 1989

White, Michael and John Gibbin. *Einstein: A Life in Science.* New York: Plume, 1994

Wolf, Fred Alan. *Taking the Quantum Leap.* New York: Perennial Library, 1989

Acknowledgments

Every reasonable effort has been made to locate the owners of rights to previously published translations printed here. We gratefully acknowledge permission to reprint the following material:

"Philosophical and Scientific Thought" by Ernst Mach appeared in *Knowledge and Error*; Dordrecht-Holland, 1976, D. Reidel Publishing Co. pp. 1–11, and is reprinted with the permission of Kulwer Academic Publishers.

"Principles of Research" and "What Is the Theory of Relativity?" by Alfred Einstein appeared in *Essays in Science*, copyright 1934 by Covici Friede Inc., published by the Philosophical Library, New York.

Chapters 9 and 10 from PHYSICS AND PHILOSOPHY by Werner Heisenberg copyright © 1958 by Werner Heisenberg. Reprinted by permission of HarperCollins Publishers, Inc.

"The Atom" by Lise Meitner is reprinted with the kind permission of Mrs. Ulla Frisch.

"The Status of Women in the Professions" by Lise Meitner appeared in *Physics Today* Vol. 13 No. 8, August, 1960, and is reprinted with the permission of The American Institute of Physics.

"Life as an Object of Chemical Research" by Adolf Butenandt. Max Hueber Verlag München, 1959.

"On Bacteriological Research" by Robert Koch appeared in *Die Ätiologie und die Bekämpfung der Tuberkulose* and is reprinted with the permission of the Verlag von Johann Ambrosius Barth (Leipzig, 1912).

"A Stroll through the Worlds of Animals and Men" by Jakob von Uexküll, is reprinted with the permission of International Universities Press, Inc. The translation by Claire H. Schiller appeared in *Instinctive Behavior: The Development of a Modern Concept* (1957).

"Habit, Ritual, and Magic" from *On Aggression* by Konrad Lorenz, copyright © 1983 Deutscher Taschenbuch Verlag, Munich, Germany; English translation copyright © 1966 by Konrad Lorenz, reprinted by permission of Harcourt, Brace & Company, and by permission of Routledge/International Thomson Publishing Services, Ltd.

© Manfred Eigen, Ruthild Winkler-Oswatitsch, Paul Woolley, and Oxford University Press 1992. Reprinted from *Steps towards Life: A Perspective on Evolution* by Manfred Eigen with Ruthild Winkler-Oswatitsch, translated by Paul Woolley, (1992) by permission of Oxford University Press.

From *From Max Weber: Essays in Sociology* edited and translated by H. H. Gerth and C. Wright Mills. Copyright © 1946 by Oxford University Press, Inc.; renewed 1973 by Hans H. Gerth. Reprinted by permission of the publisher.

"The Spirit of Language in Civilization" by Karl Vossler is reprinted by permission of Routledge/International Thomson Publishing Services, Ltd.

"Money and the Pace of Life" by Georg Simmel appeared as "The Pace of Life, Its Alterations, and Those of the Money Supply" in *Philosophy of Money*, translated by Tom Bottomore and David Frisby (1978 Routledge and Kegan Paul) and is reprinted by permission of Routledge/International Thomson Publishing Services, Ltd.

"The Concept of Law" by Gustav Radbruch, translated by Kurt Wilk, appeared in Volume IV of the *20th Century Legal Philosophy*

Series: The Legal Philosophies of Lask, Radbruch, and Dabin. Copyright © 1950 by the President and Fellows of Harvard College.

"Public Consciousness: Culture" by Carl Friedrich von Weizsäcker: from *Bewußtseinswandel.* © 1988 Carl Hanser Verlag München Wien.

THE GERMAN LIBRARY
in 100 Volumes
Select List of Titles

Wolfram von Eschenbach
Parzival
Edited by André Lefevere

Gottfried von Strassburg
Tristan and Isolde
Edited and Revised by Francis G. Gentry
Foreword by C. Stephen Jaeger

German Medieval Tales
Edited by Francis G. Gentry
Foreword by Thomas Berger

German Mystical Writings
Edited by Karen J. Campbell
Foreword by Carol Zaleski

German Humanism and Reformation
Edited by Reinhard P. Becker
Foreword by Roland Bainton

German Poetry from the Beginnings to 1750
Edited by Ingrid Walsøe-Engel
Foreword by George C. Schoolfield

Gotthold Ephraim Lessing
Nathan the Wise, Minna von Barnhelm, and other Plays and Writings
Edited by Peter Demetz
Foreword by Hannah Arendt

Immanuel Kant
Philosophical Writings
Edited by Ernst Behler
Foreword by René Wellek

Friedrich Schiller
Plays: Intrigue and Love and Don Carlos
Edited by Walter Hinderer
Foreword by Gordon Craig

Friedrich Schiller
Wallenstein and Mary Stuart.
Edited by Walter Hinderer

Johann Wolfgang von Goethe
The Sufferings of Young Werther and *Elective Affinities*
Edited by Victor Lange
Forewords by Thomas Mann

German Romantic Criticism
Edited by A. Leslie Willson
Foreword by Ernst Behler

Friedrich Hölderlin
Hyperion and Selected Poems
Edited by Eric L. Santner

Philosophy of German Idealism
Edited by Ernst Behler

G. W. F. Hegel
Encyclopedia of the Philosophical Sciences in Outline and Critical Writings
Edited by Ernst Behler

German Poetry from 1750 to 1900
Edited by Robert M. Browning
Foreword by Michael Hamburger

Karl Marx, Friedrich Engels, August Bebel, and others
German Essays on Socialism in the Nineteenth Century
Edited by Frank Mecklenburg and Manfred Stassen

German Lieder
Edited by Philip Lieson Miller
Foreword by Hermann Hesse

Arthur Schnitzler
Plays and Stories
Edited by Egon Schwarz
Foreword by Stanley Elkin

Rainer Maria Rilke
Prose and Poetry
Edited by Egon Schwarz
Foreword by Howard Nemerov

Robert Musil
Selected Writings
Edited by Burton Pike
Foreword by Joel Agee

Essays on German Theater
Edited by Margaret Herzfeld-Sander
Foreword by Martin Esslin

Friedrich Dürrenmatt
Plays and Essays
Edited by Volkmar Sander
Foreword by Martin Esslin

Max Frisch
Novels, Plays, Essays
Edited by Rolf Kieser
Foreword by Peter Demetz

Gottfried Benn
Prose, Essays, Poems
Edited by Volkmar Sander
Foreword by E. B. Ashton
Introduction by Reinhard Paul Becker

German Essays on Art History
Edited by Gert Schiff

German Radio Plays
Edited by Everett Frost and Margaret Herzfeld-Sander
Foreword by Klaus Schöning

Hans Magnus Enzensberger
Critical Essays
Edited by Reinhold Grimm and Bruce Armstrong
Foreword by John Simon